READERS' GUIDES TO ESSENTIAL CF

CONSULTANT EDITOR: NICOLAS TREDELL

Nicholas Potter	Shakespeare: *Othello*
Steven Price	The Plays, Screen Plays and Films of David Mamet
Andrew Radford	Victorian Sensation Fiction
Berthold Schoene–Harwood	Mary Shelley: *Frankenstein*
Nick Selby	T. S. Eliot: *The Waste Land*
Nick Selby	Herman Melville: *Moby Dick*
Nick Selby	The Poetry of Walt Whitman
David Smale	Salman Rushdie: *Midnight's Children –* *The Satanic Verses*
Patsy Stoneman	Emily Brontë: *Wuthering Heights*
Susie Thomas	Hanif Kureishi
Nicolas Tredell	F. Scott Fitzgerald: *The Great Gatsby*
Nicolas Tredell	Joseph Conrad: *Heart of Darkness*
Nicolas Tredell	Charles Dickens: *Great Expectations*
Nicolas Tredell	William Faulkner: *The Sound and the Fury – As I Lay Dying*
Nicolas Tredell	Shakespeare: *Macbeth*
Nicolas Tredell	The Fiction of Martin Amis
Matthew Woodcock	Shakespeare: Henry V
Angela Wright	Gothic Fiction

Forthcoming

Pascale Aebischer	Jacobean Drama
Annika Bautz	Jane Austen: *Sense and Sensibility – Pride and Prejudice – Emma*
Matthew Beedham	The Novels of Kazuo Ishiguro
Jodi–Anne George	*Beowulf*
Sarah Haggarty & Jon Mee	Willam Blake: *Songs of Innocence and Experience*
Matthew Jordan	Milton: *Paradise Lost*
Timothy Milnes	Wordsworth: *The Prelude*
Stephen Regan	The Poetry of Philip Larkin
Mardi Stewart	Victorian Women's Poetry
Michael Whitworth	Virginia Woolf: *Mrs Dalloway*
Gina Wisker	The Fiction of Margaret Atwood
Gillian Wood	Shakespeare: *Romeo and Juliet*

Readers' Guides to Essential Criticism

Series Standing Order ISBN 1–4039–0108–2
(outside North America only)

You can receive future titles in this series as they are published by placing a standing order. Please contact your bookseller or, in the case of difficulty, write to us at the address below with your name and address, the title of the series and the ISBN quoted above.

Customer Services Department, Macmillan Distribution Ltd, Houndmills, Basingstoke, Hampshire RG21 6XS, England

---

Victorian Sensation Fiction

ANDREW RADFORD

Consultant editor: Nicolas Tredell

First published 2009 by
PALGRAVE MACMILLAN

Palgrave Macmillan in the UK is an imprint of Macmillan Publishers Limited, registered in England, company number 785998, of Houndmills, Basingstoke, Hampshire RG21 6XS.

Palgrave Macmillan in the US is a division of St Martin's Press LLC, 175 Fifth Avenue, New York, NY 10010.

Palgrave Macmillan is the global academic imprint of the above companies and has companies and representatives throughout the world.

Palgrave® and Macmillan® are registered trademarks in the United States, the United Kingdom, Europe and other countries.

ISBN-13: 978–0–230–52488–0 hardback
ISBN-10: 0–230–52488–5 hardback
ISBN-13: 978–0–230–52489–7 paperback
ISBN-10: 0–230–52489–3 paperback

This book is printed on paper suitable for recycling and made from fully managed and sustained forest sources. Logging, pulping and manufacturing processes are expected to conform to the environmental regulations of the country of origin.

A catalogue record for this book is available from the British Library.

A catalog record for this book is available from the Library of Congress.

10 9 8 7 6 5 4 3 2 1
18 17 16 15 14 13 12 11 10 09

Printed and bound in China

For Lily

Contents

Appraises sensation fiction as a genre that struggled for cultural respectability due in large part to its mass market appeal. Identifies how these controversial narratives are represented by mid-Victorian opponents as both the outcome of and response to a cultural craving which mainstream society has failed to appease. Traces the social misgivings confronted and processed by literary sensationalism. Asks what this sub-genre of Gothic fiction has to offer twenty-first century readers of Victorian literature.

The Rise, Fall and Revival of Sensation Fiction

Examines H. L. Mansel's 1863 response to the mass-market appeal of sensation fiction, as well as discussing the pointed interventions of Geraldine Jewsbury, M. E. Braddon, Margaret Oliphant and George Eliot. Details the genre's apparent indebtedness to older, working-class forms of popular entertainment. Explores Winifred Hughes's seminal construction of an apparently self-contained sensational decade. Details Andrew Maunder's notion that literary sensationalism is a complex generic hybrid that defies containment within the 1860s. Explores the Modernist denigration of sensation fiction, as part of a more general rejection of Victorian aesthetics by figures such as T. S. Eliot. Offers an overview of recent research by Lyn Pykett, Patrick Brantlinger, Jenny Bourne Taylor and Tamar Heller that has led to a remarkable revival of interest in the genre.

Crime and Detection

Addresses the genre's dependency on elaborate plots that exploit intrigue, subterfuge and the solving of puzzles. Assesses Kathleen Tillotson's designation of sensation narratives as 'novels with a secret'. Scrutinizes Martin Kayman's assessment of the secret as an organizing principle of a sensation plot. Also discusses John Kucich's concept of a literary genre that portrays a culture obsessed with falsehood and fabrication. Gauges sensation fiction's preoccupation with questions of policing and the various forms of discipline outlined by D. A. Miller, Marlene Tromp and Brian W. McCuskey. Deals with the amateur sleuth or detective inspector as a notable and complex presence in sensation fiction, with reference to research by Ronald R. Thomas, Martin Priestman and Caroline Reitz.

Class and Social (Im-)Propriety

Discusses mid-Victorian reading practices and how the language of social caste imbues initial critical reactions to the genre. Concentrates on early reviewers such as Francis Paget, Margaret Oliphant and W. Fraser Rae who sought to correlate a reading class specific to sensation fiction. Gauges the threat sensation posed to clear definitions of privilege and power, as well as the genre's potential to 'contaminate' respectable readers and erode orthodox notions of 'family values'. Discusses the scholarship of Graham Law, Deborah Wynne and Cannon Schmitt in terms of how literary sensationalism interrogates social and literary decorum.

Women, Gender and Feminism

Explores critical reactions to woman as writer-subject-reader of sensation fiction. Opens by focusing on Margaret Oliphant, one of the foremost female reviewers of the period, whose interpretations identify, and deplore, women's intimate ties to literary sensationalism. Investigates the genre's repeated portrayal of women in the throes of aberrant passion and insanity. Summarizes recent interpretations of the genre by Elaine Showalter, Tamar Heller, Ann Cvetkovich and Lillian Nayder as a challenge to repressive authorities as well as the reader's ingrained passivity. Addresses the work of E. Ann Kaplan and Lyn Pykett and how maternity becomes a chief concern for female sensation writing, especially Ellen Wood's *East Lynne*.

Domesticity, Modernity and Race(ism)

Concentrates on the sensational construction of 'home' as a site of resistance, refusal and division. Discusses the genre's preoccupation with a tainted domesticity as a critique of a modern homeland vulnerable to foreign incursion. Investigates scholarly engagements with the genre's portrayal of a hectic and anxious modernity, such as Walter Phillip's designation of sensationalism as 'romance of the present'. Discusses work by Tim Dolin, D. A. Miller and Nicholas Daly on the 'shock' of sensation fiction and its staging of nervous debility. Investigates the genre's insistent mapping of metropolitan and national terrain, which raises questions about contested ideologies of Englishness. Samples debates surrounding sensational depictions of the foreign outsider in an age of expansionist foreign policy. Critics discussed include Jenny Bourne Taylor, Pamela Gilbert, Lillian Nayder, Deirdre David and Ian Duncan.

The Mutation of Sensation

Addresses how commentators have documented the sensation genre's evolution beyond its 1860s heyday. Evaluates Sheridan Le Fanu's vexed relationship with the 'sensation school', and how his hybrid narratives have been construed as a foreshadowing of late-Victorian Gothic by recent critics such as W. J. McCormack, Alison Milbank and Victor Sage. Charts the metamorphosis of the genre into myriad textual and narrative forms between 1870 and 1900. Traces an intricate genealogy of generic indebtedness on the part of canonical writers such as George Meredith, Anthony Trollope, George Eliot, Henry James and Thomas Hardy. Assesses the sensation genre as an unlikely model of inspiration for Joseph Conrad in the early twentieth century. Concludes by focusing on sensation as a tenaciously resilient genre, whose influence can be felt in contemporary fiction by Graham Swift and A. S. Byatt.

Evaluates the future for research into Victorian sensation fiction. Explains the genre as a transitional constellation of texts that divulge key Victorian preoccupations, such as the enervating limitations of bourgeois domesticity, the threat of the 'foreign' and the dangers for women of romantic fantasy. Revisits the seminal research of Andrew Maunder who argues for a more ambitious conception of literary sensationalism, given that re-evaluations of the genre too often result in the construction of a narrow alternative canon. Finally, historians of the periodical press such as Peter Sinnema and Jennifer Phegley gauge the genre's evolution beyond the bourgeois drawing-room into other localities and reading spaces.

Acknowledgements

This book has benefited from the detailed and incisive comments of Kirstie Blair, John Coyle, Rob Maslen, John Miller and the anonymous readers at Palgrave Macmillan. Christine Ferguson read drafts of the chapters and helped to make them clearer and more focused. I am grateful to the following people for answering inquiries and recommending sources: Brian Donnelly, Anthony Leyland, Mark Sandy and Ve-Yin Tee. I also wish to thank the Consultant Editor, Nicolas Tredell, for his astute and valuable suggestions, as well as Sonya Barker at Palgrave Macmillan. The Department of English Literature at the University of Glasgow have been generous in granting me the time to complete this book. And finally, I would most particularly like to thank Lily Tong for being so patient while I researched this project.

Introduction

> Two or three years ago nobody would have known what was meant by a Sensation Novel; yet now the term has already passed through the stage of jocular use (a stage in which other less lucky ones will sometimes remain for whole generations), and has been adopted as the regular commercial name for a particular product of industry for which there is just now a brisk demand.
>
> ([Anon.], 'The Queen's English', *Edinburgh Review* 70, July 1864, p. 53)

To this sardonic correspondent, writing for the 1864 *Edinburgh Review*, the 'Sensation Novel', instead of being the rich multivalent form that critics hail nowadays, was a self-evidently substandard literary category, synonymous with the swift growth of industrial capitalism and the emergence of large urban centres with newly exploding populations and new social classes. Defined by its position as an example of mass-produced popular fiction, riding the crest of 'a wave of materialism',[1] the sheer ubiquity of this genre seemed both the upshot and symptom of seismic shifts affecting mid-Victorian reading habits.[2] As we shall see in Chapter One, the genre struggled for cultural respectability due in large part to its mass-market appeal. So why was the sensation novel 'the literary rage'[3] in the 1860s, given that this subgenre of Gothic fiction does not belong exclusively to that time-period? What social misgivings and hidden fears did literary sensationalism confront and process, and what, if anything, does it have to offer twenty-first-century students of Victorian literature? These questions dominate recent criticism and this Guide will scrutinize the most trenchant interventions, as well as indicating worthwhile directions that future research into the genre might take.

'Sensationalism' becomes such a modish slogan or buzzword in 1860s periodical discourse that it takes on increasingly diffuse and perplexing connotations. However, its aura of condescending disapprobation is a keynote of countless reviews as pundits brandished the term as a means to demarcate novels deemed injurious from their more anodyne competitors. By 1867 the novelist and biographer Margaret Oliphant (1828–97) grumbled that 'all our minor novelists, almost without exception, are of the school called Sensational.'[4] *Fraser's Magazine*, reporting on the phenomenon at the apex of the vogue, noted that 'a book without a murder, a divorce, a seduction, or a bigamy, is not apparently considered worth either writing or reading; and a mystery and a secret are the chief qualifications of the modern novel.'[5] This half-appalled, half-jocose estimation, with its catalogue of scandalous and highly spiced ingredients, actually serves as a working definition of the Victorian sensation mode, one that Mary Elizabeth Braddon (1835–1915) exploited in her droll portrayal of the sensation novelist Sigismund Smith in *The Doctor's Wife* (1864). Smith remarks that his readers revel in 'plot, and plenty of it; surprises, and plenty of 'em; mystery thick as a November fog.'[6]

Though some applications of the word 'sensation' were new to commentators in the 1860s, the social trend to which they referred was perhaps more familiar. William Wordsworth (1770–1850), in the 1800 Preface to the *Lyrical Ballads*, lamented the 'craving for extraordinary incident', the 'degrading outrageous stimulation' that afflicted his countrymen. Perhaps this regrettable relish for shocks, thrills and the outlandish, Wordsworth speculated, was a peculiarly modern malaise, explained by 'the accumulation of men in cities' and 'the rapid communication of intelligence.'[7]

To contemporary reviewers and literary historians alike, the sensation novel, with its emotionally and socially provocative plots and plurality of generic affiliations, has seemed at once readily identifiable and difficult to delineate with exactitude ('fast novels', 'bigamy novels', 'crime novels', and *Punch*'s witty coinage 'arsenical novels' are sometimes equated with, sometimes distinguished from the genre). In a literary culture that fostered the merit of convenient classificatory concepts and devised an array of strategies for drawing narrow distinctions, sensationalism repeatedly called the parameters of social, textual and even organic categories into question. Indeed, the act of naming the sensation novel is an endeavour to fix something that might more usefully be surveyed as adaptable and nebulous – as a procedure designed to unsettle the concept of genre as a cluster of intrinsic textual characteristics. In spite of frequent censure of the hackneyed, cliché-ridden nature of the sensation novel, it becomes clear in hindsight that the genre's capacity to subvert sentimental and generic expectations derived substantially from its status as a multifaceted formal and ideological hybrid. The novelist, dramatist and journalist Charles Reade (1814–84) offered an early classification of sensation narrative as a 'Matter-of-Fact Romance', a term which implies how the partitions between domestic sanctuary and the public sphere of economic enterprise, propriety and indiscretion, genteel and lower-class, cannot prevent the cross-pollination of these categories, highlighting the brittleness of the markers that seem to segregate them.

Like stage melodrama, with which it had so much in common, sensation fiction was, as Charles Dickens (1812–70) wrote of *The Moonstone* (1868) by Wilkie Collins (1824–89), 'wild yet domestic'.[8] This phrase suggests the extent to which the genre employed its paraphernalia of psychic disintegration, duplicates, spectres, and transposed identities to erode the seemingly solid and respectable structures of mid-Victorian domesticity. Reviewers frequently branded sensation fiction the genre of emotional excess, not only for its dependency on heightened incident and unbalanced protagonists, but also for its stylistic mannerisms. George Henry Lewes (1817–78) was one among many who belittled popular novels for their 'detailism', a plethora of visual data that overwhelms descriptive lucidity and debunks realism's sober mimetic capacity. Indeed, as David Skilton notes of this period, 'at no time were the techniques and subject matter of fiction under more vigorous and more public debate' than in the 1860s.[9] Critics argued that the Victorian sensation novel was 'not really a distinct genre'[10] at all; rather than being a coherent literary movement it represented a strain of morbid naturalism, an English form of the racier French fiction of George Sand (1804–76), Gustave Flaubert (1821–80), Honoré de Balzac (1799–1850) and Emile Zola (1840–1902).

This Guide interrogates the cultural aspects and critical reception of the sensation controversy, surveying the pressing issues of scholarly inquiry from the genre's 1860s heyday to the present. After years of unwarranted neglect, serious attention is now devoted not only to these narratives but also to their contexts: what they disclose about the social, economic, political and discursive milieu they helped shape. The serialization of Collins's *The Woman in White* in Charles Dickens's new weekly magazine, *All the Year Round*, between 26 November 1859 and 25 August 1860 has been 'heralded as the birth of the sensation novel',[11] and was so lucrative that it created a genuine publishing bonanza, as well as a panoply of commercial spin-offs such as bonnets and dressing gowns fashioned after the dress of its title character. *The Woman in White* even inspired two new dances: a Woman in White Waltz and a Fosco Gallop.[12]

The publisher George Bentley (1828–95), summing up the literary year in his diary on the last day of 1863, noted the phenomenal success of sensation fiction generally and saluted Collins as 'king of inventors [...] the grand inaugurator of the vogue.'[13] *Vanity Fair* would publish Collins's caricature and crown him simply as 'The Novelist Who Invented Sensation' in 1872.[14] M. E. Braddon herself proclaimed that Collins was her 'literary father'[15] and that she owed *Lady Audley's Secret* (1862) to *The Woman in White*. *Punch* gave its official recognition in 1863 to the genre by producing its own sensational serial, 'Mokeanna; or, The

White Witness: A Tale of the Times.'[16] While other sensation novels, such as *East Lynne* (1861) by Ellen (Mrs Henry) Wood (1814–87), a bestseller of 400,000 copies, have remained in print, many others, such as *Hard Cash* (1863) by Charles Reade, who was acclaimed in 1867 by Margaret Oliphant as 'one of the greatest artists in the realm of fiction',[17] have vanished from public view over the years.

Concentrating on secondary scholarship, it is manifest that the re-evaluative enterprise it typifies has been both the outgrowth of and catalyst for the reissue of hitherto overlooked texts: the Oxford World's Classics and Broadview series, both useful barometers for such trends, have in the last 15 years brought out annotated editions of novels by Braddon, Wood, Joseph Sheridan Le Fanu (1814–73) and Collins. Interest in sensation fiction has radically altered the contours of a Victorian canon that once accorded the genre only 'a marginal space in the history of English letters.'[18] In 1928 for instance, the modernist poet and critic T. S. Eliot (1888–1965) offered an (in)famous appreciation of Collins which measured the author as a 'man of talent' against Dickens as the 'man of genius.'[19] But in the past decade Collins's oeuvre has undergone a literary reassessment that has prompted some pundits to place him 'nearer the first tier of Victorian novelists than he has ever been.'[20] Victorian sensation fiction is also showing signs of a popular resurgence, with film adaptations of Collins's novels *The Moonstone* and *Basil* (1852) released in 1997 and 1998.[21] The musical adaptation of Collins's *The Woman in White* by Andrew Lloyd Webber (born 1948), premiered in London in 2004, and an $11 million Broadway production opened in late 2005. As Richard Fantina and Kimberly Harrison remark in their 'Introduction' to *Victorian Sensations: Essays on a Scandalous Genre* (2006), '[t]hese Victorian thrillers, often involving themes such as bigamy, illegitimacy, drug abuse, murder, inheritance scandals, and adultery', captivated Victorians and 'continue to interest contemporary audiences.'[22]

Today, sensation narratives whether adapted for the stage, broadcast on television, premiered in cinemas, or delivered in print, are unlikely to trigger an outcry among audiences inured to graphic depictions of crime and sexuality. But this genre's 'intense appreciation of flesh and blood', according to Margaret Oliphant in 1867, provoked defensive ire and alarm on the part of religious, political and literary authorities. The Archbishop of York, William Thomson (1819–90), preached a sermon against it as one of the 'abominations' of the age in November 1864; the Dean of St. Paul's and Waynflete Professor of Moral and Metaphysical Philosophy at Oxford, H. L. Mansel (1820–71), insisted that the spawning of these vicious narratives, with their language of nervous excitability, and depictions of people almost literally taken out of themselves in moments of shock and awe, was a species of decadent drug potent enough to corrode the reader's morally contemplative responses. H. F. Chorley (1808–72), reviewing Collins's *Armadale* (1866) for the *Athenaeum*, found in the popularity of sensation novels undeniable evidence that he lived 'in a period of diseased invention' of which 'the coming phase [...] may be palsy.'[23]

There has always been and still remains an acute difficulty in classifying the genre, enclosing its dimensions and its chief practitioners, as evidenced by the frustrations of Victorian reviewers who grappled with tenuous distinctions among a plethora of fictional modes. Charles Reade averred that sensation was the constitutive facet of all compelling fiction: 'Without [it] there can be no interest.'[24] Was Dickens really a lowbrow sensation author masquerading as a fastidious practitioner of high art, as some declared after reading *Bleak House* (1852–53) and *The Mystery of Edwin Drood* (1870)? *Belgravia* claimed him as the 'founder' of the sensation school,[25] while Margaret Oliphant in *Blackwood's* reviewed *Great Expectations* (1860–61) along with all the other current sensation novels, judging it markedly inferior to Collins's *The Woman in White* as a specimen of the genre: 'With the most fantastic exaggeration of means, here is no result at all achieved, and no sensation produced upon the composed intelligence of the reader. [...] In every way, Mr. Dickens's performance must yield precedence to the companion work of his disciple and assistant.'[26] Was Thomas Hardy (1840–1928) a secret member of the sensation school? Ellen Wood? Wood's stories of dislocated individuals prompted the *Athenaeum* to tag her, rather than Wilkie Collins, as the 'originator and chief of the sensation school of English novelists.'[27] Yet, in other investigations of her oeuvre, Wood was construed as an elegantly restrained and fortifying proponent of domestic realism, whose novels were distributed as Sunday School Prizes, cultivating a different mode of fiction from that of her 'fast' rival M. E. Braddon.

Chapter One appraises the 'Rise, Fall and Revival' of the sensation genre. I begin with H. L. Mansel's condemnation of these 'electrifying' narratives in 1863, which was 'a landmark year for sensation fiction in Britain', according to Christine Ferguson.[28] For Mansel and many other 1860s reviewers, these novels became the focus of interrelated social tensions, confusions and disputes. Was sensationalism a *cause* of socio-cultural decay, or a *symptom* of a deterioration that was already happening? If a key aim of realism was to teach its readers to see with mature and measured detachment, the contrasting role of sensation, according to Mansel, was to generate a lurid spectacle that would physically stimulate its readers while simultaneously eroding the barrier between their bodies and those of the central protagonists. Though mid-Victorian commentators tended to situate sensation fiction as one of numerous subgenres within the fluid category of popular literature, sensation narratives were often showcased in the same periodicals that serialized what Victorian readers deemed as 'substantial' and 'wholesome' literature. Sensation fiction was also judged in these journals, albeit frequently in terms of derogatory comparison. As Jonathan Loesberg remarks, in his 1986 essay 'The Ideology of Narrative Form in Sensation Fiction', '[b]ecause the genre, at least at first, was as much a creation of the literary journals who grouped the novels together as it was of the novels themselves', classifying it 'solely in terms of internal features presents classic problems' of either characterizing it 'too broadly or too narrowly.'[29] What Margaret Oliphant designated as a new school in fiction was in fact an incredibly broad church. My first chapter evaluates how, and why, these novels fell so drastically out of favour by the early-twentieth century. In addition I chart the continuing critical implications of the initial, often stinging reviews for those who have contributed to the genre's rehabilitation as a field of academic research, inquiry and exposition.

Chapter Two canvasses the obsession with crime and detection in Victorian sensation fiction, and to what degree these novels are, according to Thomas Boyle, 'riddled with details which recall widely reported criminal occurrences of the time.'[30] I begin by showing how the typical sensation narrative has been assessed as a 'novel with a secret' in which the solving of puzzles becomes a principal ingredient in its extraordinary commercial impact. The chapter goes on to consider the questions of transgression and containment, or discipline, which have engrossed late twentieth-century criticism. In literary terms, Victorian sensation fiction is often perceived as 'the cradle of detective fiction'[31] and I conclude with the figure of the 'private eye' or amateur sleuth, who is an enigmatic presence in many of these texts, and whose intervention in the diurnal rhythms and rituals of the middle-class home implies the permeable boundaries between private and public space.

Given that the 1860s was the decade of a second Reform Bill, with widespread discussion on expanding the Parliamentary franchise, primarily in terms of working-class men, as well as the establishment of the National Society for Women's Suffrage (1866), it is no surprise that shifting or disintegrating class identity is a core theme of sensation fiction. The language of caste, including metaphors of stratification, pervades the critical reception of the genre at a historical juncture when cheaper methods of printing made it increasingly feasible to disseminate more texts to a larger reading public. Moreover, literacy itself was no longer a guarantee of 'social standing.' In Chapter Three I address the sensation novel's reflection of contemporary arguments about unstable or porous class boundaries, again through the lens of both mid-Victorian reactions and current analyses of the genre as an ardently contested site of literary value during the 1860s and 1870s, so that 'the literature of the Kitchen [becomes] the favourite reading of the Drawing-room.'[32] Here is a deep-seated cultural unease about the rapid and prolific production of sensation fiction, which imperils the social regulation that safeguards rigid class divisions.

Proclaiming the sheer enjoyment of reading *Lady Audley's Secret*, *The Times* (18 November 1862) contended that '[t]his is the age of lady novelists, and lady novelists naturally give the first place to the heroine.'[33] Chapter Four gauges the critical response to woman as writer-subject-reader of sensationalism. Heated debates surrounding gender have distinguished the genre's signal impact from the beginning. Pamela Gilbert, in *Disease, Desire and the Body in Victorian Women's Popular Novels* (1997), follows the lead of many mid-Victorian and current commentators to aver that 'sensation novels as a genre are perceived as feminine'[34] in that, even in fiction produced by male writers such as Collins, the vital focus is on forceful, venturesome and assertive women. Much recent scholarship documents how this 'sensational heroine' affronts the nineteenth-century discourses of women as weaker vessels or compliant conduits of a transcendent notion of femininity.

The chapter goes on to evaluate the female body as a specific site of cultural uncertainty in these novels, as well as the particular traits in the 'sensational heroine' that mark her off as more dangerously free-spoken and intransigent than those figures drawn by canonical writers such as Dickens, William Makepeace Thackeray (1811–63) and Anthony Trollope (1815–82). Were representations of the 'ill-regulated' or aberrant female protagonist as discomfiting to the reading public as we might assume? An early study, *Corrupt Relations: Dickens, Thackeray, Trollope, Collins and the Victorian Sexual System* (1982) by Richard Barickman, Susan MacDonald and Myra Stark, implies one way in which this comparative question might be scrutinized. Another might be to test whether sensationalists evinced 'a conservative modernity', in that they queried the laws governing marriage as a form of legal servitude for women but psychologically were unable – or unwilling – to progress towards a more outspoken and demanding stance.[35]

Among the more ephemeral titles of the period that reflect authors' resolve to portray female sexuality with unprecedented candour – *Woman Against the World* (1864), *Which Shall it Be?* (1866), *Hidden Fire* (1867) – it is *Treason at Home* (1865) which supplies the 'bridge' to Chapter Five. The elaboration of the female body as a source of corruption in sensation fiction also expresses disquiet about the mid-Victorian 'body politic' and the security of the 'homeland'. Here I explore a range of approaches to the dizzying modernity and topicality of sensationalism, and how 'the presence of the present',[36] in Richard Altick's memorable phrase, affects the genre's ominous delineation of the domestic sanctuary. The deployment of nervousness in these texts – revealed in its protagonists, elicited in its audience – is a complicated reaction to a metropolitan experience of cognitive dissonance in the face of radically reconfigured relations among urban, national, and global terrains as imperial rapacity fused with nineteenth-century capitalism. The chapter concludes by focusing on the sensation novel's coding of the foreign interloper at a time when empire building was at the very forefront of public consciousness.

Chapter Six furnishes a chronological reading of the sensation novel's influence throughout the latter half of the nineteenth century. This chapter opens by considering the strange case of Joseph Sheridan Le Fanu, whose novel *Uncle Silas: A Tale of Bartram-Haugh* (1864), published at the height of the sensation vogue, has been viewed as both a single-minded continuation of an older Gothic tradition and a harbinger of *fin-de-siècle* uncanny strategies. David Punter and Neil Cornwell assert that Le Fanu, rather than following an existing literary fad, actually instigated a new technique of writing about psychological terror that pushed the sensation genre towards the symbolist novel and the later fiction of Henry James (1843–1916).[37] This makes Le Fanu an especially rewarding case study in a wide-ranging account of the sensation legacy.

Andrew Maunder counsels against talking of 'sensation fiction as though it were all of a single type or of equal merit'.[38] This work encourages us to think about the problems of labelling, and how the genre becomes a phantom presence in novels by more established late-Victorian writers. We can locate sensational echoes in the writings of George Meredith (1828–1909), Anthony Trollope, George Eliot (1819–80), Thomas Hardy, Rhoda Broughton (1840–1920), Ouida (Mary Louise de la Rame or Ramée 1839–1908), and Dora Russell (1874–1907). This survey of the mutation of sensation is brought into the early-twentieth century via Joseph Conrad (1857–1924) who impeaches the social, political and ethical relevance of the genre. My final chapter ends by gesturing towards the genre's resurgence in the work of contemporary authors, especially the so-called neo-sensation school.[39] The proliferation of fictional accounts of the Victorian period in the last few decades constitutes an ambitiously diverse and textured portrait of an era that continues to captivate the contemporary imagination.

CHAPTER ONE

The Rise, Fall and Revival of Sensation Fiction

The genesis of sensation

> A class of literature has grown up around us, usurping in many respects, intentionally or unintentionally, a portion of the preacher's office, playing no inconsiderable part in moulding the minds and forming the habits and tastes of its generation; and, doing so principally, we had almost said exclusively, by 'preaching to the nerves.' [...] works of this class manifest themselves as belonging [...] to the morbid phenomena of literature – indications of a widespread corruption, of which they are in part both the effect and the cause; called into existence to supply the cravings of a diseased appetite, and contributing themselves to foster the disease, and to stimulate the want which they supply. [...] No divine influence can be imagined as presiding over the birth of [the sensation writer's] work, beyond the market-law of demand and supply; no more immortality is dreamed of for it than for the fashions of the current season. A commercial atmosphere floats around works of this class, redolent of the manufactory and the shop. The public wants novels, and novels must be made – so many yards of printed stuff, sensation-pattern, to be ready by the beginning of the season.
>
> ([H. L. Mansel], 'Sensation Novels', *Quarterly Review*,
> 113, April 1863, pp. 495–96)

In April 1863, Henry Longueville Mansel launched in the pages of the *Quarterly Review* (a solemn repository of reactionary sentiment) one of the most wide-ranging and vehement attacks on sensation fiction published in the 1860s. The *OED* first attributes the term 'sensation novel' to Mansel, but it had appeared in print earlier.[1] Mansel asserts that the secularized mysteries of sensationalism – 'preaching to the nerves' – are threatening the claims of orthodox religion. While he mentions a few sensation novels that deal directly with religious subjects (e.g., *Philip Paternoster: A Tractarian Love Story* [1858] by Charles Maurice Davies [1828–1910]), his larger point is that religious discourse imbues the genre less as content and more as form. The rhetorical persuasions of the pulpit are now displaced onto the pages of these sensational sermons – exercises in habitual stimulation 'moulding minds', 'forming tastes and habits.' This fiction triggers, according to Mansel, the same embodied nervous responses in its readers that the protagonists registered in sensational episodes.

Mansel's judgement indicates, among other things, deep misgivings about cultural production and the cross-fertilization between sanctioned modes of Victorian realism – exemplified by the novels of W. M. Thackeray and George Eliot for instance – and illegitimate fiction rising from underclass print culture. For Mansel, literary sensationalism stimulates a 'craving' for escapist solace that dissolves any distinction between the light reading habits of a leisured, overwhelmingly middle-class female audience on the one hand and the coarse mass entertainment of a newly literate working-class audience on the other.[2] As Chapter Three will show, the sober rationality associated with middle-class manners was acutely vulnerable to the 'lower' appetites characteristic of the inner-city proletariat. Mansel goes on to explain that the circulating libraries, railway bookstalls and serial publication were primarily to blame for this 'disease' of compulsive, indiscriminate reading.

For Mansel and other watchdogs of dominant culture, sensation fiction, with its accents of 'market-law' desire and 'shop-talk' idiom, implicates 'works of this class' within a system of cultural stratification. His magisterial disavowal of material conditions in the context of the literary rehearses the elevation of culture above political ambition and commercial acumen, a view endorsed by Matthew Arnold (1822–88), John Ruskin (1819–1900), and Thomas Carlyle (1795–1881). Like the hierarchical classification of Western and primitive peoples, Mansel connotes that the 'sensation-pattern' is promulgated by a lesser species, whose aggressive ignorance and 'morbid' tendencies must be monitored with tireless rigour. While he treats the sensation novel as ephemeral output, mechanical and manufactured writing, it paradoxically exerts a formidable and agitating influence over the populace, 'preaching to the nerves' its message of moral atrophy.

In Mansel's account the addictive drug of sensationalism is an index of a collective cultural nervous debility, since responses to it produce a network of associations that fuse its deleterious physiological effect on readers and its unsavoury narrative strategies. A sign of the 'commercial atmosphere' that 'floats' around these works is the subordination of character motivation to fluidity of plotting which is calculated to excite overwrought feelings. To G. H. Lewes, this genre depends not only on trite manoeuvres, but also on a 'breathless rapidity of movement; whether the movement be absurd or not matters little, the essential thing is to keep moving.'[3] Mansel concurs, since a sensation novel

> ■ abounds in incident. Indeed, as a general rule, it consists of nothing else [...] The human actors in the piece are, for the most part, but so many lay-figures on which to exhibit a drapery of incident. Allowing for the necessary division of all characters of a tale into male and female, old and young, virtuous and vicious, there is hardly anything said or done by any one specimen of a class which might not with equal fitness be said or done by any other specimen of the same class. Each game is played with the same pieces, differing only in the moves.[4] □

Mansel focuses on the needlessly complicated unravelling of 'incident' hinging upon improbable coincidence and chance. What he views as the genre's reliance on shop-soiled histrionics was combined with its unwholesome interest in deviant figures to elicit a heightened uneasiness from the audience. In a charge typical of attacks on popular culture, then as now, Mansel accuses the sensation genre of being numbingly dull (as lacking in all variety) at the same time as he decries it as hyper-stimulating. So the only differences among such novels, he avers, lie in the species of sensation at which they aim:

> ■ A great philosopher has enumerated in a list of sensations 'the feelings from heat, electricity, galvanism, &c.' together with 'titillation, sneezing, [...] shuddering, the feeling of setting the teeth on edge, &c;' and our novels might be classified in like manner, according to what sensation they are calculated to produce. There are novels of the warming pan, and others of the galvanic battery type – some which gently stimulate a particular feeling, and others which carry the whole nervous system by steam.[5] □

Like pornography or its more naive twin, melodrama, the sensation novel was thought by Mansel to conjure up a corporeal rather than a cerebral response in the reader. Alison Winter's notion in *Mesmerized: Powers of Mind in Victorian Britain* (1998) that 'the route from page to nerve was direct'[6] conveys how these sensations bypass an intermediary stage of mental reflection to dismantle the border between fiction and physiology. Nor did the pornographic connection go unmade: Margaret Oliphant, as Chapter Four indicates, believed that representing the 'appetite' for 'sensuous raptures' among the female protagonists of these novels 'as the natural sentiment of English girls' was an unhealthy and pernicious 'practice'.[7] Indeed, *Punch* devised a parodic prospectus for an invented journal called *The Sensation Times*. The sensational 'product' was described as: 'devoted to Harrowing the Mind, making the Flesh Creep [...] Giving Shocks to the Nervous System, Destroying Conventional Moralities, and generally Unfitting the Public for the Prosaic Avocations of Life.'[8]

Punch's impish wit plays on several key moments in sensation fiction: before his fateful meeting with Anne Catherick on the road to London, Walter Hartright in Collins's *The Woman in White* is already, like many of the novel's other characters, in a 'restless frame of mind and body';[9] the conniving anti-heroine of Collins's *Armadale* (1866), Lydia Gwilt, also seems to suffer in this way, asking her accomplice, Mother Oldershaw, to send her laudanum to stop her grinding her teeth in her sleep. Lady Audley, in Braddon's *Lady Audley's Secret,* is 'nervous' to the point of madness, and ends her days in a private nursing home. Doctor Downward in *Armadale* at one point voices a sentiment that is amply borne out by the genre as a whole, that they 'live in an age when nervous derangement' is 'steadily on the increase.' This insistent appeal to the nerves which forms the centrepiece of Mansel's scornful survey of sensationalism became a trademark of the genre according to D. A. Miller in *The Novel and the Police* (1988): 'The genre offers us one of the first instances of modern literature to address itself primarily to the sympathetic nervous system, where it grounds its characteristic adrenaline effects: accelerated heart rate and respiration, increased blood pressure, the pallor resulting from vasoconstriction, and so on'.[10]

Henry Mansel's terms shaped much antagonistic contemporary criticism of the genre: the *Christian Remembrancer* argued that sensation fiction was capable of 'drugging thought and reason [...] stimulating the attention through the lower and more animal instincts.'[11] In the *Athenaeum*, Geraldine Jewsbury described these narratives as 'fantastic and unwholesome as the smoke which curls up from the puffing pipe of the smoker of hashish.'[12] The 1866 *Westminster Gazette* registered with unfeigned dismay the emergence of a 'Sensational Mania' that was little better than an atavistic throwback to forms of medieval madness:

> ■ There is no accounting for tastes, blubber for the Esquimaux, half-hatched eggs for the Chinese, and Sensational novels for the English. [...] Just as in the Middle Ages people were afflicted with the Dancing Mania and Lycanthropy, sometimes barking like dogs, and sometimes mewing like cats, so now we have a Sensational Mania. Just, too, as those diseases always occurred in seasons of dearth and poverty, and attacked only the poor, so does the Sensational Mania in Literature burst out only in times of mental poverty, and afflict only the most poverty-stricken minds.[13] □

Mansel's judgement – like these other pundits – is rooted in a wilful misapprehension of the core themes and aims of sensation novelists. In Mansel's opinion, writers such as Braddon and Collins merely assail 'the nerves' of the 'public'. But the 'craving' that Mansel deplores was symptomatic of something more profound and far-reaching than the malicious boredom and 'diseased appetite' of mid-Victorian writers and readers. As Chapter Two of this Guide will demonstrate, these novels dramatised domestic upheaval and transgressions at a time when the laws governing marriage and divorce in England were subject to searching critique and drastic reform.

The sensation genre, along with its conspicuous commercial success noted by Mansel, seemed to be a mushroom growth on the literary scene, emerging as 'a distinctly novel kind of novel' according to John Sutherland's essay 'Wilkie Collins and the Origins of the Sensation Novel' (1991).[14] However, M. E. Braddon's *The Doctor's Wife* (1864) asserts the mongrel nature and demotic origins of a genre that had been in circulation for much longer than its name:

■ That bitter term of reproach, 'sensation', had not yet been invented for the terror of romancers in the fifty-second year of this present century; but the thing existed nevertheless in divers forms, and people wrote sensation novels as unconsciously as Monsieur Jourdain talked prose [... These] highly-spiced fictions enjoyed an immense popularity amongst the classes who like their literature as they like their tobacco – very strong [...] a public that bought its literature in the same manner as its pudding – in penny slices.[15] □

Braddon's wry assessment was reinforced by the 1863 article 'Not a New Sensation' in *All the Year Round*:

■ It is much the fashion now to dwell with severity on certain morbid failings and cravings of the grand outside Public – the universal customer – the splendid bespeaker, who goes round every market, purse in hand, and orders plays, poems, novels, pictures, concerts and operas. Yet this taste for fiery sauces and strongly-seasoned meats and drinks is of very ancient date, nay, with the public – so long as it has been a public – it has been a constant taste.[16] □

The 'morbid cravings' noted here evoke Mansel's polemical assault on the sensation novel as the opiate of leisure hours. However, in her articles for *Blackwood's Edinburgh Magazine*,[17] Margaret Oliphant claimed that the Brontë sisters – especially, she thought, Charlotte Brontë (1816–55) – were the true progenitors of the female sensationalism of M. E. Braddon, Rhoda Broughton and Ellen Wood. Reviewing *Great Expectations* in the May 1862 *Blackwood's*, Oliphant opined that Charles Dickens had inspired the genre's male practitioners, Collins and Charles Reade, whose work Dickens's periodical *All the Year Round* had published.

Though Oliphant's rhetoric is more restrained than that of Mansel, she shares his concern about the capacity of this genre to 'stimulate' an appetite for unnatural spectacle. As long as it occupied the limelight, the sensation novel's exploitation of murders, madness and vice for plotting would have a disastrous effect on the readership:

> ■ The rise of a Sensation School of art in any department is a thing to be watched with jealous eyes but nowhere is it so dangerous as in fiction, where the artist cannot resort to a daring physical plunge, as on the stage, or to a blaze of palpable colour, as in the picture gallery, but must take the passions and emotions of life to make his effects withal. We will not deny that the principle may be used with high and pure results, or that we should have but little fault to find with it were it always employed with as much skill and self-control as in the 'Woman in White'; but that is an unreasonable hope; and it seems but too likely that Mr Wilkie Collins, in his remarkable novel, has given a new impulse to a kind of literature which must, more or less, find its inspiration in crime, and, more or less, make the criminal a hero.[18] □

The 'new impulse' that Oliphant identifies connotes an electrical stimulus, and the 'electrical novel' was another label for the work of the sensationalists, appealing irresistibly below the level of mind to jolt the readers' nervous systems with turbulent feelings of trepidation and exhilaration. Underlying Oliphant's comments is a construction of leisure as a potentially hazardous time for the reader, when the brain is comparatively passive, the critical faculties dulled, and dubious narrative absorbed without being properly judged or sifted. In 1867, the *Contemporary Review* accused sensation novelists of 'studiously and of set purpose, seek[ing] to awaken our sympathies for certain types of characters by involving us in such circumstances as tend to set us in active opposition to some conventional moral regards.'[19]

To a bemused George Eliot, writing in a letter of September 1860 to the publisher John Blackwood (1818–79), the current craze for sensation meant that her own work was being edged out of public favour by slipshod exponents of 'trash' such as Braddon, whose novelistic debut *The Trail of the Serpent* (1861) was selling well:

> ■ I sicken again with despondency under the sense that the most carefully written books lie, both outside and inside people's minds, deep undermost in a heap of trash. I suppose the reason my 6/– editions are never on the railway stalls is [that they] are not so attractive to the majority as 'The Trail of the Serpent'; still a minority might sometimes buy them if they were there.[20] □

The lucrative market for six-shilling editions, available in railway waiting rooms, and for the even more avidly purchased two-shilling yellow-back editions of novels, was dominated by sensation writers.

Eliot's patronising disapproval of the genre, partially fed by material disappointment, was also anchored in aesthetic criteria. By categorising sensation fiction as 'trash' (Mansel also impugns the genre as 'mere trash') Eliot explicitly dismisses it from the realm of realist art that she had endeavoured so punctiliously to recreate in *Adam Bede* (1859) and *The Mill on the Floss* (1860). Eliot was by no means alone among Victorian authors in succumbing to what might seem today a mild fit of career envy.

Eliot's contemptuous remarks epitomize a widespread sense that the pull of sensation fiction was proving irresistible to the 1860s audience – the 'hard-won respectability'[21] of the realist novel was under assault. As Lillian Nayder points out, sensationalism tended to be construed as 'an artful literary mode'[22] and its apparent indebtedness to older (working-class) forms of popular entertainment led to its being perceived as a retrograde, but also as an incendiary, form. Eliot's letter signals how the sensation genre's wide appeal across the classes disqualified it as serious writing; nor did its frequent association with pre-packaged pot-boilers of crime, mystery, romance and the supernatural help matters. Patrick Brantlinger argues that 'the development of the sensation novel marks a crisis in the history of literary realism. At the same time that George Eliot was investing the novel with a new philosophical gravitas the sensationalists were breaking down the conventions of realist fiction.'[23]

Eliot's 'despondency' at the profitability of Braddon's work sheds light on how from the very outset, the sensation novel provoked heated debate and even hysteria among contemporary commentators for its debunking of the mimetic standards of 'Realism' in its original, nineteenth-century sense. To G. H. Lewes 'Art always aims at the representation of Reality, i.e. of Truth.'[24] Detractors of the sensation genre castigated the 'unnatural', 'artificial', 'false' and 'grotesque apparitions' which masquerade as characterization in these novels, invoking a naïve and narrow form of verisimilitude. It becomes the highest tribute to a novelist's skill to think of his characters as 'real, living, breathing' men and women, with whom the reader feels 'intimately acquainted.'[25] Without this 'intimacy' and this trait of lifelikeness, the characters fail, and with them the novels they populate. Braddon's creations are cited as evidence of 'her entire ignorance of human nature and mental processes'; Olivia Marchmont, of *John Marchmont's Legacy* (1863), is 'but a creature of Miss Braddon's imagination [...] unreal as a hobgoblin', while Lady Audley is 'scarcely a human being', though 'she may be a fine conception.'[26] Ultimately, 'when the characters in a novel cease to be true to nature, they lose their chief interest'[27] for 1860s reviewers who want companionable presences rather than literary constructs. W. Fraser Rae (1835–1905) in his essay 'Sensation Novelists: Miss Braddon' (1865) argues that

> ■ [i]nto uncontaminated minds they will instil false views of human conduct [...] A novel is a picture of life, and as such ought to be faithful. The fault of these novels is that they contain pictures of daily life, wherein there are scenes so grossly untrue to nature, that we can hardly pardon the authoress if she drew them in ignorance, and cannot condemn her too strongly if, knowing their falseness, she introduced them for the sake of effect.[28] □

At stake here is the preservation of the fictional illusion, so dear to the realist reviewers, presupposing grand laws that operate to ensure the order and significance of 'life-as-it-is.'[29] This realist vision, for Rae, is essentially a moral one. For these hostile witnesses to the sensation phenomenon, 'truth' and 'human nature' are constants; not only do they have an objective existence that can be scrutinized minutely and imitated by artists, they also obey certain innate principles, predictable and immutable. The 'fault' of sensation fiction, as Rae sees it, is to undermine the prevailing Victorian worldview, irresponsibly tampering with the perception of 'reality' and so recalibrating its traditional meaning.

Formally then, the sensation novel is a 'mixed mode',[30] demotic in provenance and democratic in its appeal. Neither realist nor idealist – 'neither exact nor exalting', according to the reviewer in *Temple Bar* – the genre 'represent[s] life neither as it is nor as it ought to be.'[31] However, as early as 1863, a contributor to Dickens's *All the Year Round* deplored how the term 'sensation' had acquired the quality of an instrument of the literary establishment, an 'orthodox stone' to hurl 'at any heretic author who is bold enough to think that life has its tremendous passes of anguish and crime, as well as its little joys and little sorrows, its strange adventures and vicissitudes, as well as its daily progresses from Brixton to the Bank.'[32] The defenders of sensationalism invoked the precedent of stage tragedy to justify the novelist's enterprise, which is 'to excite' in equal measure, 'all the strong and deep emotions that traditionally belong to the playwright'[33]

> ■ If any one writes a novel, a play, or a poem, which relates anything out of the ordinary experiences of the most ordinary people – some tragedy of love or revenge, some strange (though not impossible) combination of events, or some romance of guilt or misery – he is straightway met with a loud exclamation of 'Sensational' ! [...] life itself is similarly sensational in many of its aspects, and Nature is similarly sensational in many of her forms, and art is always sensational when it is tragic.[34] □

If the sensation vogue provoked some of the shrillest literary criticism of the period, it also inspired some of the most impassioned and provocative debate. The mere existence of the sensation novel, at the apex of the trend towards realism, raised fundamental critical problems for contemporary observers. Its amazing popularity alone challenged the critics to uphold, and, in the process, to reconfigure their own most basic assumptions and beliefs about the purpose of the mid-Victorian novel: its relation to the sensuous immediacy of felt experience and to observable fact, its non-mimetic components and appropriate aesthetic structures. Beneath the bluster of Henry Mansel's much-quoted review, is an initial and tentative search for concepts, a sculpting of critical vocabulary, so as to begin canvassing with new subtlety and precision the novel as a distinct form of literary art.

The 1860s: a sensational decade?

Some would have it an age of Sensation,
   If the age one of Sense may not be –
The word's not *Old* England's creation,
   But New England's, over the sea –
Where all's in the high-pressure way,
   In life just as in locomotion,
And where, though you're here for today,
   Where tomorrow you'll be, you've no notion.[35]
                    (*Punch*, Saturday July 20 1861)

Punch's light-hearted verse claims that the 'age of Sensation' was inaugurated by America's fascination for the new-fangled, in all its chaotic and gaudy splendour. However, George Augustus Sala (1828–95) construed sensationalism as 'that Cry of cries'[36] for 1860s Britain struggling to address the solemn implications of its own disorienting and febrile modernity. This was the primary sense in which Margaret Oliphant utilized the term in her 1862 review article, in *Blackwood's Edinburgh Magazine*, of three sensation novels: Collins's *The Woman in White*, Dickens's *Great Expectations*, and Ellen Wood's *East Lynne*. Oliphant registered how beneath the much-vaunted equipoize of mid-century, a fictional phenomenon had emerged which articulated the confused despair of an insipid and secularized culture, in which 'we recognise the influence of a system which has paralysed all the wholesome wonders and nobler mysteries of human existence.' Consequently, sensation was essentially made through grotesque exaggeration, as opposed to common sense experiences that occur naturally.

■ We who once did, and made, and declared ourselves masters of all things, have relapsed into the natural size of humanity before the great events which have given a new character to the age [...] It is only natural that art and literature should, in an age which has turned [out] to be one of events, attempt a kindred depth of effect and shock of incident.[37] □

Here Oliphant links the sensation novel with an anticlimactic retreat from an epoch of national self-congratulation and unqualified belief in progressive enlightenment, both moral and technological, that the Great Exhibition (1851) had typified at the start of the previous decade. Oliphant's articles for *Blackwood's* express a mood of lost faith under the 'shock' of renewed conflict, particularly the Crimean War (1853–6) and the American Civil War (1861–5).

Oliphant is also alert to how this fiction took its label from the contemporary theatre's 'sensation drama' and the accompanying displays of intense emotion and physical spectacle this encompassed.[38] According to Richard Altick, the direct source for the modern use of sensation is the term 'sensational scenes', introduced from America into the London theatrical vocabulary in 1860 to summarize the spectacular effects achieved in contemporary popular melodramas by the elaborate mechanical paraphernalia refined in the Shakespearean drama.[39] The sensation novel repaid its debt to the stage in adaptations of the most successful novels, but the new novels also lent themselves to stage parody: a burlesque based on Collins's novel, *The Woman in Mauve* by Watts Phillips (1825–74), appeared at the Haymarket in 1865.[40] Michael Booth's 1981 book *Victorian Spectacular Theatre, 1850–1910* supports Lyn Pykett's sense in *The Sensation Novel* (1994) that the 'mode of amplification and excess', the stylised dramatic tableaux and fevered emotions of melodrama, became 'a mode of producing the *material* world.'[41]

■ this was an age of increasingly spectacular 'special effects', exploiting dioramas, panoramas, intricate lighting systems and machinery of all kinds. Theatrical illusion and the Victorian machine culture combined in a new technology of representation. In short, this decade was a moment of consolidation in the 'era of the spectacle' – inaugurated by the French Revolution [1789–99], and consolidated by the Great Exhibition of 1851 and the International Exhibition of 1862.[42] □

When the sensation novel burst onto the literary scene at the start of the 1860s, it did so, according to Winifred Hughes's *The Maniac in the Cellar* (1980), in the character of a theatrical phenomenon, akin to 'a travelling-circus exhibition – prodigious, exciting, and agreeably grotesque'.[43]

■ The new sensationalism, judged more pernicious than its gothic and romantic ancestors, grafted a progressive approach to the Victorian bêtes noires of sex and violence onto the primitive and even childish formulas of stage melodrama, already tattered and threadbare. [...] The new genre had no perceptible infancy; its greatest triumph, as well as its masterpieces, coincided with its initial appearance. It sprang full-blown, nearly simultaneously, from the minds of Wilkie Collins, Mrs. Henry Wood, and M. E. Braddon [...] As long as it occupied the limelight, the sensation novel – brash, vulgar, and subversive – was viewed with undeniable justice as something of a literary upstart.[44] □

This account lends credence to John Sutherland's misleading later claim that the three iconic novels by Collins, Braddon and Wood 'exploded' on the Victorian literary scene in 1860–62 'like a bombshell.'[45] However, Collins's earlier novel *Basil* (1852) is a complex forerunner of sensation fiction, and other early works such as *Hide and Seek* (1854) and *The Dead Secret* (1857) might also be situated in this category. Wood and Braddon had likewise begun their careers in the early 1850s, writing tales of criminal intrigue and bigamy for monthly and weekly magazines, long before they secured popular acclaim in the 1860s. In that decade they refined their craft with a keen awareness of themselves not as publishing in a vacuum but as part of a wider and diverse community with deep roots in the literary field.

Hughes's seminal construction of a seemingly self-contained sensational decade underestimates how a significant number of very different kinds of Victorian novels can exist and co-exist but still be classified as 'sensational'. This raises the issue of which writers and texts are scrutinized, and of an accompanying tendency to associate the genre with the 1860s. Andrew Maunder's *Varieties of Women's Sensation Fiction: 1855–1890* (2004) amplifies our conception of what the sensation novel encompasses, as well as reminding us of the vast unexplored hinterland of literary endeavour which is rarely broached. A main feature to emerge from Maunder's extensive research is that there were myriad kinds of sensation novel, and the genre appeared 'hydra-headed' to its original critics.[46] *Lucretia* by Edward Bulwer Lytton (1803–73), loosely based on the career of forger and poisoner Thomas Wainewright (1794–1847), had scandalized readers in 1846;[47] bigamy novel by Sophia Crawford, *A Double Marriage*, appeared in 1851, its topicality cemented with a key scene set in the Great Exhibition; Noell Radecliffe published *The Secret History of a Household* in 1855; the same year that the career of Caroline Clive (1801–72)as a best-seller began with *Paul Ferroll* (1855), the story of an outwardly genteel man who has murdered his wife. Emma Robinson (1814–90) published *Mauleverer's Divorce*, a tale of marital abuse and syphilis in 1857, while *A Life for a Life* by Dinah Craik (1826–87), about a young man who kills yet manages to hide his secret, appeared in 1859, the story being told through diary entries in a way which pre-empted the more acclaimed *Woman in White*. The key point here, as Maunder eloquently establishes, is that the sensation novel resists glib containment within the single decade.

Although Hughes's *The Maniac in the Cellar* portrays the triumvirate of Collins, Braddon and Wood as exemplary sensation writers with recognizably individual temperaments, whose stylistic and representational techniques were much copied, it is not clear that all Victorian readers and critics were struck by the iconoclastic verve and novelty of their work as forcefully as Hughes and others have proclaimed.[48] In 1868, George Augustus Sala, writing in the *Belgravia* magazine (edited by Braddon), contended that,

■ The only wonder is that the charitable souls [some of Dickens's critics] have failed to discover that among modern 'sensational writers' Mr. Charles Dickens is perhaps the most thoroughly, and has been from the very outset of his career the most persistently, 'sensational' writer of the age. There is sensation even in [*The Pickwick Papers* (1836–37).] *The Old Curiosity Shop* [1841] is replete with sensation, from the extravagant pilgrimage of Nell and the old man to the death of Quilp. *Barnaby Rudge* [1841] begins with the sensation of an undiscovered murder, and ends with the sensation of a triple hanging [...]. In *Nicholas Nickleby* [1839] the end of Mr. Ralph Nickleby and the shooting of Lord Frederick Verisopht by Sir Mulberry Hawk are sensational enough to suit the strongest appetite.[49] □

Sala's catalogue illustrates how broadly the term had come to be applied by that time, and his comments throw into relief Mirella Billi's recent research into Dickens as the father of literary sensationalism:

■ [Dickens] undoubtedly created the genre, though there are differences between him and his contemporary 'rivals', whose work nevertheless he anticipated and decisively influenced, making the sensation mode an authentically new fictional form, away from the trend towards conventional realism [...] As early as 1837, after the success of *Pickwick Papers* (where ghost stories and plenty of sensational elements were inserted!), in *Oliver Twist* [1839] all the sensation elements are already present: intrigue, crime, mistaken or denied identities, the theft and hiding of papers, victims and persecutors. Everything originates in the 'respectable' family, the middle-class home, and the society of which it is the centre (the beginning of the novel is a grim description of a workhouse), which proves as cruel and violent as the London underworld, its inherent and complementary double. The two worlds are in fact inextricably connected by correspondences and oppositions on which the novel is tightly structured.[50] □

Billi proposes that Dickens furnishes the blueprint for 1860s sensation-alism, especially in his vivid evocation of an apparently irreproach-able and settled domestic existence where moral judgement, and any solution of the central mysteries, is vague, sketchy and ambiguous; obliquity and uncertainty are not completely dispelled by conventional or generally unpersuasive happy endings; identities – particularly fem-inine – are rarely definite; and the distinction between the domestic angel and the devious malefactress becomes blurred. Billi shows that the idealized family is disrupted by intrigue, lies, greed, persecution and murder, and if restored to peace and respectability, this often hap-pens by recourse to the law and after spectacular and devastating tri-als. Billi's key concern is to demonstrate how all of this is achieved through a sophisticated fusion of elements that strongly appealed to 1860s sensationalists, who continued Dickens's elaboration of literary modes: realistic narrative; journalism; melodrama; popular and street magazines; Newgate novels; stage melodrama; Gothic and fantastic tales; and domestic fiction.[51]

Billi's portrait of Dickens as the originator of sensationalism in the 1830s suggests how a full comprehension of this genre requires that we look throughout the Victorian period and not only to Hughes's conception of the 'sensational sixties.' This notation was partially fostered by those middlebrow magazine reviewers who were keen to publish obituaries of the genre towards the end of the decade. As early as 1868, one correspondent was already observing that 'sensationalism, as manifested of late years in fiction, has not so much been written down as written out. People have not so much protested against it as turned away from it in sheer weariness.'[52] Three months later, the *Saturday Review* professed to see in the latest sensation novels 'an unpleasant tendency to read like parodies.'[53] While the main practitioners, Wilkie Collins, Ellen Wood and Mary Elizabeth Braddon, continued to publish novels through the rest of the nineteenth century, and Collins, at least, continued to be widely reviewed and treated with a measure of polite respect, by 1870 the genre of sensation fiction itself seemed to have lost its capacity to stir up controversy.

While reviewers of Collins's later novels endeavoured to address his intricately structured and melodramatic plots, they ceased to wonder if those qualities were part of a general trend that was debasing the currency of literary taste, and more or less considered them as repre-sentative of Collins's own peculiar artistic vision. That the end of the genre is made to coincide with the end of the decade in these journalis-tic accounts has undoubtedly had an adverse effect on the way current scholars gauge Collins's post-1870s fiction.

In November 1889, just over a month after Collins's death, a lengthy retrospect by Algernon Charles Swinburne (1837–1909) appeared in the *Fortnightly Review*. Surveying the trajectory of Collins's career, Swinburne extolled the novelist's narrative ingenuity but

> ■ there are many, I believe, who think that Wilkie Collins would have a likelier chance of a longer life in the memories of more future readers if he had left nothing behind him but his masterpiece *The Moonstone* and one or two other stories [...] In some but by no means in all of his later novels there is much of the peculiar and studious ability which distinguishes his best: but his originally remarkable faculty for writing short stories had undergone a total and unaccountable decay. □

Swinburne deprecates 'the extreme clumsiness and infelicity' with which Collins plays the role of 'dramatic teacher and preacher'[54] after 1870. Swinburne paints a picture of a writer who compensates for diminished creative gifts by engaging in specific topical debates and probing the workings of modern institutions. Norman Page, writing almost a century later, emphasizes the story of a writer who suffers irreversible imaginative atrophy after the end of the sensational sixties:

> ■ More than a dozen novels were to appear during the last seventeen years of Collins's life, and about the decline in the quality of his work – variously attributed to ill-health, massive drug-taking, and over-productivity – there can be little disagreement. The view that he slipped into obscurity, forgotten by readers and critics alike, is quite unacceptable, however: there is no shortage of evidence that he enjoyed a continuing popularity during the 1870s and 1880s. Nevertheless, the legend was to grow up which presented a pathetic picture of the ageing novelist, lonely and forgotten, compulsively scribbling tenth-rate stories which no one cared to read.[55] □

This assessment prompts us to ask: why has sensation fiction, until recently, been dismissed by Patrick Brantlinger and others as an irretrievably 'minor subgenre of British fiction that flourished in the 1860s only to die out a decade or two later'?[56]

The demise of the genre

In 1863 Henry Mansel reluctantly conceded that sensation fiction was a 'great fact' in the literature of its day. Thomas Arnold the younger (1823–1900) observed in 1866 that 'the jaded palate of the habitual reader of fiction in our day requires more stimulating food [...] murder, theft, [im]personation, forgery, and the like.'[57] Arnold was struck by the rise of a new 'convulsional school' represented by the 'spicy' fast-paced narratives of Wilkie Collins, Braddon, *Recommended to Mercy* (1862) and *Such Things Are* (1863) by Mathilda Houston (1824–92) *Respectable Sinners* (1863) by Mary Brotherton, *Miriam May* (1863) by Arthur Robins (18??–1900) and Ouida's *Held in Bondage* (1863), a story of bigamy, adultery and imposture set in 'high' society. These were the books by depressingly 'like-minded writers' which had attained 'an unprecedented circulation' among the 'great and growing middle class'. Arnold saw no immediate sign that they would disappear from the literary landscape. Writers like Eliot and Thackeray were being unceremoniously elbowed aside, whilst readers were eager to forage for their 'mental food' in a new 'crop' of 'clever' novels.[58]

Thomas Arnold's snapshot of the mid-Victorian literary marketplace is intriguing, given that for most of the twentieth century almost all of the writers he enumerates as beneficiaries of huge popular praise were rarely featured on university lecture lists and all but vanished from library bookshelves. Andrew Maunder notes how Arthur Robins, chaplain to the Prince of Wales, was construed as one of the most confrontational novelists of the day, as was Mathilda Houston. Between 1860 and her death in 1915, Braddon published 85 novels under her own name and was lauded by Henry James as 'a soldier in the great army of constant producers.'[59] Yet, in the years following their deaths, 'they became ready candidates for critical oblivion.'[60] Moreover, the fact that so few of the second-generation Victorian sensation novelists cited above are remembered today obviously raises more questions about the virtual disappearance from literary history of a particular body of fiction, and inevitably about the way literary canons are moulded.

Collins was widely reckoned the 'Master of constructive fiction', who, as critics noted, counted statesmen among his devotees.[61] But thereafter Collins was identified as a writer of 'middlebrow' fiction, whose sizeable and diverse output met with 'inconsequent praise.'[62] This process of effacement began to function during Collins's own lifetime, as the writer himself realised when he scrutinized the biography of Dickens by John Forster (1812–76). Forster avidly underscored his own relationship with Dickens and downplayed the Collins link. Viewing himself sidelined in this manner irritated Collins and he referred to the biography as 'The Life of John Forster, with occasional anecdotes of Dickens.'[63]

While Forster almost systematically erases Collins from this biography of Dickens, it is the unquiet spirit of Dickens that haunts more recent 'appreciation' of Collins. T. S. Eliot exemplifies this approach in his long review in the *Times Literary Supplement* in 1927, 'Wilkie Collins and Dickens.'[64] Eliot is nostalgic for a more literary culture and the essay is as exercised by the baleful influence of the cinema as it is with calibrating Collins's artistic achievement. Eliot identifies 'the replacement of dramatic melodrama by cinematographic melodrama, and the dissociation of the elements of the old three-volume melodramatic novel into the various types of the modern 300-page novel.'[65] This dissociation of sensibility contrasts with Eliot's concept of a 'golden age' when

> ■ The best novels *were* thrilling; the distinction of genre between such-and-such a profound 'psychological' novel of today and such-and-such a masterly 'detective' novel of today is greater than the distinction of genre between *Wuthering Heights* [1847], or even *The Mill on the Floss*, and *East Lynne*, the last of which achieved an enormous and instantaneous success.[66] □

To appreciate Wilkie Collins, Eliot contends, it is necessary to 'reassemble the elements which have been dissociated in the modern novel.' In the nineteenth-century novel, drama had coexisted with melodrama and a comparative study of the novels of Collins and Dickens does much 'to illuminate the question of the difference between the dramatic and the melodramatic in fiction.'[67] All of this, on a cursory reading, appears favourable to Collins, but in the opposition he refines, Eliot privileges drama. To a great extent this dramatic quality captures the essence of the Dickensian novel and it is the imaginative fecundity of Dickens that becomes a cultural yardstick with which to measure, and ultimately belittle, Collins's art. The 'greatest novels' will always be read but, Eliot concedes, 'it is not pretended that the novels of Wilkie Collins have this permanence.' As far as Eliot is concerned, Collins's melodramatic narratives are really of importance only as an antidote to the gaudy excesses of the cinema and he is grudging even in this regard:

> ■ In *The Moonstone* Collins succeeds in bringing into play those aids of 'atmosphere' in which Dickens (and the Brontës) exhibited such genius, and in which Collins has everything except their genius. For his purpose, he does not come off badly. Compare the description of the discovery of Rosanna's death in the Shivering Sands – and notice how carefully, beforehand, the *mise-en-scène* [the setting] of the Shivering Sands is prepared for us – with the shipwreck of Steerforth in *David Copperfield* [1850]. We may say 'There is no comparison!' but there *is* a comparison; and however unfavourable to Collins, it must increase our estimation of his skill.[68] □

Eliot's response to Dickens reflects perhaps how novels such as *David Copperfield* cannily adopt many sensational narrative strategies while maintaining their canonical status as multifaceted and deeply pondered realist masterpieces. As Philip O'Neill notes in his book *Wilkie Collins: Women, Property and Propriety* (1988), 'Eliot is really a poor ally of Collins and the faint praise may have done more to condemn Collins to the critical twilight than would a sustained and polemical dismissal of his novels.'[69]

Joan De Jean and Nancy K. Miller's 'Introduction' to their study of canon formation, *Displacements* (1991), suggests myriad complex reasons why the majority of Victorian writers labelled 'sensational' were so little cherished in the first half of the twentieth century. De Jean and Miller register the profound shifts in aesthetic taste and comprehension expressed by how 'social preferences of a given cultural moment are erased, forgotten, and re-written by later generations.'[70] Suzanne Clark, in *Sentimental Modernism: Women Writers and the Revolution of the Word* (1991) construes this cleansing as much in evidence at the outset of the 'modernist' era:

> ■ Lest we think that the modernist separation of literature from the kitchen was politically innocuous, at worst resisting the influence of a mass culture that was all too powerful outside the domain of literature, consider what else was lost, along with the sentimental. The modernist exclusion of everything but the forms of high art acted like a machine for cultural loss of memory.[71] □

This 'cultural loss of memory' noted by Clark also informs David Goldie's account, in his monograph *A Critical Difference* (1998), of a widespread sense after the Great War of a desire for 'a fresh start' which 'helped accelerate the next generation's repudiation of its literary inheritance.'[72]

This disavowal was particularly strident in relation to female sensation writers, who struggled to adapt and find effective publishing venues after the decline in the 1880s and 1890s of the three-volume publishing format, which had been so ascendant at mid-century.[73] Elaine Showalter suggests in *Sexual Anarchy* (1992) that by the final decade of the nineteenth century the literary intelligentsia is striving to 'reclaim the kingdom of the English novel for male writers, male readers and men's stories.'[74] This perspective is elaborated by Gaye Tuchman and Nina Fortin, whose book *Edging Women Out: Victorian Novelists, Publishers and Social Change* (1989) identifies the years 1880–99 as 'The period of redefinition', when men of letters, including critics, actively redefined the nature of a good novel and a great author. They preferred a new form of realism that they associated with 'manly' literature – that is, great literature'.[75]

Tuchman and Fortin chart how this process effectively excluded women from a profession in which they had prospered during the 1860s and 1870s. Oliver Elton in his 1920 *Survey of English Literature* (1861–1945) judges that the varieties of women's sensation novel epitomized a 'species of absurd fiction' marred by 'simple-minded plots' and a 'governess mentality.'[76] In the middlebrow *Daily Mail* of 1924, H. H. W. Seaman, assessing the sensational legacy of the novelist Marie Corelli (1855–1924), felt that her accomplishment, such as it was, had been rendered redundant by history. Seaman's thesis reminds us that the sensation novel has been perceived, almost from the moment of its inception, as a peripheral, asinine and short-lived form, a genre so much the product of its 1860s context that it was unable to transcend that historical moment: '[Corelli] belonged to a great company of story-tellers, but the world they wrote about is gone. If the fame of some of them is forgotten it is because they wrote not for all times but for their own times. And times have changed'.[77]

Seaman's estimate reflects a highly charged literary climate of reinvention, stern rejection and partial salvaging of the literary past in which the sensation genre typified exactly the kind of negligible 'pulp fiction' that many members of Bloomsbury and the new literary cognoscenti of the 1920s and 1930s yearned to distance themselves from. The sensationalists' literary experiments were categorized as jejune and fustian; the authors themselves wickedly caricatured as cynical hacks, mired in the accoutrements of a sterile Victorianism and unable to speak eloquently and pointedly to a questing modern sensibility.

Malcolm Elwin (1903–73) in his *Victorian Wallflowers* (1934), intended as 'a panoramic survey'[78] but reading like a post-mortem of once-popular nineteenth-century writing, is a signal example of this process of haughty renunciation. Elwin (like T. S. Eliot) called for Collins to be acknowledged as 'an important novelist', whose *The Moonstone* was 'an ancestor of the modern detective story', but who possessed 'only the facile talent of the born story-teller' content 'to appease the popular appetite with works of competent mediocrity.' However, the 'literary merit' of female sensation writers 'was little above the level of the penny press':[79]

> ■ Collins, Mrs. Wood, and Ouida were novelists who successfully capi-
> talised the degenerate taste of the uncultured public [...] The end of
> Ouida's career is symbolic of the end of the Victorian era; she died in
> 1908, a tawdry, bedraggled scrap of derelict wreckage, defiantly wearing
> her tattered and old-fashioned finery in surroundings of accumulating
> ruin while raucously vociferating the wisdom of her superficial cynicism
> and ludicrously confident of her suppositious genius.[80] □

Andrew Maunder indicates that Wood's oeuvre has been almost completely shunned by scholars because it is construed as smugly moralistic and sprawling, too conservative, and thus 'unworthy of sustained critical attention.'[81] Elwin confirms that this view was established very early in the twentieth century when he refers to Wood as 'the most intrinsically representative woman novelist of the mid-Victorian era' who 'made no pretension to pose as a literary artist; she was simply a storyteller.'[82] However, as Maunder points out, Wood deserves more considered scrutiny precisely because of the striking 'contrast between her public and private faces.'[83] In reading Wood's novels, audiences consumed not just vivid and fast-paced narratives but also an iconic and carefully stage-managed construction of feminine authorship, one with momentous implications for subsequent generations of readers and writers of women's popular fiction.

Despite the fact that Malcolm Elwin's book was intended to rehabil-itate the work of these obscure Victorian novelists, he had no hope that they would ever be anything other than a touchstone of tawdry oppor-tunism in the literary marketplace. Obsessed by royalty cheques, ful-some reviews and ample audiences, their 'derelict' status was glaringly obvious. For later generations of scholars, Elwin's testimony implies, the sensation school could be little more than a dusty museum piece, or a bizarre episode in the stuttering development of public taste.

Critical rehabilitations

In the 1860s Henry Mansel reflected on the butterfly existence of liter-ary sensationalism: '[w]ritten to meet an ephemeral demand, aspiring only to an ephemeral existence.' On the whole, literary history has tended to validate Mansel's derisive evaluation. This was particularly true, as Lyn Pykett notes, of the women's sensation novel, given the propensity for popular texts by female authors to sink without trace within a generation of their first appearance. However, empirical research and the theoretical innovations of the last thirty years have not only redrawn the map of nineteenth-century writing but have also led to what Andrew Maunder calls 'an astonishing revival' in the anal-ysis of sensation fiction.[84] This project has been boosted by an accel-erating interest in 'popular' cultural forms such as genre fiction, and also by the emergence, since the mid-1970s, of a generation of seminal feminist commentators who have recalibrated the history of the British novel, resuscitating 'lost' women writers whose non-canonical status has been exacerbated by the difficulty of obtaining their work in fully annotated and affordable editions.

The genre is no longer perceived as irremediably irrelevant in nineteenth-century fiction but as a dynamic and dissident articulation of a new side to the mid-Victorian literary landscape. In *Sensational Designs* (1985), Jane Tompkins argues that the early twentieth-century scorn for what was construed as mawkish sentimentality, moral earnestness and melodrama in popular fiction by women, ignores the centrality of these conventions and their role in 'expressing and shaping the social context that produced them.'[85] The reappraisal has also involved moving beyond the potentially reductive assumption that 'the non-canonical text must be legitimated as subversive in order to be considered worthy of study.'[86]

The task of reassessing sensation novels with more concentration of focus was initiated by Kathleen Tillotson's 1969 essay, 'The Lighter Reading of the 1860s' in which she situated *The Woman in White* in relation to a range of contemporary sensation writing, much of it by women, which had long since vanished from critical view. Another early work, P. D. Edwards's pamphlet *Some Mid-Victorian Thrillers: the Sensation Novel, Its Friends and Foes* (1971) furnished a similar account of the sensation decade, examining the extreme critical response to the best-selling novels to ascertain why these writings engendered a cultural phenomenon.[87] Patrick Brantlinger's 1982 essay, 'What is "Sensational" about the "Sensation novel"?' synthesizes and extends, but also deviates from these earlier accounts in several key respects. Brantlinger does not analyse the genre (which he proposes is an evanescent and 'minor subgenre') in order to restore it to its rightful place in a literary tradition from which it has been unfairly disqualified by critical misprision. His interest is in documenting the history of a particular cultural symptom. The term 'sensational' for Brantlinger pinpoints partly a specific kind of fictional content (bigamy, theft, adultery, murder), and partly a repertoire of structural components, such as the blending of domestic melodrama with Gothic romance, the refinement of techniques involving narrative secrecy and the subordination of character to plot.

■ At the same time that the narrator of a sensation novel seems to acquire authority by withholding the solution to a mystery, he or she also loses authority or at least innocence, becoming a figure no longer to be trusted. Just as character is subordinated to plot in the sensation novel, so the narrator is diminished by no longer communicating with the reliability of the tellers of more forthright tales.[88] □

Brantlinger scrutinizes the sensation novel from three 'different but complementary perspectives': historical, structural and psychological. These standpoints, singly or in diverse combinations, have imbued the bulk of subsequent research. Tracing the sensation novel's genealogy and status as a cultural fusion of different kinds of 'lower-class' forms, such as the 'Newgate' narrative,[89] as well as the 'silver fork' novel of criminal 'high-life'.[90] Brantlinger invites us to see this generic hybridity through the 'law of genre' of Jacques Derrida (1930–2004), which is a 'law of impurity and contamination', according to which the core element of any genre is impatience with, and a drive to undermine and destabilize, its own generic conventions. However, Brantlinger concludes that the mysteries of sensation narrative 'do not connect with anything outside of themselves', which leaves this 'minor subgenre' stranded, only at best mimicking 'aspects of serious fiction': on the wrong side of the cultural divide between great art and its formulaic, threadbare counterpart.[91]

Brantlinger's 1982 essay highlighted an issue that has dominated criticism since: the sensation novel's relationship to the tradition of mimetic realism which left its indelible stamp on the nineteenth-century novel. Brantlinger argues against the view promulgated by Winifred Hughes, and later by Jenny Bourne Taylor and Tamar Heller, that the Victorian sensation novel is a productively subversive riposte to bourgeois hegemony and the literary mode it selects to represent itself best. For Brantlinger, any subversion in this 'minor subgenre' is timorous and trivialising, with its writers' 'backing away from the deepest truths in their stories.'[92]

Winifred Hughes's *The Maniac in the Cellar* (1980) and Thomas Boyle's *Black Swine in the Sewers of Hampstead* (1989) were the first long studies of the genre and probed issues that also resonate through Brantlinger's seminal essay: how did mid-Victorian reviewers specify the 'propriety' of a literary text? How did labelling a narrative as 'sensational' marginalize, manage or contain its transgressive potential, precluding it from sustained scrutiny? How were the novel form, class ideology, and, often more surreptitiously, debates about national belonging and the fervour for imperial expansion entangled in nervous mid-Victorian reactions to these nagging questions?

Hughes's *The Maniac in the Cellar* reads Collins's fiction alongside that of M. E. Braddon and Ellen Wood in relation to mid-Victorian critical controversies and literary strategies. However, despite the genre's indebtedness to the discursive modes noted by Brantlinger, Hughes gauges it as a unique experiment, and anchored in 'propinquity', that is, the setting is in the time and place of the intended readership: 'What distinguishes the true sensation genre, as it appeared in its prime during the 1860s, is the violent yoking of romance and realism, traditionally the two contradictory modes of literary perception'.[93]

Through its 'violent yoking' of opposites, Hughes contends that the sensation novel operates as an audacious assault on the hypocritical and stagnant traditions of mid-Victorian gentility. Boyle, on the other hand, implies there may be less of a gulf between sensation fiction and its contemporary discourses of actuality. He chronicles his surprise, in the initial stages of his project, to find that a standard mid-Victorian newspaper 'was sensational to say the least, certainly not supportive

of an image of domestic tranquillity. *The Times* of January 3, 1857 [...]
featured an account of "The Double Murder of Children in Newington";
a lead article on "Robberies and Personal Violence"; an extended rendi-
tion of "A Week of Horror." '[94]

Boyle's book denotes that the 'sensational' was more complexly
embedded in mid-Victorian culture's comprehension of itself than
had been acknowledged hitherto. His enterprise endorses Charles
Reade's perception that sensational novels were, to a significant
degree, 'studies from the life', elaborating the popular newspapers
which were as graphically explicit in their rendering of sexuality and
bloodshed as their fictional counterparts, often even more so. Richard
Altick concurs, arguing in *Victorian Studies in Scarlet* (1970) that fiction,
'however sensationalised, could be regarded as a faithful transcript
of contemporary life: there were the newspapers to prove it. They
added verisimilitude to extravagance, and thus made the extravagant
credible.'[95] As a result, these novels owed their imaginative verve to
other factors than that of being the only refuge from the stultifying
norms of mid-Victorian decorum.

Boyle and Altick address how sensation fiction, couched in the
popular frames of marital abandonment, domestic abuse and bigamy,
explicitly treated themes that were eschewed by so-called morally
stringent, 'realist', 'high' literature. Both critics evaluate this generic
taxonomy by reappraising the dichotomies that situate sensation
beyond the pale of and antagonistic to 'truth', positing a much closer
relationship between the genres, exploring the ways in which sensation both emerged from and reconfigured realist narrative. This is
not Patrick Brantlinger's concept of a crisis in literary realism, but a
salutary revision of realist procedures, that long outlasted sensation's
ostensibly transient and tenuous hold over public appetite.

Hughes's *The Maniac in the Cellar* gave prominence to women
writers of sensation fiction, following Elaine Showalter's *A Literature
of Their Own* (1977), which argued that women's sensation fiction was
a 'genuinely radical protest against marriage and women's economic
oppression.'[96] Showalter and Hughes, along with Sally Mitchell's *The
Fallen Angel* (1981) and Ellen Miller Casey's essay 'Other People's
Prudery' (1984)[97] have become standard sources for feminist investigations of the sensation genre. During the 1980s, an increasing
number of specialists began to refine cultural and gender-based
interpretation of the novels, which changed our perception of what
is peripheral and what is core, developing the relationship of – and
boundaries between – high and low (popular) art. In addition to
these revisionist readings, D. A. Miller, in a 1986 essay on *The Woman
in White*, applied queer theoretical approaches to sensation fiction, by
noting the 'homosexual component given to readerly sensation by

the novel', pointing to both male homoerotic and lesbian elements in the text.[98]

It is a testament to the sensation genre's growing academic legitimacy that these scholars have become less concerned with the inherent or 'timeless' value of literature, and more absorbed in the ideological work that it performs, confronting urgent contemporary issues such as urban crime, alcoholism, class unrest, and fiery debates over women's domestic function and responsibilities. As Ann Cvetkovich points out in *Mixed Feelings* (1992): '[t]he sensation novel, and sensationalism more generally, makes events emotionally vivid by representing in tangible and specific terms social and historical structures that would otherwise remain abstract.'[99] Feminist accounts of the genre also supply a context for Jenny Bourne Taylor's incisive critique of Wilkie Collins's employment of the sensation narrative to negotiate the contradictions of contemporary discourses about consciousness, identity and the social formation of the self.

In the 1990s, research by scholars such as Tamar Heller, Catherine Peters, Lyn Pykett, Cvetkovich and Lillian Nayder, continues to further our knowledge of the genre, its authors, and the cultural contexts to which they reacted. Andrew Maunder's excellent series, *Varieties of Women's Sensation Fiction, 1855–1890* (2004), issues up-to-date critical editions of out-of-print novels by Florence Marryat (1837–99), Felicia Skene (1821–99), Rhoda Broughton, Mary Cecil Hay and Dora Russell (1874–1907), who all became household names in the latter half of the nineteenth century but who continue to suffer severe critical and popular neglect, having been effectively 'written out of histories of Victorian fiction',[100] even though their work offers a multifaceted response to women's disenchantment with their limited gender roles within the family and in society at large. Maunder avers in his 'General Introduction' that recent investigation has helped consolidate the genre's place in a more diverse canon of nineteenth-century fiction:

> ■ It is now acknowledged that if sensation fiction is cut out of the picture it is impossible to gain an accurate sense of nineteenth-century historiography and of what the Victorian novel meant to the Victorians, not only the reading public but also in terms of cross-influences between writers, as well as our knowledge of the development of mass market [...] fiction. Sensation fiction and the critical furore it provoked is now seen as a key event in the nineteenth century, involving some of the wider cultural and social preoccupations of the mid-Victorian period.[101] □

Maunder chronicles the extent to which the study of sensation fiction has benefited from an array of twentieth-century methodologies as scholarly tools – the resurgence of Marxist criticism as a mode of intellectual inquiry; psychoanalysis; post-colonialism; the readings of crime and punishment developed from the ideas of Michel Foucault (1926–84), gender studies – whilst being analysed for their historical significance and the contemporary ideas they can be seen to contain. Deconstruction, which canvasses the collapse and transgression of boundaries, asking about the place of these functions in discursive procedures, is well suited to gauge the sensation novel's frequently mischievous disruption of social and legal codes. Clear evidence of the rehabilitation of sensation fiction as a 'key' literary 'event' is afforded by the fact that nearly a dozen of Collins's novels have been marketed in the Oxford World's Classics series. A complete collection of his short fiction appeared in 1995, and two volumes of his letters in 1999. Andrew Gasson's *Wilkie Collins: An Illustrated Guide* (1998) gives readers an encyclopaedia of information about Collins and his oeuvre that rivals those devoted to Dickens and George Eliot.[102] As Lillian Nayder remarks, 'whether his novels are defended as canonical "masterpieces" or used to explore the contradictions and complexities of Victorian culture, Collins has emerged from the shadow of the "inimitable" Charles Dickens and come into his own.'[103] Arguably the most notable sign of Collins's newfound academic prestige was the decision of Princeton University Press in 1999 to bring out an edition of Collins's first and hitherto unpublished novel *Iolani; or Tahiti as it was. A Romance*, written in 1844 and rejected by Longmans and Chapman and Hall in 1845.

Wilkie Collins is not the only author to prosper from this diligent recovery work. Jennifer Carnell's Sensation Press provides scrupulously annotated editions of lesser-known novels by M. E. Braddon and evangelical controversialist David Pae (1828–84). Essay collections published in the twenty-first century, such as Kimberly Harrison's and Richard Fantina's *Victorian Sensations: Essays on a Scandalous Genre* (2006) attest that sensation fiction 'continues to offer' us 'a plethora of research questions' as we endeavour 'to better understand the fiction that generated both a strong critical and popular response.'[104]

The initial focus of this Guide upon the contemporary reception of sensation has revealed that the genre's identification by its supposedly insidious habit of 'preaching to the nerves' was clinched during the height of its huge popularity in the early 1860s. Despite this awareness of a new 'convulsional' school of fast-paced writing, there lingered a contemporaneous disquiet about the plurality of traditions that fomented the genre, especially its aesthetic provenance in an earlier school of Gothic romance, as well as 'penny blood' publications and Newgate narratives, stage melodrama and the sensational journalism that reported criminal cases and divorce proceedings. As the following chapters of this Guide indicate, the Victorian sensation novel cannot be fully disentangled from these other literary and dramatic sources and forms, upon which it gleefully feeds to generate that 'plethora' of 'research questions' noted by Harrison and Fantina.

Returning to H. L. Mansel's anti-sensation diatribe which opened this chapter, it is apparent that the depiction of transgression denotes one of the most crucial 'research questions'. If 'a crime of extraordinary horror figures among our *causes célèbres*' Mansel remarked in 1863, 'the sensationist is immediately at hand to weave the incident into a thrilling tale, with names and circumstances slightly disguised'.[105] 'Murder, conspiracy, robbery, fraud, are the strong colours upon the national palette', observed Margaret Oliphant the same year, and, it seems, the popular novelists were keen to exploit the widespread proclivity.[106] Wilkie Collins's training as a barrister cemented an enduring fascination with legal matters; while Ellen Wood, according to her son, evinced a fervent interest in real murder cases.[107] M. E. Braddon was blasé about her own improper fiction and would even characterise it as 'most piratical stuff': 'The amount of crime, treachery, murder, slow poisoning, and general infamy required by the Halfpenny reader is something terrible. I am just going to do a little parricide for this week's supply.'[108] Mansel saw himself patrolling the boundaries of decorous taste; a custodian of civilized values against fiction whose relentless stress on – even glorification of – vice and scandal had to be curtailed at all costs. Andrew Mangham, in *Violent Women and Sensation Fiction* (2007), explains that theories of deviant behaviour, newspaper reports of turbulent events in the Victorian courtroom and popular sensational narratives had a massive impact on one another.[109] My next chapter explores these issues in detail, first of all by tracing the genre's obsession with secrets, and how this relates to crime, detection and policing – as well as the function of these latter activities in 'discipline'.

CHAPTER TWO

Crime and Detection

Secrets and lies

> Shall I trust you with his [Ozias Midwinter's] story? Shall I tell you his real name? Shall I show you [...] the thoughts that have grown out of my interview with him? [...] Or shall I keep his secret as I promised? And keep my own secret too, by bringing this weary long letter to an end at the very moment when you are burning to hear more!
>
> (Wilkie Collins, *Armadale* (1866), ed. Catherine Peters, Oxford: World's Classics, 1989, p. 603)

Lydia Gwilt in *Armadale* is, like her creator Wilkie Collins, an adroit manipulator of intricately plotted suspense, teasing the reader by delaying the anticipated revelation of secrets. Patrick Brantlinger calls this tactic of producing and prolonging mystery a type of 'narrative hide-and-seek': 'The best sensation novels are [...] as Kathleen Tillotson points out, 'novels with a secret', or sometimes several secrets, in which new narrative strategies were developed to tantalize the reader by withholding information rather than divulging it.'[1]

Thomas Hardy specified four key components of the sensation narrative in his description of his own foray into the genre, *Desperate Remedies* (1871): 'Mystery, entanglement, surprise and moral obliquity'. The 'moral obliquity' noted by Hardy is just one of the consequences of the sensation narrative's focus on what is hidden by the 'smooth varnish of cant'[2] – varying proportions and combinations of duplicity, disguise, fraud, forgery (often of a will), blackmail and bigamy, murder or attempted murder. *Punch*'s 1863 serial parody of sensationalism, 'Mokeanna', derided what it perceived as the emptiness behind this obsession with labyrinthine, cloak-and-dagger plots: 'Do you know that you remind me of a sensation novel; when the secret's out there's nothing in it?'[3] Lady Janet in chapter 9 of Collins's *The New Magdalen* (1873) hates 'all mysteries [...] And as for secrets' she deems them 'to be one of the forms of ill-breeding.'[4] Yet we collude with the culture of spying and subterfuge that pervades *Armadale*, which, according to

Hughes's *Maniac in the Cellar*, 'more than any other sensation novel [...] depicts an entire populace down on its knees before its neighbours' keyholes.'[5]

The secret in sensation fiction is more difficult to uncover given the habit of writers, according to *Temple Bar*, of substituting 'characteristics for character, and palming off the one for the other.'[6] Henry James diagnoses M. E. Braddon's Lady Audley as 'a non-entity, without a heart, a soul, a reason. But what we may call the small change for these facts – her eyes, her hair, her mouth, her dresses, her bedroom furniture, her little words and deeds – are so lavishly bestowed that she successfully maintains a kind of half-illusion'.[7]

James notes how speech, action, sartorial detail and demeanour bear the weight of character exposition in a genre that was specifically concerned with aberrant behaviour and extreme passions. Hatred, jealousy, fear and illicit love are worked to maximum effect without the benefit of disclosure of their internal processes. James, like many contemporary reviewers, felt cheated by a genre that specialized in practicing an elaborate fraud on readers through the exaggerated concealment of crucial data. But as Martin Kayman argues in *From Bow Street to Baker Street: Mystery, Detection and Narrative* (1991), secretiveness is not simply the source and subject of a sensation plot, but an intricate ordering principle as well:

■ [A]lthough secrets are indisputably an important ingredient in many sensation [...] stories, it is not true that they are the necessarily mechanical or specious centre. *Lady Audley's Secret* is an obvious case in point. If a sensation novel starts with a concealed secret, explores its dramatic consequences, and ends with its transformation from a disturbing lacuna to a plenitude of clarity and order, what, one might ask, *is* Lady Audley's secret? [...] Rather than being dissipated by the plot, the secret simply proliferates, denying us a signified which will exhaustively fill the gap it opens. Lady Audley's secret is, like [...] Collins's moonstone, most basically a sensational signifier, an absence which generates nervous and discursive reaction in the characters and the reader.[8] □

Kayman posits that the classification of certain kinds of writing as 'sensation' or 'detective' literature in the Victorian period emerged as a reaction on the part of the hegemonic force of nineteenth-century reformist zeal. As the novel's claims to the status of 'serious' literature began to depend more and more on the suppression of sensational subjects like transgression and psychopathology, writing that took up these subjects was subordinated and snubbed. Kayman maintains that these topics survive as the residual relics of deep cultural mysteries that could not be assimilated by the reformist codes of moral management (law and medicine) and stood as an affront to those codes. Kayman construes 'Lady Audley's Secret', for example – as he does Collins's moonstone – as an encrypted and dissident potency that fractures the cultural authorities dedicated to neutralizing the forces of misrule.

Kayman's argument evinces that Henry James's impatience with the genre derives from what is actually the efficacy of Victorian sensationalism in portraying how secrecy emerges from the opposition of public and private spheres, becoming, as Chapter Three will suggest, the founding principle of middle-class existence. Collins's narrator in *Armadale* reflects: 'We live [...] in an age eminently favourable to the growth of all roguery which is careful enough to keep up appearances.'[9] From the outset, reviewers commented upon the genre's presentation of criminals as seemingly refined and reliable members of civilized society. As the *Saturday Review* observed in 1864, 'the murderers and forgers and bigamists and adulterers are people like ourselves, such as we might meet any day in society.'[10]

Elaine Showalter, in her 1979 essay on 'Guilt, the Shadows and *Little Dorrit*', focuses on Dickens's distrust of his function as narrator and how it relates to the disappearance of a 'knowable community', the type of community that could be held together and comprehended by a single consciousness. The growth of the Victorian metropolis and shifting methods of conceptualizing social life eroded this totalizing standpoint.[11]

■ As the inquirer, the novelist, he felt frustrated by the 'profound secret and mystery' of the human personality. To be aware, as one walks through the city, that every house contains a myriad of secrets – a persistent theme in Dickens's later novels – is to be constantly teased by what Hillis Miller calls 'the opacity of other people.' Yet Dickens also feels a horror of the surveillant, of the intimate intruder who violates individual privacy.[12] □

Showalter indicates that the sensation genre, because of its tendency to undermine concepts of 'reality' by which 'truth' and human nature seem discernible and predictable, divulges an entire range of misgivings about the principles of openness and privacy, and the implication that everyone, no matter how socially privileged, has something to hide.

Towards the end of Braddon's *Lady Audley's Secret* the eponymous protagonist retires to her dressing room after a day of unusually busy criminal activity.

■ Amongst all privileged spies, a lady's-maid has the highest privileges. It is she who bathes Lady Theresa's eyes with eau-de-cologne after her ladyship's quarrel with the colonel; it is she who administers sal-volatile to Miss Fanny when Count Beaudesert, of the Blues, has jilted her. She has a hundred methods for the finding out of her mistress's secrets. She knows by the manner in which her victim jerks her head from under the hair-brush, or chafes at the gentlest administration of the comb, what hidden tortures are racking her breast – what secret perplexities are bewildering her brain. That well-bred attendant knows how to interpret the most obscure diagnoses of all mental diseases that can afflict her mistress; she knows when the ivory complexion is bought and paid for – when the pearly teeth are foreign substances fashioned by the dentist – when the glossy plaits are the relics of the dead, rather than the property of the living; and she knows other and more sacred secrets than these.[13] □

Feigning a headache, Lady Audley sends her maid from the room because she shares with her contemporary readers 'a mounting anxiety about the eyes and ears of servants in the home.'[14] 'Everything that you do and very much that you say at home', cautions an 1853 *North British Review* article, 'is related in your servants' families, and by them retailed to other gossips in the neighbourhood, with appropriate exaggerations, until you almost feel that you might as well live in a glass house or a whispering gallery.'[15] Through servants' curiosity and whispered innuendo, the private affairs of the family could become public knowledge. In *Domestic Crime in the Victorian Novel* (1989), Anthea Trodd asserts that 'the householder's outraged sense of routine invasion of privacy by his domestic staff expressed itself in the production of crime plots in which servants, so often inconspicuous in other kinds of fiction, routinely play highly visible and sinister roles.'[16] For Trodd

> ■ [s]ervants are perceived as the weak link in the maintenance of the privacy of the home, both as internal intruders and as publicists to the outside world. In the crime plots of the period this idea of endangered privacy is formulated as the household's dark secret which the servant may control or reveal. Such popular topics in journalism as the problems of household management and the role of the young housewife are sensationalised in fiction as the problems of controlling a household of spies and criminals.[17] □

While Lady Audley's secrets are especially incriminating, nineteenth-century periodicals and household manuals warn even the most genteel homeowners to beware the spying and eavesdropping of servants who could spread scurrilous rumour and lies to the populace. Trodd shows the degree to which sensation fiction plays upon middle-class fears about circumstantial evidence – the almost imperceptible traces and residues left in the wake of even minor transgressions. Anne Gaylin, in *Eavesdropping in the Novel from Austen to Proust* (2002) remarks of *The Woman in White*:

■ Eavesdropping – an improper activity on the border between inside and outside, private and public – figures transgression in [*The Woman in White*]. An eavesdropper steals the secrets of private life and controls their dissemination in the public realm; by withholding or disclosing people's secrets, the eavesdropper determines their social identity. In *The Woman in White*, illicit overhearing stages anxieties about and pleasure in the complex relations between gender, identity, and narrative and social agency.[18] □

Gaylin suggests that eavesdropping servants can exercise their own police powers. Mid-Victorian household manuals tried to counter these potential invasions of privacy by exhorting valets and chambermaids to hold the secrets of the family sacrosanct – or preferably, to ignore and forget those secrets altogether. *The Lady's Maid* (1877) broaches the very problems that it asks its servant readers to deny: 'If your master should be unfortunate in his temper, or in any of his habits, if you should hear harsh words, or see your mistress in distress, you are bound in honour to be as silent upon the whole matter, whether you are so desired or not, as if it were a secret committed to your keeping.'[19] James Williams, author of *The Footman's Guide* (1847), advises that there are

■ times and seasons in all establishments, particularly in a numerous family, when the domestics are bound by every consideration of honesty and honour to act with the greatest circumspection and prudence; when they must not observe what they cannot help but see, must not notice what they cannot help but hear, and when, although present, they must consider themselves absent.[20] □

Ironically, in warning servants not to 'observe', these manuals acknowledge and articulate precisely those guilty secrets – alcoholism, illness and domestic brutality – that middle-class households were so determined to suppress and which are woven into the imaginative fabric of sensation fiction.

If the home has a right to safeguard its privacy in an age when information culture is making speedy advances, an external intervention also becomes imperative to expose family secrets to the corrective force of public opinion. Sergeant Cuff in *The Moonstone*, believed to be a master of detective 'science', recollects of a recent case: 'At one end of the inquiry there was a murder, and at the other end there was a spot of ink on a tablecloth that nobody could account for. In all my experience along the dirtiest ways of this dirty little world, I have never met with such a thing as a trifle yet.'[21] In the most inconsequential of details, in the most ephemeral of moments, a power relentlessly exerts itself in the interests of discipline and order, revealing guilt and punishing squalid self-interest, corruption and chicanery. Collins, in *No Name* (1862), perceives this power as a force of nature, and even of providence itself: 'Nothing in this world is hidden for ever [...] Look where we will, the inevitable law of revelation is one of the laws of nature: the lasting preservation of a secret is a miracle which the world has never yet seen.'[22]

Who has the authority and influence to keep safe the secrets of the middle-class is a major question imbuing John Kucich's monograph *The Power of Lies: Transgression in Victorian Fiction* (1994). Distinct from studies such as Nina Auerbach's *Private Theatricals* (1990), Kucich's project considers deceit not as a mode of higher truth but, by maintaining truth and lies as separate ethical categories, as an 'arbitrary overcoding of one forbidden aspect of experience with psychic value.'[23] Kucich is not so much preoccupied by gauging how truth was produced for the Victorians as he is in determining who clinches the privilege of adjusting and finessing it. Instead of looking to the wrongdoing of a criminal underclass, Kucich focuses on the professional elite, social initiates, aesthetes and others who, through their exceptional 'dexterity with the truth' consolidate a position of prestige and patronage within the ranks of the bourgeoisie. Extending the insights into the sociology of knowledge furnished by Alexander Welsh's *George Eliot and Blackmail* (1985),[24] D. A. Miller's *The Novel and the Police* and W. David Shaw's *Victorians and Mystery: Crises of Representation* (1990), Kucich posits that 'the transgression of distinctions between honesty and dishonesty was pivotal in struggles for middle-class cultural authority.'[25] He presents an ostensibly truthful culture suffused in and addicted to fabrication and falsehood and asks, 'why did the Victorians *say* so insistently that they repressed lying?'[26]

■ Victorian fiction is as interested in the qualities, the categories, and the productivity of lying as it is in celebrating honesty. In a culture so preoccupied with truth-telling, an affirmation of lying – or a blurring of this ethical distinction – could be a powerful symbolic gesture. Rather than being simply the dark underside of official ethics, lying came to have an enormous range of positive cultural values for the Victorians and was crucial to Victorian thinking about the nature of power in a number of different areas. Lying was seen, variously, as a fundamental form of resistance to social control, as a way to recognise the presence and the force of desire, and [...] as a way to rethink the distribution of power across lines of social or sexual difference.[27] □

Building on Peter Stallybrass and Allon White's *The Politics and Poetics of Transgression* (1986), Kucich maintains that the much-vaunted

Victorian valorization of truth-telling, probity and confession was complicated and problematized by an intricately shifting and bitterly contested terrain of justified lying. Pairing writers of detective and sensation fiction such as Collins and Ellen Wood with 'realistic' novelists like Anthony Trollope and Elizabeth Gaskell (1810–65), Kucich demonstrates how all these texts participate in the endorsement of a moral and epistemological subtlety that redefined stable moral groupings without overthrowing altogether the categories of truth and mendacity – in actions such as Walter Hartright's adept manipulation of legal documents to establish the identity of Laura Fairlie and himself as her spouse in *The Woman in White*. This is an instance of what Kucich calls 'transgressive authority', greatly prized as a means of social resistance for certain emerging classes and which 'ultimately laid a new foundation for modernism's delicate appropriations of scientific and technical authority.'[28]

Justice and the law

In Ellen Wood's *East Lynne*, the solicitor hero Archibald Carlyle articulates what comes to be the definitive statement on the law's potential for error, oversight and caprice: 'justice and law are sometimes in opposition'.[29] Wood's novel stages a series of displacements – from courtroom to servants' hall – designed to wrest policing and judicial capabilities away from the assize courts at Lynneborough and reconstitutes those functions within the diurnal rhythms and rituals of the local community itself. Vagaries of the legal system indirectly initiate the two major plot complications of Wood's novel: Lord Mount Severn dies without making provision for his daughter Isabel, who is left penniless and vulnerable; Richard Hare finds himself wrongly accused of murder, convicted by 'the odium of circumstances.'[30] To underscore the erratic nature of the law, Wood presents a most outlandish example early in its story: Lord Mount Severn's creditors arrest his corpse for debt, a move that confounds even Carlyle's legal acumen.

East Lynne's narrative trajectory reflects the degree to which sensation fiction generally shadowed and foreshadowed the Victorian reformulation of attitudes to crime, and examined how the parameters of the new criminal system were delineated and violated throughout this period. This is evident in the complex legal plots to do with wills and the inheritance of property,[31] and with issues arising from women's lack of legal identity and rights: for example, the inability of married women to own property, and the inequitable nature of the divorce and child custody laws. Lyn Pykett, along with Jonathan Loesberg[32] and

Stephen Knight,[33] persuasively contend that the narrative structure of those three novels – *The Woman in White, Lady Audley's Secret,* and *East Lynne* – whose grouping together by Victorian reviewers produced the sensation genre and thus also the framework for critical discussion, reveals much about legal-political debates over parliamentary reform in the late 1850s and 1860s. Financial insecurity, fears about the chimerical nature of Victorian speculative capitalism, and worries that the seemingly solid material trappings of elegant middle-class life might have an all too brittle base are played out in numerous plots concerning deception and bankruptcy.

Traditionally, critics have argued that there were two types of sensation novel in its heyday. Firstly, what was sometimes termed 'newspaper sensationalism' frequently, though not exclusively, associated with male novelists; secondly, 'domestic sensationalism', linked with female authors. In *Black Swine in the Sewers of Hampstead: Beneath the Surface of Victorian Sensationalism* (1989), Thomas Boyle indicates that sensation novels of the first kind echoed the format of the earlier 'Newgate' novels (based on actual crime stories appearing in the *Newgate Calendar*). Boyle explores how the details of domestic poisonings, divorce proceedings, impersonation and bigamy trials were communicated to the ever-widening readership of the rapidly expanding newspaper press by the sensational reportage then enjoying a vogue, from *The Times* and the *Daily Telegraph* to early crime tabloids such as the *Illustrated Police News*.[34] Both Collins's *The Woman in White* and Charles Reade's *Hard Cash* draw on the contemporary furore over wrongful incarceration in lunatic asylums. Henry Mansel's 1863 article 'Sensation Novels' reflects on newspaper sensationalism and the growing dialogue between fact and fiction throughout Victoria's reign.

■ From vice to crime, from the divorce court to the police-court is but a single step [...] Let [the sensation author] only keep an eye on the criminal reports of the daily newspapers, marking the cases which are honoured with the especial notice of a leading article, and become a nine-days' wonder in the mouths of [...] gossips; and he has the outline of his story not only ready-made, but approved beforehand as of the true sensation cast.[35] □

Mansel assumes the tone of a judge passing sentence on sensation fiction's slavish dependency upon newspaper headlines and slogans as a source of titillation, offering readers a chance to live vicariously through the exploits of others. This reliance on sensation journalism negates any claim the novelist might have to narrative originality, given that avid crime reporters have already sketched out the plotline. The 1866 *Saturday Review* correspondent agreed with Mansel: 'the clever ladies who supply our circulating libraries' now 'reflect in their writings the change in the spirit and taste of the age, and go to Bow Street and the Divorce Court for their inspirations.'[36] Mansel highlights how the gimmickry of these novels furnishes 'close representations of events passing around us' and he cites as another example Mathilda Houston's novel *Such Things Are* (1862), and its indebtedness to 'the Road murder and the Glasgow poisoning.' Here Mansel refers to the cases of Constance Kent (1844–1944), 15 year old daughter of a customs official living at Road, in Kent, suspected of stabbing her three-year old brother to death before hiding his body in the family privy (1860); and Madeleine Smith(1835/6–1928), daughter of a Glasgow architect, who poisoned her lover by putting arsenic in his cocoa (1857).[37]

In 1862 Margaret Oliphant, halfway through the run in *Blackwood's Magazine* of *Salem Chapel*, a serial novel about the relations between a dissenting minister and his congregation, sought to enhance its popularity by making the minister's teenage sister chief suspect in a murder case. Oliphant's plot detail had clear echoes of the Road Murder, and Anthea Trodd has shown in *Domestic Crime in the Victorian Novel* what influence this investigation had on 1860s fiction generally.[38] Oliphant's recourse to the kind of police intrigue associated with the sensation genre was curious for she was a persistent and vociferous opponent of the genre. As Oliphant observed of Braddon's *Lady Audley's Secret* the 'fashionable' crimes of sensation fiction 'could only have been possible to an Englishwoman knowing the attraction of impropriety, and yet loving the shelter of law.'[39]

By 1862 the new police force created by Sir Robert Peel (1788–1850) in 1829 had been in existence for over a quarter of a century, and the fiction of this period suggests not only the accommodations, but also the deep resistances in middle-class attitudes to the force. Trodd asserts that Oliphant's *Salem Chapel* offers an especially striking demonstration of an anxiety about police intrusion into middle-class homes. If the sensation genre catered to a growing public fascination with crime and punishment, it also evinced a deep suspicion of the power that police officers wielded, as in Ellen Wood's novel *Mrs. Haliburton's Troubles* (1862). Hearing wild screams proceeding from a well-appointed home the constable on the beat enters the premises 'possibly to gratify his curiosity, possibly because he thought his services might be in some way required.'[40] Trodd explores the contemporary debates about the sensation genre's obsession with the role of the law in organizing and controlling the family.

■ [The confrontation] between a [...] policeman, intruder into the sanctuary of the home, and a young lady, representative of that home's sanctities [...] is significant in the fiction of the period. [...] concern with these two areas and the relationship between them extended well beyond the sensation novel proper. Gaskell, Dickens and Trollope, as well as Braddon and Wilkie Collins, explored these new possibilities of relation between the domestic and public spheres, and in their treatment of the encounters between policemen and ladies expressed the anxieties these new possibilities evoked. The encounter was fraught with problems for the writer. At one level these problems concern etiquette, uncertainties about the social status of the policeman, and the conversational peculiarities of being interrogated by a kind of higher servant or lower tradesman. Most significantly, the encounters betray deep fear about the threat to the world of domestic innocence posed by the new police world of subterfuge and surveillance.[41] □

Although the Detective Department of the Metropolitan Police was founded in 1842 with a membership of eight (two inspectors and six sergeants) and had risen to 15 by the time of its reorganization in 1870, its slow growth evidences, according to Trodd, the unease surrounding its creation. The whole Road case affronted the popular conception of the domestic sanctuary in the most violent manner imaginable. Trodd addresses a complex problem in sensation fiction: does this literary category thrive on bringing criminality and middle-class neighbourhoods into unprecedented and disturbing proximity? Or is it intent upon sanitizing and framing hectic disorder, so that readers might scrutinize the lurid spectacle – and surreptitiously enjoy it – from a cozy distance? At a time when fears about the possible police threat to the middle-class home had seemed to be receding, the Road Murder revived and strengthened that dread.

According to Trodd, Oliphant's *Salem Chapel* signifies that domestic disputes, however acrimonious, are best resolved within the family. In the police intrigue of *Salem Chapel*, Oliphant is able to express her anxieties about the kind of moral and social threat which she felt 'sensational' material represented, especially through its portrayal of the baleful influence of police detectives, who are little more than officious and misguided interlopers. The sensation novel is, Oliphant suggests, a literary institutionalization of the habits of mind of the new police force. Both the new genre and the new profession encourage the construction of ingenious hypotheses about the private lives of others, and regard their private agonies as a frivolous diversion. Elizabeth Gaskell made a similar case against the police authorities in *Mary Barton* (1848):

■ There is a pleasure in unravelling a mystery, in catching at the gossamer clue which will guide to certainty. This feeling, I am sure, gives much impetus to the police. Their senses are ever and always on the qui vive [on the alert], and they enjoy collecting and collating evidence, and the life of adventure they experience; a continual unwinding of Jack Shepherd romances[42] always interesting to the vulgar and uneducated mind, to which the outward signs and tokens of crime are ever exciting.[43] ☐

For sensation novelists seeking to present to the middle-class reading public a coherent image of the police as both resourceful and amenable there were difficulties to confront. In *Henry Dunbar* (1864), Braddon felt compelled to apologize for her detective:

■ If there is anything degrading in the [detective's] office, that degradation had in no way affected him [...] If, in the course of his duty, he had unpleasant things to do; if he had to affect friendly acquaintance with the same man whom he was hunting to the gallows; if he was called upon to wormout chance clues to guilty secrets in the careless confidence that grows out of a friendly glass; if at times he had to stoop to acts which, in other men, would be branded as shameful and treacherous, he knew that he did his duty, and that society could not hold together unless some such men as himself [...] were willing to act as watch-dogs for the protection of the general fold.[44] ☐

One problem lay in the working-class origins of the members of the force. Trodd contends that the challenge for Collins and others was to find a way to reassure their readers that the police could indeed neutralize the enemy without and within, but that their miraculous skills of surveillance posed no danger to the middle-class householder. Another problem lay in the police detective's continued availability for public hire. Trodd uses Sergeant Cuff, in Collins's *The Moonstone*, as a fictional example of this uneasy transition from private employee to public servant. He is personally requested from Scotland Yard and dismissed from the unsolved case with a generous cheque. He does then express a profound anxiety to pursue his investigations despite the opposition of his employers, but when he eventually returns to the case it is not from Holmesian zeal but to pay off Lady Verinder's cheque.

Collins's complex attitude to 'the Law' and its traditional custodians has dominated literary scholarship, especially since the publication of U. C. Knoepflmacher's 1975 essay 'The Counterworld of Victorian Fiction and *The Woman in White*.' Knoepflmacher makes a persuasive case for portraying Collins as a writer who revels in an 'anarchic and asocial counterworld as a powerfully attractive alternative to the oppressively formal and civilised world of conventional belief.'

■ Unlike Dickens, who would later urge his friend to respect the sensibilities of his Victorian audience, Collins never disguised his fascination with the amorality of the counterworld. In *A Rogue's Life: From His Birth to His Marriage*, a five-part novella published in *Household Words* in 1856, three years before the serialisation of *The Woman in White* in *All the Year Round*, he depicted with great relish a transported young convict's supposed confessions. Like the satirical Becky Sharp [in Thackeray's *Vanity Fair* (1848)], Frank Softly [...] shares his creator's delight in puncturing the pretensions of conventional society. [...]

In *A Rogue's Life*, Collins [...] teases the appetite for sensationalism of readers who belong to the same middle-class society that exiles Frank.[45] ☐

Dickens, who serialized much of Collins's work in his weekly journals, often felt the need to censor Collins's writing, and deplored his friend's 'tendency' to be 'unnecessarily offensive to the middle class.'[46] In Knoepflmacher's polemical scheme, Collins is figured as repeatedly antagonizing self-righteous reviewers by extending his authorial sympathies to quick-witted villains and villainesses such as Captain Wragge in *No Name* and Lydia Gwilt in *Armadale*. This critical perspective challenges the tendency to generalize Victorian middle-class pieties as absolutely hegemonic, by disclosing the covert or encoded rebellion in Collins's rendering of legal and juridical proceedings in his fiction.

Drawing on Knoepflmacher's essay, Winifred Hughes expresses her appreciation of the 'subversive ironies' and genial villains of Collins's fiction, which 'explores forbidden territories and releases hidden sources of energy.'[47] However, Knoepflmacher's identification of *The Woman in White* as a fiercely 'subversive' text that espouses the decadent, unruly 'counterworld' of Count Fosco and his belief in the fragility of social and moral identity is peculiarly problematic. In claiming Fosco as an enabling embodiment of the defiant nihilist so as to consolidate Collins's place in the literature of insurgency, Knoepflmacher oversimplifies the gender politics of *The Woman in White*. In the novel Fosco is actually *denigrated* for his exploitation of frail women such as Laura Fairlie and Anne Catherick, and for the subjugation of his once-venturesome wife, whom he converts from an independent feminist campaigner before her marriage into a mute and submissive automaton, mute and submissive.

For Walter M. Kendrick, in 'The Sensationalism of *The Woman in White*' (1977–78), Collins's novel is neither reactionary nor oppositional, but seems instead 'a landmark of ambivalence' which 'marks a tentative breach' of the laws of mid-Victorian realism:

■ The major sin of the sensation novelists was their breach of this realistic faith. By focusing the reader's attention on the chains that constitute a novel's plot, they made of fiction merely a game, an activity which dictates its own rules and which stands to the real world in at best an arbitrary relation.[48] ☐

Kendrick's critical methodology fuses a literary-historical contextual approach with a formalist fascination with the relation between plot, events, and narration. He argues that *The Woman in White* is distinguished from other fictions in the genre by its self-consciously puckish narrative that exploits the strategies of sensationalism while simultaneously demanding to be read as if it studiously follows 'respectable' realistic conventions.

Most recently, however, literary critics have contested Knoepflmacher's view of Collins the lone rebel, arguing instead that his fiction is not subversive enough. Since the publication of *Corrupt Relations* in 1982 – the collaborative project of Richard Barickman, Susan MacDonald, and Myra Stark – most studies of Collins have underlined his abiding political ambivalence while calling attention to the circuitous methods and 'strategies of indirection' he employs to package and qualify his social critique.[49] With the publication in 1988 of *The Novel and the Police* by the Foucauldian scholar of the nineteenth-century novel D. A. Miller, the conception of Collins as a 'dissident moralist',[50] and even Walter Kendrick's rendering of *The Woman in White*'s teasing and self-referential play with its own textuality, was not simply modified, but replaced by the image of Collins the strict social disciplinarian, whose novels serve a penitential and policing function despite their seeming capacity for impudent daring and dissent.

In *Discipline and Punish* (1975) Michel Foucault explores the shift from corporeal violence to juridical regulation through self-monitoring. The polemical momentum of the first volume of Foucault's *The History of Sexuality* (1976) resides in showing how proclamations of sexual dissidence, subversions of the supposed outlawing of deviant desire, are contained within the larger discourse of sexuality. Foucault, for whom the Victorian period affords the launching site for much of his research, contends that bold emancipatory pronouncements work with, not against, censorship and prudishness to bolster the proliferation of sexualities. These apparent opposites, he argues, 'are doubtless only component parts that have a local and tactical role to play in a transformation into discourse, a technology of power.'[51] For Foucault the formidable reach and efficacy of the discourse of sexuality is generated by its capacity to exploit both repression and sedition. This notion implies that Collins's challenge to the establishment may have been re-contained within it. Just such an argument becomes a core component of Miller's *The Novel and the Police*. Collins's *The Woman in White* and *The Moonstone* operate, as indeed the novel as a cultural institution does, 'to confirm the novel-reader in his identity as 'liberal subject', a term with which I allude not just to the subject whose private life [...] is felt to provide constant inarguable evidence of his constitutive 'freedom', but also to [...] the political regime that sets store by this subject'.[52]

Collins's fiction uses subversion better to accomplish this enterprise, according to Miller, who maintains that *The Moonstone*'s disavowal of the figure of Sergeant Cuff – and, by implication the national apparatus of governmental policing he embodies – furnishes a spectacle of subversion at one level to camouflage a reinstallation of Cuff at another: 'the move to discard the *role of the detective* is at the same time a move to disperse the *function of detection* [Miller's italics].'[53] *The Moonstone* enacts in miniature the sensation genre's general transmutation from being something that seamlessly weaves police work into its imaginative fabric to being something that operates like the police. Subversion here functions, as Foucault proposes it does in the discourse of sexuality, as an elaborate cover for the relentless amplification of 'discipline'. Foucault identifies 'discipline' as a diffuse and largely invisible mode of power that began to permeate European societies towards the end of the eighteenth century. Discipline is not enforced by any particular institution or leader, but rather consists of 'instruments', 'techniques' and 'procedures' and is thus impossible to resist. To illustrate the diffusion of 'discipline', Foucault describes the plans of the philosopher Jeremy Bentham (1748–1832) for the Panopticon, a prison organized around a central watchtower. In this prison, the prisoner is permanently visible, but uncertain of when he is being observed; as a result, 'he inscribes in himself the power relation' of prisoner and guard, and 'becomes the principle of his own subjection.'[54] Refining these ideas, Miller's book argues how the classification and marginalization of popular forms like the sensation and detective genres are effects of the culture of knowledge and power that generated them.

One of the strengths of Miller's concept of the 'radical *entanglement* between the nature of the novel and the practice of the police'[55] is the way it shifts the focus from appraising the opposition between 'high' Victorian realism on the one hand and the dissident 'other Victorian' literary underworlds of gothic, detective and sensation fiction on the other, to registering all these manifestations of the novel as continuous expressions – even agents – of a pervasive culture of social discipline. Rather than announcing the sensation genre as 'the illegitimate child of the realistic and the biographical novel',[56] this analysis confers upon it the status of a redoubtable literary and cultural project that imbues and secretly occupies those more traditionally revered forms. Miller juxtaposes readings of what have come to be considered 'standard detective texts'[57] (*The Moonstone* or *Bleak House*) with a classic work of Victorian realism (Anthony Trollope's *Barchester Towers*) and a seminal Victorian autobiographical novel (*David Copperfield*). Without disavowing the differences between such texts, Miller posits their essential equivalences in deploying 'representational technologies' that internalize in the novel-reading public (and more broadly in the nineteenth-century bourgeois self) the social practices of surveillance and regulation associated with the police force. Narrative form is given a disciplinary sway that is dispersed, disseminated and lacking a definable centre. Miller suggests that the detective plot displaces and effaces seemingly intractable social problems by rewriting them in simpler terms; once good and evil become readily identifiable entities, evil can be exorcized. Miller draws on the ideas of the Russian literary theorist Mikhail Bakhtin (1895–1975) to pinpoint in the workings of *The Moonstone* a 'monologism' that conveys the illusion of the resolution of ambiguities that is integral to the novel's discourse on and of power:

> ■ Unlike the majority of Victorian novels, *The Moonstone* is not related by an 'omniscient narrator', whose unimpeachable authority imposes itself on the reader. Instead, the story is told in a succession of narratives written by some of the characters and organised through their limited point of view [...] however, the 'unreliable' and 'contradictory' narrative structure of *The Moonstone* works only as a ruse [...] To use Mikhail Bakhtin's term, the novel is thoroughly *monological* – always speaking a master-voice that corrects, overrides, subordinates, or sublates all other voices it allows to speak [...] the monologism of the narration is exactly analogous to the work of detection in the representation. Just as a common detection transcends the single efforts of various detective figures, a common narration subsumes the individual reports of various narrators. The world resolves its difficulties, and language finds its truth, according to the same principle of quasi-automatic self-regulation.[58] □

In *The Moonstone*, Collins writes a novel in myriad voices, from a range of class positions, appearing to embrace subjectivity, unreliability and a sceptical relativism. Yet the dialogism of the novel proves to be a convoluted ploy, in Miller's opinion: Collins may utilize diverse narrators each with his or her own foibles, but all are subsumed in and corrected by 'a master-voice.' Miller's analysis has contributed to a notable revisionist enterprise which divulges various 'crimes' of elision and effacement in Victorian culture, namely the domestic incarceration of women; the denial of casual brutality and sexuality among the patrician and middle classes; a gullibility about the pseudo-scientific basis of the detection process itself; and the reactionary bias and elegiac nostalgia implicit in the return to order of the typical sensation plot finale. Like John Bender's *Imagining the Penitentiary* (1989), a study of eighteenth-century English fiction that 'sets out from Foucault',[59] Miller's book deplores the shortcomings of what he implies is a literary criticism that unwittingly promotes, and pays tribute to, the ideology of the work under scrutiny.

Miller's inventive approach has prompted significant interest in Collins's representation of law and order over the past 20 years, placing his best-known novels under the spotlight of a seminal theory of narrative, as well as giving Collins scholarship a trenchant and theoretical boost. As Ronald R. Thomas demonstrates in *Detective Fiction and the Rise of Forensic Science* (2004), much of this research has deepened and complicated our apprehension of the social and epistemological revolutions that moulded the nineteenth century. It has also helped explain how the recent representational technologies of satellite surveillance, DNA fingerprinting, and crime-scene computer simulation affect our view of our place in civic society.

However, Foucauldian appraisals of Collins's depiction of policing institutions have their own grievous shortcomings, gaps and omissions, failing to address how Collins figures gender as one of the primary avenues of power exchange and management. Lillian Nayder remarks that '[p]erhaps more clearly than any other recent study of Victorian fiction, Miller's *The Novel and the Police* suggests both the pleasures and the pitfalls of reading the English novel through the eyes of Michel Foucault.'[60] Lois McNay notes in her 1993 monograph *Foucault and Feminism: Power, Gender, and the Self*:

■ Despite Foucault's theoretical assertion that power is a diffuse, heterogeneous and productive phenomenon, his historical analyses tend to depict power as a centralised, monolithic force with an inexorable and repressive grip on its subjects. This [...] arises, in part, from the fact that Foucault's examination of power is one-sided; power relations are only examined from the perspective of how they are installed in institutions and they are not considered from the point of view of those subject to power.[61] □

Miller's ideology critique stresses what Collins fails to accomplish in his fiction rather than what he manages to envisage and achieve. In Miller's case, this emphasis is necessitated by the Foucauldian foundation on which his criticism is based, disclosing the 'facelessness of a system where it is generally impossible to assign responsibility for its workings to any single person or group of persons.'[62] In the panoptical society that Miller inherits from Foucault, novelists such as Collins and politicians cannot effect reform because of the dissemination of power in the modern state: 'the diffusion of discipline's operations precludes locating them in an attackable centre', and hence robust opposition to authority is impossible.[63]

For reasons such as these, *The Novel and the Police*'s contentions have themselves been queried and reprogrammed by scholars, including those most obviously influenced by his project. Elisabeth Rose Gruner, in her essay 'Family Secrets and the Mysteries of *The Moonstone*' (1991) argues that *The Moonstone* divulges a social vision markedly different from the one that Miller advances about Collins's literary tactic of reproducing and upholding the laws of bourgeois respectability. Gruner counters by proposing that Collins subjects class, gender and imperial ideologies to scathing critique.Like Anthea Trodd in *Domestic Crime and the Victorian Novel*, Gruner pursues some of the implications of *The Moonstone*'s similarities to the 1860 Road Murder case to indicate that the mysteries of both are based on the family's impulse to conceal, and on the secrecy which is integral to the 'fabled privacy of the domestic sphere':

■ Cuff's failure to solve the crime on his own, like Whicher's failure in the Road Murder, clearly implies that there are family secrets which the police cannot penetrate – secrets not perhaps worse than murder or theft, but more difficult to reveal. [...] The lesson of *The Moonstone*, like the lesson of the Road Murder, is that the family is complicit in the failings of the larger society; murder and robbery are not invasions from without but manifestations of societal tensions – involving especially the dangerous desires of greed and sexuality – within.[64] □

Gruner's interest in Collins's sardonic dissection of the social, sexual and psychological makeup of the family also revises the orthodox view that the Victorian country house crime thriller invariably shows the stalwart defenders of conservative English precepts imperilled by but ultimately triumphing over a foreign incursion. In *The Moonstone* by contrast, the family, as site and source of threat, is eventually undermined by its own dissensions, petty vanities and squalid self-interest. Once the privacy that it jealously guards is removed, the family has to confront the extent of its own dysfunctional drives.

In *The Private Rod: Marital Violence, Sensation, and the Law in Victorian Britain* (2000) Marlene Tromp while acknowledging Miller's theoretical rigour, also shows how his arguments tend to overlook a vital fund of sensation fiction's contestatory brio. She probes his claim that *The Woman in White* merely authorizes 'as a cultural value [...] privacy, the determination of an integral, autonomous, "secret" self under constant surveillance.'[65] Rather, the novel campaigns for the exposure of secrets that are not always explicitly disclosed, highlighting contradictions in the mainstream social and legal conceptions of marital violence:

■ the alternative representations in sensation novels challenged the solidity and impermeability of the legal and cultural understanding of violence in the home [...] By identifying [this site] as vexed, the novels challenged the identification of the law as a coherent, seamless text that provided unity to social articulations of violence, gendered identity, and social control. They exposed the law as a scripted social text and contested the justifications of the law's articulation and functioning as natural, godly, and inherently true.

Reducing the law to the level of myth threatened to confound its authority as well as that of its manufacturers.[66] ☐

Tromp asserts that the evocation of marital conflict in sensation fiction prompted a push for 'juristic control' of the issues addressed, a process that persisted and flowered in legislation late into the century. To illustrate this 'conversation between novelistic text' and 'parliamentary debate' Tromp demonstrates how Collins's *The Woman in White* took up the tensions embedded in the 1857 Divorce Act. Tromp portrays the novel as an interrogation of the rhetoric of violence in the domestic space, foreshadowing and setting the frame for later debates, especially the Married Women's Property Act (1870) and the initial endeavours to repeal the Contagious Diseases Act (1857–70), which carried with them the same anxieties of the policing of gender, class and sexuality as the Divorce Act had.

Tromp allows us to treat Collins's oeuvre as providing essential opportunities for re-envisioning the cultural constructions of issues such as domestic brutality and gender, making a range of behaviour and attitudes, which had previously remained beyond the ambit of polite social conversation and so outside the boundaries of legislation, 'subject to prescription.' Sensation fiction sees through the grievous limitations of realist discourse to offer a disruptive reading of 'the decentred subject' – not the Caucasian middle-class gentleman, but 'his bruised and battered wife.'[67]

Tromp's *The Marital Rod* offers precisely the kind of concentration on social and legal context that is lacking in *The Novel and the Police*. Cannon Schmitt, in his 1997 book *Alien Nation*, shares Miller's scepticism about the debunking capacity of *The Woman in White* but complains that

■ For Miller, [...] the novel confirms one type of subject and one type of politics endlessly. The lack of historical grounding with which he is often and accurately charged, then, appears not only understandable but symptomatic. He fails to provide any extra-novelistic history not as an oversight but because it is in a sense irrelevant, in that each novel he treats interpellates one and only one subject, enforcing a regime of the same.[68] ☐

Schmitt proclaims that 'for Foucault discourse works not merely to ensure the continuous reproduction of the same [...] but to harness subversion in order to produce difference.'[69] Indeed, Foucault's research expresses a discourse of sexuality that, in both its repressive and liberatory guises, has effected 'a dispersion of sexualities, a strengthening of their disparate forms, a multiple implantation of "perversions."'[70] Jenny Bourne Taylor's book *In the Secret Theatre of Home: Wilkie Collins, Sensation Narrative, and Nineteenth Century Psychology*

(1988) seeks to 'historicize [...] the formation of psychological and fictional conventions' of subjectivity in a genre which, she reminds us, has all too often been refracted through the anachronistic lens of psychoanalysis. Taylor expresses the 'process of historical transformation' through which concepts of subjectivity are fashioned by looking not at social conditions or class relations but at the 'set of discourses' on subjectivity.

The primacy Taylor gives to 'discourse' contributes to a lively debate within literary Foucauldianism over whether context is best specified in terms of relations of power (disciplinary, policing modes of social control), or relations of knowledge (discursive, conceptual forms of definition). Taylor responds to *The Moonstone* and its solution to the diamond's theft by foregrounding a radical ambiguity that is more flexible and variegated than Miller's reading and avoids what she calls the 'monolithic implications' of Foucault's power analysis:

■ There are at least five distinct cognitive frameworks that are set up within their own terms in the novel [...] There is Betteredge, voice of English common sense [...] Bruff, 'immersed in Law, impenetrable of Medicine'; Cuff, working by logical inference, based on the speculative interpretation of empirical evidence; Murthwaite and Jennings, both cognitively liminal figures; and Blake, a palimpsest of clashing methodologies. These overlap with the specific function of the actual narrators in the novel, who, like the specific narrators of *The Woman in White*, are asked to keep within the perimeters of their own experience, but whose equally important function [...] is to highlight the shifting and provisional nature of evidence, the arbitrary and unreliable nature of memory, so that the reader reads simultaneously through and against their testimony.[71] □

Taylor reminds us that in discussing *The Moonstone*, Miller mentions neither the Prologue nor the Epilogue, the narrative framework that dramatises the British plunder of the sacred Hindu diamond and its eventual restoration, which commentators sometimes cite as a reflection of Collins's anti-imperialist position. Taylor reveals how Miller's arguments that *The Moonstone* is monological and that, 'in every crucial case, all readers [...] pass *the same judgement*'[72] are among his least persuasive since Collins's novel consistently fashions interpretive conflicts, tensions and hesitations about criminality and guilt, and is deliberately designed to do so. And few commentators have uncritically endorsed Miller's account of the solution to the crime (there is not simply one crime in this novel, since the diamond is purloined repeatedly in the course of the narrative): 'The diamond has been stolen not by Rachel or Rosanna (whose suspicious behaviour is only intended to screen Franklin Blake, the man they love and think has stolen it), but by Godfrey Ablewhite, who needs ready cash to pay off his debts.'[73] Although Miller identifies Godfrey Ablewhite as *the* thief, Colonel Herncastle is guilty of this crime as well, and Collins refers to him as the 'Honourable John', the nickname of the East India Company. Furthermore, the 'hero' Franklin Blake, though provided with an excuse for his own theft of the diamond, is not exonerated as comprehensively as Miller proclaims. Elizabeth Rose Gruner explains in her incisive article on family secrets in *The Moonstone*: 'we establish that Godfrey is both a philandering debtor and a thief, but we never really establish that Franklin is neither.'[74] For all its flair and perspicacity, Miller's analysis tends to downplay these ambiguities, excluding potentially subversive material from consideration and precluding the possibility of genuine resistance on Collins's part.

Sensation novels, according to Brian W. McCuskey's essay 'The Kitchen Police: Servant Surveillance and Middle-Class Transgression', (2000) explicitly stage a conflict between two detective agencies, the servants and the police, the former subject to the will of the private family, the latter aiding the drive towards public order.

■ *The Moonstone*'s conspicuous employment of servants as house detectives demands that Miller's claims about the novel be reconsidered. Miller's vision of a Foucauldian nineteenth century, ruled by the totalising logic of discipline, has been questioned most frequently by feminist and cultural critics who insist upon the political ambivalence of Victorian novels. The examination of servant figures in Victorian fiction suggests a different but complimentary line of counter-argument: Foucauldian readings of the novel, even when they are most persuasive, refuse the Victorians much awareness of the conditions of power in their own century. Such Foucauldian claims about disciplinary power, the novel, and nineteenth-century culture must be tempered and complicated by attending to the ways in which the Victorians themselves both recognised the nature of that power and negotiated their relation to it.[75] □

For McCuskey, *The Moonstone*'s employment of servants as police can be comprehended as a reaction to the very dispersal of a microscopic disciplinary potency that Miller delineates. By investing servants with a policing function, the novel and its middle-class community refigure that energy so as to make it palpable, visible, distanced and psychologically bearable. There is little doubt, as Laurie Langbauer admits, that 'criticism inspired by Foucault' has asserted its 'dominance'[76] in analysis of Victorian sensation fiction, as in literary studies generally, in recent years. As Paul Cantor notes in his 1989 essay 'Stoning the Romance', critics of Victorian literature such as Miller are increasing in number and demand 'ideological purity' from the writers they dissect.[77] Current commentators on literary sensationalism continue to read the police presence in various ways – historical, psychoanalytic, formalistic – and to represent Collins as a maverick libertarian presence as well as a social disciplinarian, a writer as eager to expose class and gender inequities as he is to validate them.

The Private Eye

> ever since I read the 'Moonstone' [...] I have been longing to meet a detective – a real detective.[78]
>
> (M. E. Braddon, *His Darling Sin* (1899), p. 112)

D. A. Miller's *The Novel and the Police* has occasioned debates over the moral and literary virtues of the sensation novel's twin – the detective narrative, its status as a literary genre, its ideological affiliations, and its evolution as a mode of popular culture. Miller's monograph is not principally concerned with fashioning another account of the detective genre's history, arguing a case for its peculiarities as an identifiable form, or even setting it aside as a special category of literature. He is more struck by the signal importance of the detective's invisibility in the Victorian novel rather than his appearance in it. The detective is most present when he is least observed or remarked upon. *Bleak House* and *The Moonstone* are given a privileged place in this analysis since they most conspicuously chronicle the very process Miller identifies – not only portraying but also enacting a regime of self-policing.

By framing questions about the proper place of detective fiction in discussions of generic priority and influence in the Victorian novel, Miller has played a seminal role in questioning what Ronald R. Thomas calls the 'ghettoization'[79] of detective fiction as a literary subgenre, a project extended by Martin Priestman's *Detective Fiction and Literature: The Figure on the Carpet* (1991) which considers 'classic' detective texts from Edgar Allen Poe (1809–49), Collins and Conan Doyle alongside works by ancient Greek writers – the philosopher Aristotle (BC 384–22) and the playwright Sophocles (c. BC 496–06) – and by Henry James. Priestman explores the amorphous and unstable boundary between popular and serious literature, arguing that a dialectical relation exists between the two in which each debunks, appropriates and domesticates the energies and rhetorical mannerisms of the other. Together with Richard Maxwell's *The Mysteries of Paris and London: Detective Fiction and Literature* (1992), we are forcibly reminded that generic distinctions and cross-contaminations cannot be construed as purely formal matters, but are themselves intricate historical and sociological events.

■ The 'reinvigorated' historicist approach to 'the genealogy of popular genres' has been taken up by scholars who have moved in new and more sophisticated directions the treatment of detective fiction as an 'exceptional force' in late-Victorian literary and cultural history. □

Thomas (1996), p. 372.

Although T. S. Eliot saw Collins's *The Moonstone* as 'the first and greatest of English detective novels'[80] he was not the first to make this claim: G. K. Chesterton (1874–1936) had written in 1912 that *The Moonstone* is 'probably the best detective tale in the world.'[81] Dorothy L. Sayers (1893–1957) espoused this estimation of the novel in a discussion of *The Moonstone* first published in 1929, two years after Eliot: 'Judged by the standards of seventy years later [...] *The Moonstone* is impeccable. What has happened, in fact, is that *The Moonstone* set the standard, and that it has taken us all this time to recognize it.'[82] It did indeed take time to recognize, and Anthea Trodd, in her 1982 introduction to *The Moonstone,* argues to what extent Collins's novel 'fathered' detective fiction.[83] However, the majority of Victorian authors and pundits regarded detective plots with a disapproving eye. As Ronald R. Thomas points out, 'some of the most ardent articulations of the aesthetic and moral attributes of high Victorian realism were occasioned by anxiety over the cheap effects and immense popularity of nineteenth-century detective and sensation fiction.'[84] Anthony Trollope castigated the unrealistic preoccupation with narratives that were too tortuously involved and characters that were too crudely schematic. Henry James saw these fictions not so much as 'works of art' as 'works of science.'[85] Margaret Oliphant, in her 1862 article 'Sensation Novels' for *Blackwood's,* warned:

■ We have already had specimens, as many as are desirable, of what the detective policeman can do for the enlivenment of literature: and it is into the hands of the literary Detective that this school of story-telling must inevitably fall at last. He is not a collaborateur whom we welcome with any pleasure into the republic of letters. His appearance is neither favourable to taste nor morals.[86] □

One positive outcome of recent alertness to the 'literary Detective' has been greatly to complicate what we mean by the term 'detective fiction' and to liberate it from the exclusive hold of popular culturists. A. D. Hutter's 1975 essay, 'Dreams, Transformations and Literature: The Implications of Detective Fiction' is an early example of this bracing realignment, which posits *The Moonstone* as the 'prototypical detective novel':

■ Detective fiction involves the transformation of a fragmented and incomplete set of events into a more ordered and complete understanding. As such it seems to bridge a private psychological experience, like dreaming, and literary experience in general. And like a psychoanalysis, the detective story reorders our perception of the past through language. Although psychoanalysis and detective fiction are so different in conscious design and intent, they share a significant structural relationship, just as they share a close historical relationship: *The Moonstone* (1868) was the first full-length English detective novel, and it preceded Freud's first work on hysteria by less than twenty-five years.[87] □

Hutter not only uses post-Freudian psychoanalytic theories to develop a model of assessing the tactics of detection, but he also foreshadows Jenny Bourne Taylor's endeavour to read Collins in the context of Victorian notions of and about psychology and psychologists. Scholarship of this kind has promoted the integration of the literary detective into broad interdisciplinary discussions of Victorian fiction, reconfiguring awareness of Victorian realism and its sensational offshoot. So Hutter examines *The Moonstone* in the context of the research of Dr William Benjamin Carpenter (1813–1885) and Dr John Elliotson (1791–1868) on preconscious thought, memory, and the related effects of drugs, mesmerism and hypnosis. Hutter not only shows how the outcast Ezra Jennings employs the theories and methods of Carpenter and Elliotson to such sensational effect, but he also appraises Jennings as the novel's shrewdest detective – a perception of Jennings that D. A. Miller's *The Novel and the Police* and Tamar Heller's *Dead Secrets: Wilkie Collins and the Female Gothic* (1992) would elaborate. For Hutter, Jennings is a nascent psychoanalyst in his capacity to decode Dr Candy's abstruse utterance, but also a highly 'sensitive subject' whose mind transcends the rules of merely rational inquiry and wrests from apparently random details the most dazzling insights. This gift, according to Hutter, marks Jennings out as the beneficiary of a synthesising and transforming Romantic imagination.

Like Mark Hennelly in his 1980 essay 'Reading Detection in *The Woman in White*', Hutter is concerned to distinguish Collins's contribution to the detective genre from that of his contemporaries Edgar Allan Poe and Sir Arthur Conan Doyle . Hutter contends that the Poe-Doyle version of the genre calls into question dispassionate and logical forms of perception by means of its valorising of the detective's subjective and intuitive vision, ultimately revealing the objective/rational and subjective/intuitive to be two sides of the same coin. The narrative structure of *The Moonstone*, on the other hand, is thoroughly subjective and untrustworthy, which compels the reader to fashion a rational solution from the partial testimonies while avoiding the false clues that litter our path and lend various misleading appearances to a single action or event.

This is one facet of Hutter's argument with which D. A. Miller takes issue in *The Novel and the Police*. Hutter links the rise of the detective novel to the collapse of 'the older orders of self-policing' that existed in the rustic hinterland or earlier forms of urban existence when towns were smaller and communities more 'knowable'. The German writer Walter Benjamin (1892–1940) described the fictional preoccupation with surveillance, detection and incarceration as a peculiar symptom of urban modernity. Of nineteenth-century Paris he observes that 'in times of terror, when everyone is something of a conspirator, everybody will be in a situation where he has to play detective.'[88] Like many historians of detective fiction he construes the genre as one of the defining outcomes of metropolitan modernity because the new detective police were needed to 'read' a city that had grown far beyond the easy knowledge of its inhabitants. Miller, by contrast, posits that one of the most significant features of *The Moonstone* is precisely the failure of the new detective police, in the person of Sergeant Cuff. This failure, Miller suggests, is essential to the ideology of the shape of the detective story, which is geared towards producing a 'social innocence' based on the perception that everyday life is basically beyond the regime of police power. In Miller's Foucauldian conception of the surveillance society, every individual polices him or herself in a neighbourhood of voluntary spies who report on one another's activities; the fever for detection that breaks out in *The Moonstone* is merely an extension of normative social customs and models of behaviour.

Like Miller, Peter Thoms, in *Detection and its Designs* (1998) asserts that detective literature has a covert project of its own, namely 'to exert control over others.'[89] The influence of Foucault and Miller is especially evident in that Thoms devotes two of his five chapters to *The Moonstone* and *Bleak House*, texts also foregrounded in *The Novel and the Police*. Thoms proclaims that the detective's 'desire for authorial mastery disturbingly resembles the oppressive deeds of the criminal', for the detective 'threatens the autonomy of individuals as he invades their privacy and attempts to define their identities.'[90] Detective literature demonstrates this ambiguity about the purposes of detection by repudiating both 'the recovery of order' and 'the imposition of closure' in its narratives. However, Thoms resists spelling out here how the rival oppositional and collaborative tendencies in detective narrative relate to each other, and which tendency is privileged in the end. In the wake of Thoms's research, critical opinion has divided over whether the detective figure underwrites or subverts the social and epistemological orders that shape literary sensationalism. Marie-Christine Leps, in *Apprehending the Criminal: The Production of Deviance in Nineteenth-Century Discourse* (1992) and Martin A. Kayman's *From Bow Street to Baker Street: Mystery, Detection and Narrative* both aver that Miller's judgement of the sensation novel, and by implication detective fiction, too quickly rejects its capacities for exposure, resistance, and transgression.

Collins's tendency both to guy and re-inscribe the inequities he represents in his fiction is more fully addressed in a number of works on detection in his novels. Tamar Heller, Lillian Nayder and Ann Cvetkovich concern themselves directly with the relation between detective and sensation narratives, and contribute equally to the scholarship in both genres, building on the foundations provided by seminal accounts such as Ian Ousby's *Bloodhounds of Heaven* (1976), Stephen Knight's *Form and Ideology in Detective Fiction* (1980) and Dennis Porter's *The Pursuit of Crime* (1981). Ousby prefaces his study on the detective in English fiction with a pointed reference to the Latin derivation of the verb, 'to detect' (*detegere*, to unroof) and his argument shows the godlike or devilish capability of the detective in the Victorian novel to enter the private house and to divulge its guilty secrets.[91]

Tamar Heller's *Dead Secrets: Wilkie Collins and the Female Gothic* (1992), which Lillian Nayder calls 'perhaps the most significant critical study of Collins to appear in the 1990s'[92] acknowledges the critical tradition which lauds *The Moonstone* as Collins's 'most seamless transformation' of the predominantly feminine genre of the Gothic into the more robustly masculine detective novel, a genre that 'brings to light and banishes the buried secrets so prominent in the Gothic.' Heller's *Dead Secrets* probes Collins's relation to 'the female Gothic', a dissident tradition that dramatizes the victimization of women and the abuses of hegemonic patriarchy. As Heller demonstrates, Collins both associates himself with the female Gothic, which gives him 'a way of being a social critic', yet distances himself from it in order to establish his professionalism as a male writer.[93] Thus his fiction repeatedly 'evade[s] the full implications of a feminist critique', as acts of feminine revolt and transgression become 'the dead secrets in the text': 'Collins's novels, in fact, are often paradoxically Gothic plots that end with the containment of the Gothic as the site of subversion and literary marginality.'[94] However, Heller's examination of the 'detective work' performed in *The Moonstone*, as well as the baffling 'gaps and silences' which puncture its narrative of revelation and rational scrutiny, indicates that the novel 'is Collins's great cover up' and 'simultaneously expresses and suppresses' the ideological and generic complexities that had imbued his fiction from the outset of his literary career.

■ The tension between Gothic and detective fiction in the novel is symptomatic of Collins' continued and heightened ambivalence about his literary project. [...]

The central image in this narrative, the theft of the Moonstone, represents an exposé of Victorian culture that recognises the links between types of domination – of the colonizers over the colonized, of men over women, and of the upper over the lower classes. Yet the novel also papers over the traces of its own exposé, an erasure attested to by its obsession with buried writing.[95] □

Heller identifies Ezra Jennings, the social pariah with a secret past, as a figure for Collins, and the detective's decision to take his writings with him to the grave expresses 'the novel's tendency at once to diffuse its social criticism and to draw attention to its own self-censorship.'[96] Finally the stress Heller places on 'containment' may itself contain the subversive impetus of the novel.

What Tamar Heller terms the 'ideological doubleness' which causes a detective novel like *The Moonstone* 'to speak in two voices'[97] is the subject of several important critical essays, including the second chapter of Lillian Nayder's monograph *Wilkie Collins* (1997). Here, Nayder explains that while thefts, murder, and suicides sometimes occur in his detective fiction, the transgressions that Collins most frequently depicts include violations of gender norms and class boundaries, rather than criminal violence:

■ Despite our association of detective fiction with sensational murders and thefts, such novels as *Hide and Seek* (1854), *The Dead Secret* (1857), and *The Law and the Lady* (1874–75) have a different focus. Using transgressive figures to uncover family secrets, they call attention to acts of seduction and fraud, and enable Collins to investigate the grounds of social identity in Victorian England and to simultaneously challenge and reinforce gender boundaries and class lines. [...] In their own ways, and to varying degrees, each of these works questions the assumption that gender and class distinctions are grounded in nature, while also treating sexual differences and class distinctions as innate and naturally determined.[98] □

Nayder convincingly contends that the 'transgressive figures' in these novels are not drawn from a criminal underworld but tend to be 'the detectives' themselves, working-class men and middle-class women who assume the prerogatives of their social betters, and themselves become objects of surveillance and deep suspicion.[99] While these detectives can be seen to discredit overly restrictive class and gender norms in the course of their investigations, they are eventually returned to their proper, subordinate places as the novels draw to an end.

Ann Cvetkovich's *Mixed Feelings: Feminism, Mass Culture, and Victorian Sensationalism* (1992) is a revisionist project whose eclectic critical strategy includes feminism and Marxism while also drawing heavily on Foucault. By centring on feeling as 'the politics of affect' with which women are associated in domestic ideology, Cvetkovich supplies an incisive corrective to the tendency to regard sensation fiction as simply expressing oppositional impulses. The link between sensational literature and bodily affect is, like Victorian sexuality, a politically interested construction – a disciplinary apparatus with a traceable history. Cvetkovich assesses acts of detection in *Lady Audley's Secret* and *The Woman in White* so as to demonstrate that the mad or hysterical woman becomes a scapegoat for the more general insanity manifested broadly across gender lines by British middle-class society.

Cvetkovich is particularly interested in probing the disciplining of a feminine affect that is culturally determined. In sensation fiction, 'scenarios of repressed or silenced affect' result inevitably in 'strategies of containment' and ultimately the 'structures of bourgeois life [...] are reinforced rather than challenged by the intimate scrutiny of the internal landscape of women's lives'[100]

■ The construction of Lady Audley as the repository of dangerous secrets and impulses mobilises Robert Audley's detective work, which controls the intrusions of this deceptive woman; he has the power to discover truth and administer the law. [...] Read according to Miller's model, the detective plot in *Lady Audley's Secret* operates to explore and defuse domestic anxieties.

At the same time, however, detection and the family intersect differently in *Lady Audley's Secret* than they do in *Bleak House*. Miller argues that *Bleak House* uses the detective plot to create an alternative to the interminable processes of Chancery. The detective police represent an institution of power that, unlike Chancery, is containable and that guarantees the possibility of a sphere outside of the jurisdiction of the law, such as the family. [...] In contrast, *Lady Audley's Secret*, for all its simplifications, doesn't separate detection from the family, producing no thematic or formal difference between private and public realms, or between realist and detective narratives.[101] □

Because detection occurs in its midst, the family can no longer serve as a refuge and instead becomes the scene of discord and unease. And rather than being a figure with untroubled authority, like Inspector Bucket in *Bleak House*, Robert Audley, the detective, doubts his knowledge, efficacy and motives. In terms of individual novels, Cvetkovich's thesis means that for nearly every powerful and threatening sensationalized woman there is a stalking, controlling and disciplining male detective figure, often a young man whose path to prosperity and social prestige is temporarily impeded by female affect. *Mixed Feelings* is especially astute at analyzing these villainess-detective (or victim-detective) relationships and exposing the men's hidden agendas. In her reading of *Lady Audley's Secret*, Cvetkovich notes that Braddon's novel can be appraised as either a 'fantasy of rebellion' or as a 'fantasy of control' by underlining the role of the sensitive but finally self-serving young 'detective' Robert Audley.[102] For Cvetkovich, the core question sensation novels raise is how the community can best locate and construct the detective's power so as to make its presence both tolerable and manageable.

Like Cvetkovich, Caroline Reitz in *Detecting the Nation* (2004) takes up D. A. Miller's challenge by examining *The Moonstone* as a text that evinces a complex configuration of crime, empire, and political repression. Indeed 'The England of [Dickens and Collins] displays' according to Reitz, 'the messiness of a new imperial world that makes the detective necessary':

■ what *The Moonstone* illustrates, as a definitive English detective novel, is that the tradition of detective fiction is by no means a domestic genre [...] critics have written abundantly on the imperial issues at the heart of the novel, but none of these otherwise important readings have linked the imperial issues to the work of detection that organises the novel [...] *The Moonstone* is able to remain a detective story [...] because knowledge imported from the imperial periphery keeps the investigation in play [...] D.A. Miller's influential reading of the novel argues that the text in fact demonstrates the lack of necessity for the professional detective [...] Because so many critics, like Miller, focus on what Cuff, the novel's professional detective, fails to do, it is important to recover what it is that Cuff actually does. Cuff's ultimate return to the narrative is far from 'incidental.' While it might not signify his necessity for solving the literal investigation (an arguable point), it shows his necessity to the story being told about detection itself and its evolving relationship to national identity in 'an age of progress.'[103] □

Reitz underscores the dialectical relationship between narratives of policing at home and the policies of imperialism abroad. The sensation genre, and its outgrowths into detective narratives of the 1890s, both uphold and sabotage emerging scientific theories of criminal physiology which serve to categorize foreign contaminants from remote colonial outposts. Reitz reveals how anthropological data and fictional narrative merge to craft a system of knowledge and a 'story' of 'detection' that not only afforded psychological reassurance about the stability of life and property at home, but also disclosed and managed – however imperfectly – nagging cultural misgivings in Victorian Britain about the consequences of empire in Africa, India and beyond.

What is often lacking from these otherwise discerning studies is a concept of how the private or official female sleuth operates in the sensation genre, bringing together, for instance, Collins's Valeria Woodville in *The Law and the Lady* (1875),[104] Anthony Trollope's Marie Goesler in *Phineas Redux* (1973), Jessie Dunbar in Mary Hatch's

The Bank Tragedy (1890) and the early crime novels of Grant Allen (1848–99) featuring lady detectives, *What's Bred in the Bone* (1891) and *Recalled to Life* (1891).[105] This oversight is a 'crime' that Anne Humpherys identifies in recent scholarship on the Victorian detective: 'an obsessive return to a handful of canonised texts by three male writers – Charles Dickens, Wilkie Collins, and Arthur Conan Doyle' – while 'the majority of such fiction (a good deal written by women)'[106] still awaits reclamation from the long shadows cast by this select canon.

Heidi H. Johnson's essay 'Electra-fying the Female Sleuth' (2000), like Joseph A. Kestner's 2003 monograph *Sherlock's Sisters: The British Female Detective, 1864–1913*, reinserts Braddon's later novels into the history of the emerging genre of detective fiction, directing attention to her female amateur sleuths who uncover secrets on their fathers' behalf. Johnson focuses on *Eleanor's Victory* (1863) and *Thou Art the Man* (1894) in the light of Braddon's recurrent theme of the daughter's desire to overcome an overly dependent and protracted attachment to the father:

■ Though the protagonists of *Eleanor's Victory* and *Thou Art the Man* are not criminals but women who identify that criminality in others, their sleuthing leads them to the same psychic hurdle in the father [...] A frequently recapitulated scenario of the daughter who detects to discover the secret of her father's death or, conversely, whose detection reveals his culpability.[107] □

Johnson avers that the enigma which fuels the female sleuth's 'quest' in these narratives is more complicated than merely explicating 'a single guilty act'[108] or dispelling a mystery which clouds family honour. Braddon's female sleuth is committed to uncovering the 'secret' of her father's fearsome authority, demystifying his status as an idol for the Victorian family. Johnson's conception of these calm and canny heroines shows how the process of detection is less about restoring social equilibrium and more about salvaging a means of personal growth without the stifling interference of the Victorian patriarch or the deforming constraints of domesticity. Instead of identifying with the father's ambitions while sacrificing her own, Braddon's female sleuth is, according to Johnson, looking to inaugurate her own autonomous selfhood.

Johnson's treatment also signifies how Braddon's *Thou Art the Man*, whose title echoes that of Edgar Allan Poe's 1844 short story, re-inflects the motif of female madness from *Lady Audley's Secret*, by portraying a psychically damaged and homicidal masculinity. The dread of hereditary madness, passed from mother to daughter in *Lady Audley's Secret*, takes the form of Brandon Mountford's epilepsy in *Thou Art the Man*, which he fears in its advanced stages will progress to sudden violent impulses that could lead to murder. What is an irregular and aberrant female proclivity in Braddon's 1862 novel is radically redrawn as a male instability in her later detective plot.

Johnson's essay adumbrates a fruitful new direction for studies of Braddon's overlooked detective fiction, especially those novels which foreground women as the determined pursuers of criminals – for example, *Under the Red Flag* (1886) and *The Fatal Three* (1888). This approach also clarifies so-called unseemly female behaviour within literary sensationalism, and raises questions regarding class identity and participatory citizenship, which inevitably implicate issues about the ideological nature of the state and the operations of civil society. My next chapter focuses on the genre's tendency to probe orthodox assumptions about caste and social propriety, especially through a portrayal of the bourgeois clan as an embattled enclave, or as a site of coded ambiguity and moral duplicity.

CHAPTER THREE

Class and Social (Im-)Propriety

Sensation as a genteel pleasure?

'Let us then consent to a little unharnessing from the go-carts of life', appealed the progressive periodical *Meliora* in 1864, in its meditation on the place of recreational reading in the greatly expanded world of bourgeois leisure.[1] For Francis Paget (1806–82) however, a moral 'unharnessing' had already caused an educated reading public to succumb to the intensely acquisitive diet of sensation fiction: 'incalculable mischief has been done among the upper and middle classes, through their insatiate perusal, for years past, of all this pernicious nonsense.'[2] Paget's account foregrounds the class and gender inflections of contemporary debates about morality, civilized culture, 'breeding' and dangerously seductive forms of the imagination. He explicates the sensation genre as a heady 'stimulant', whose amalgamation of tabloid reportage with the grisly narratives of cheap penny dreadfuls, corrodes literary standards and profoundly unsettles domestic tranquillity, the sustaining myth of bourgeois life:

> ■ [M]any of our day, who make books their stimulants, think themselves at liberty to read anything that amuses them; and they take no account whatever of the time which they so employ. In the absorbing interest of literary dram-drinking, all higher studies are neglected, and the duties of life left unfulfilled. There are not a few young persons who seldom read anything but sensational novels, yet they are reading continually; – that is, in very plain language, they wallow from day to day, amid filth of the most defiling kind. The subjects which, of dire necessity, occupy the mind of the Judge of a Divorce Court, occupy theirs of free and deliberate choice. And their appetite grows by what it feeds on, just as the opium-eater requires stronger and stronger doses of the drug that destroys him.[3] □

Paget's 1868 spoof on sensation fiction, the epistolary novel *Lucretia; or The Heroine of the Nineteenth Century*, chronicles the misadventures of the easily duped Lucretia Frummage, an inveterate reader of the genre whose immersion in its stylistic overload causes her to become embroiled in a series of awkward, though not ultimately damaging, encounters. Paget compares the aficionado of these novels to an 'opium-eater', an addiction metaphor that signifies overmastering 'appetite', leading 'young persons' away from the austere 'duties of life' which keep passions in check by promoting discriminating, decorous taste.

Paget portrays a supposedly responsible and prosperous social group neglecting its 'higher studies' to purchase forbidden texts that are both the realization and provenance of a disorderly desire for literary 'filth of the most defiling kind.' By devising this category Paget subsumes print culture within a class structure, so that some forms of reading are deemed less productive and 'lower' than others. In *Distinction: A Social Critique of the Judgement of Taste* (1984) the French sociologist Pierre Bourdieu (1903–2002) notes that 'the definition of art, and through it the art of living, is an object of struggle among the classes.'[4] Sensation fiction can be perceived in these terms of class conflict. For the literary establishment, positioning this genre along a trajectory of 'defiling' fiction, below so-called authentic and genuine culture, is a means of fending off shifting class relations by reinforcing existing categorical containers. However, as Paget concedes, with sensation fiction, a tainted mass entertainment has already infiltrated, and now masquerades as, edifying elite culture, while the 'literary dram-drinking' of genteel readers mirrors the tawdry pastimes of the underclass, with its penchant for the brazen and the bizarre.[5] Paget's reaction implies how the critical uproar surrounding 'sensation' derails the politics of sentiment, a correlation between feeling and social status.

Paget's locutions echo the vituperative critical reviews which deploy a lexicon of ordering – 'high' and 'low' – to highlight the sensation genre's ignominious class affiliations. Margaret Oliphant writes in her 1862 *Blackwood's* article 'Sensation Novels':

■ To combine the higher requirements of art with the lower ones of a popular weekly periodical and produce something that will be equally perfect in snatches and as a book, is an operation too difficult and delicate for even genius to accomplish, without a bold adaptation of the cunning of the mechanist and closest elaboration of workmanship.[6] □

Oliphant, like Paget, indicates how the lowliness of this genre removes it utterly from the sublime domain of art, situating it instead in the grimier echelons of manufacturing and commerce, which can only incite a 'lower' order of feeling among the reading clientele. E. S. Dallas (1828–79), writing in *The Gay Science* (1866), construed 'the craving which exists among us for sensation' as 'but the reaction from over-wrought thinking'; these febrile but facile pleasures function as a partial release from a debilitating 'age of thought.'[7] Ruskin believed the dispiriting monotony of inner-city existence played a key role in making sensationalism a viable escapist antidote. What modern fiction does, in its 'fouler' embodiment, is to anatomise these gruesome new forms of moral disease, 'purporting thus to illustrate the modern theology that the appointed destiny of a large average of our population is to die like rats in a drain, either by trap or poison.' 'Normal evil' as Ruskin terms it, traditionally dependent on physical vigour, has been replaced by urban 'decrepitude', by 'aberration, palsy, or plague.'[8]

This rhetoric of pathology and incessant addiction to strong 'stimulants' extends Henry Mansel's hyperbolic terms about insatiable hunger in an epoch of vulgar surfeit and democratic capitalism run amuck. He too laments that the 'Newspaper Novel' now apparently commands the middle-class reader's irresistible and restlessly craving fascination:

> ■ There is something unspeakably disgusting in this ravenous appetite for carrion, this vulture-like instinct which smells out the newest mass of social corruption, and hurries to devour the loathsome dainty before the scent has evaporated. When some memorable crime of bygone days presents features which have enabled it to survive the crown of contemporary horrors, and, by passing into the knowledge of a new generation, has in some degree attained to the dignity of history, there is much to be said in defence of a writer of fiction who sees in the same features something of a romantic interest which makes them available for the purposes of his art; but it is difficult to extend the same excuse to the gatherer of fresh stimulants from the last assizes. The poet or the philosopher may be allowed to moralise over the dry skeleton turned up to view in the graveyard or the battlefield, but we doubt whether the strongest-stomached medical student would find a theme equally poetical or equally instructive in the subject laid out in the dissecting room.[9] □

Just as 'carrion' and waste fosters disease in poverty-stricken neighbourhoods with overcrowding and poor sanitation, so 'social corruption' engenders sensationalism, a tacky lower-class commodity at root yet audaciously exported to more well-appointed localities. Mansel envisages himself not only as a judicious custodian of aesthetic purity but also as a sanitary inspector with a solemn and onerous task to police consumption and make the sensational commodity safer for the middle classes. Sensational 'stimulants' are hazardous because they gratify common needs and afford a mode of distancing which gives repressed emotions a form that is assumed to be publicly palatable and that makes them a source of pleasurable recreation. Mansel signifies how it is bad enough that a newly literate popular audience should demand this pungent and immediate diversion in return for its shilling. That this penchant for the 'loathsome dainty' should infect the bourgeoisie was symptomatic of imminent social, moral and cultural dissolution, a situation which demands the most diligent scrutiny, according to G. H. Lewes: 'the vast increase of novels, mostly worthless, is a serious danger to public culture, a threat which tends to become more and more imminent, and can be arrested by an energetic resolution on the part of the critics to do their duty with conscientious rigour.'[10]

Peter Brooks, following Susan Sontag (1933–04) and Roland Barthes (1915–80), has investigated the issue 'of our compulsions to read', the erotic appeal of following a narrative to its conclusion.[11] While Brooks's psychoanalytical methodology sheds little light on the social and cultural milieu of the 1860s, it does imply both the power of reading and the strategies that were passionately debated by mid-Victorian pundits to counteract its 'poisonous' effects.[12] Valerie Pedlar has described how the sensation novel 'drew on the reader's own experience of life and invited a thrilling involvement that highminded commentators felt was not quite commensurate with moral standards.'[13] In 1860, *Fraser's Magazine* noted that neither the original impetus of the sensation novel nor its specific narrative techniques had been refined within the constraints and regulations of middle-class moral management. Despite the shielding censorship of the circulating libraries, *Fraser's* expressed concern about plot-driven novels that played so directly and aggressively upon the senses, influencing a callow audience at a time when the memory is still fresh: 'The growing independence of the young people of the present day, and the very slight supervision exercised by parents or guardians over what they read [...] render such books as we allude to even more dangerous than they would have been twenty years ago'.[14]

Fraser's portrays 'young people' – and by implication young ladies – as a social group whose moral standard is largely fluctuating, volatile and unreliable; and experience has not yet instilled a criterion by which to distinguish 'accurate' representations of life from that which flouts modest decorum in both language and incident.

Mid-Victorian reviewers, keen to certify a cultural hierarchy within Britain, tried repeatedly to correlate a reading class specific to sensation fiction, and yet the audience for these novels represented a point at which categories of difference collapsed into one another. Thomas Arnold, in an 1866 article entitled 'Recent Novel Writing' for *Macmillan's Magazine*, proffered an account of the social and economic origins of 'the reading class':

■ But let us consider the circumstances of the reading class. It swells every day, owing [...] to the immense and continual expansion of our industry. Every new row of suburban villas [...] every railway [...] every factory that is built, betoken an increase, not only in the class of those who [...] are making their fortunes, but also in the class of intelligent ministrants to these, such as clerks, book-keepers, surveyors, engineers, merchant-captains, and the like.

Now both these classes of persons – not only they but their wives and families – as their numbers increase, directly swell the reading class.[15] □

Arnold catalogues this mushrooming 'reading class' by citing the sensation genre as the 'mental food' of the new lower-middle-class which has become M. E. Braddon's principal audience: 'There is a crowd of clever people waiting to read what she writes; to whom culture is unknown, who miss nothing, feel no void, because the work that fillips them is not noble, is constructed upon no elevated and consistent plan.'[16] Foreshadowing Matthew Arnold's distinction between popular reading and 'the best that is known and thought' in the world, here the concept of 'culture' itself is implicitly evolutionary, a potency that will, according to this pundit, raise 'us from a lower level to a higher.'[17] Thomas Arnold's concept of the 'swelling' of this 'reading class', having seized the circumscribed possibilities for upward mobility engendered by industrial capitalism, evinces an anxiety not only about the unbridled and random growth of a suspect audience, but more importantly about cultural miscegenation of readerships: sensation novels, circulating both in cheap and expensive editions, are hybrid narratives in which ostensibly distinct modes of literature commingle. The project to demarcate and rank overlapping genres as part of a campaign to separate out mass entertainment 'trash' from culturally approved authors would be thwarted if one could not discern class identity through reading habits.

Jenny Bourne Taylor's monograph *In the Secret Theatre of Home* (1988) scrutinizes these misgivings: 'The sensation novel was seen as [...] a morbid addiction within the middle class that worked directly on the body of the reader and as an infection from outside, continually threatening to pollute and undermine its boundaries through this process of metaphoric transference and analogy'.[18]

As Taylor proceeds to argue, the sensation novel, like the emergence of Gothic romance in the eighteenth-century, elicited 'panic' about the general public's nervous systems, and how such phenomena were tied to a sense that class-based cultural barriers were being dismantled by the technological sophistication of new methods of production and circulation.[19] Taylor is alert to those mid-Victorian reviewers who sought to forestall the conflation of supposedly discrete literary genres fostered by the advent of serialized sensational bestsellers enjoyed across 'boundaries' of gender and class-specific readerships. She proposes that these issues highlight worries about the longer-term development of generic conventions and cultural practices. The obsession with the kind of 'enjoyment' reading sensation fiction supplies, played out in 1860s journalism, raised questions about whether this school of writing epitomized an updated version of earlier Gothic narratives or a wilful distortion, even betrayal, of a dominant mode. Unlike the multiplied perception created by the exotic scenarios of earlier Gothic romance, in which highly strung nerves function as what Taylor calls 'delicate moral mediators', the nervous response elicited by sensation fiction derailed orthodox morality, and so is rendered morbid 'by becoming more directly sensualized.'[20]

Subverting social propriety

To a young Henry James, surveying M. E. Braddon's sensation fiction from across the Atlantic in 1865, Braddon is privy to notions that

■ betray an intimate acquaintance with that disorderly half of society which becomes every day a greater object of interest to the orderly half. They intimate that, to use an irresistible vulgarism, Miss Braddon 'has been there.' The novelist who interprets the illegitimate world to the legitimate world, commands from the nature of his position a certain popularity. Miss Braddon deals familiarly with gamblers, and betting-men, and flashy reprobates [...] She knows much that ladies are not accustomed to know, but that they are apparently very glad to learn. The names of drinks, the technicalities of the faro-table, the lingo of the turf, the talk natural to a crowd of fast men at supper, when there are no ladies present but Miss Braddon, the way one gentleman knocks another down – all these things – the exact local colouring of Bohemia – our sisters and daughters may learn from these works.[21] □

Braddon was construed by her detractors as a parvenu writer who encourages other sensation novelists to haunt the 'sinks and sewers of society', in order to render minutely the 'obscene birds of night.'[22] Such reading will inevitably destabilize 'our sisters and daughters' by making them emotionally vulnerable and dissatisfied with ordinary domestic duties and everyday life. Not only does Braddon imaginatively map what James calls 'the exact local colouring of Bohemia', but she looks on with amused indulgence at the 'fast' figures who populate it, according to the 1865 *North British Review*:

■ The moral of the story [*Eleanor's Victory*] seems to be, that to cheat an old man at cards and to forge a will are no impediments to attaining distinction in the world, and, indeed, are rather venial offences [...] Few other novelists could have invented anything so diabolical as the murder [in *Henry Dunbar*], or have depicted with seeming complacency the after-life of the criminal. The impression made is, that the murderer was a clever man, and was very hardly used.[23] □

At the core of all these attacks, pinpointed by Margaret Oliphant, was woman's 'one duty of invaluable importance to her country and her race which cannot be overestimated – and that is the duty of being pure. There is perhaps nothing of such vital consequence to a nation.'[24] If Oliphant's ideal middle-class family is rooted in the cornerstone of womanly purity, then the equivocal and imprudent protagonists of the sensation novel not only compromise the worthy practice of reading fiction generally, but also scoff at the entire social and moral fabric of mid-Victorian Britain.

Reflecting on the sensation genre's ostensible concentration on the risqué topics outlined by Henry James, the 1864 *Christian Remembrancer* proposes that the 'fundamental change in the working of society' that the sensation genre both delineates and promulgates, is an 'unnatural' attempt to breach traditional hierarchies of power, patronage and privilege:

■ The 'sensation novel' of our time, however extravagant and unnatural, yet is a sign of the times – the evidence of a certain turn of thought and action, of an impatience of old restraints, and a craving for some fundamental change in the working of society. We use the popular and very expressive term, and yet one much more easy to adopt than to define. Sensation writing is an appeal to the nerves rather than to the heart [...] The one indispensable point in the sensation novel is, that it should contain something abnormal and unnatural; something that induces, in the simple idea, a sort of thrill.[25] □

Another contemporary critic interpreted the 'thrill' of sensational extremes, an appetite for 'fiery sauces' and 'strongly seasoned meats and drinks',[26] as a consequence of material deprivation: 'People working face to face with the primitive powers – people in whose understanding poverty does not mean a smaller house or fewer servants, or a difficulty about one's butcher bill, but means real hunger, cold, and nakedness – are not people to be amused by abstractions.'[27] Exploiting a link between the underprivileged and the 'primitive', the correspondent associates aesthetic sensibility with material advantage and declares, in effect, that those belonging to the 'lower' orders do not possess the intellectual resources to savour the 'abstractions' of elite culture due to the primacy of physical want governing their quotidian lives: 'hunger, cold, and nakedness.' This cultural determinism, harmonising class status and aesthetics, wilfully ignores the extraordinary appeal and accessibility of sensation fiction to a significant cross-section of Victorian society.

As Dallas Liddle has recently noted, one of the things which made the genre 'thrilling', guaranteeing it a popularity inexplicable and disturbing to prevailing ideologies, was the way it 'implied that both personal and class identity in contemporary Britain were fluid and unstable rather than secure, and thus potentially subject to manipulation, misrepresentation, and outright theft.'[28] The content and implications of the genre, far more than those of the popular domestic romance in which it was anchored, tended to deviate from or even undermine the social order by perverting human nature, social actuality, the relations between the sexes and orthodox conceptions of gender. Mid-century sensationalism had to be perceived, according to the 1864 *Westminster Review*, in the context of smothering respectability, and the extremes of the writing articulate a desperation and dissent that the contributor defended: 'We are so thoroughly impressed with the conviction that art and morals alike suffer by the prudish conventionalities of our present English style, that we are inclined to welcome rebellion against it merely because it is rebellion.'[29] For this correspondent, the merging of social distinctions, witnessed in daily life in the mild form of a shared literary taste, becomes more overt and insistent in the world of sensation novels themselves. The patrician and bourgeois characters not only associate freely with their inferiors but they begin to ape lower-class behavioural mannerisms and practices, most strikingly in such matters as irregular morals or 'domestic relations of an exceedingly peculiar nature.'[30]

Contemporary commentators sifting for evidence of the sensation genre's incitement to social impropriety had to look no further than its provenance in the cheap publications for the masses; these are identified by Mansel as 'the original germ, the primitive monad, to which all the varieties of sensational literature may be referred, as to their source.' This virus of blatant commercialism is 'spreading in all directions, from the penny journal to the shilling magazine, and from the shilling magazine to the thirty shillings volume.'[31] Working-class fiction and penny part fiction, known as 'penny bloods', were thought to have conditioned respectable serials and three-volume novels. W. Fraser Rae (1835–1905) in his 1865 article, 'Sensation Novelists – Miss Braddon' commented that:

> ■ Others before her have written stories of blood and lust, of atrocious crimes and hardened criminals, and these have excited the interest of a very wide circle of readers. But the class that welcomed them was the lowest in the social scale, as well as in mental capacity. To Miss Braddon belongs

the credit of having penned similar stories in easy and correct English, and published them in three volumes in place of issuing them in penny numbers. She may boast, without fear of contradiction, of having temporarily succeeded in making the literature of the Kitchen the favourite reading of the Drawing Room.[32] □

Despite their saturation of the mainstream market, the basic plotlines of these novels were, according to Rae and others, all too often indistinguishable from those of the crudest broadsides: 'But (as many of our readers will know)', remarked *Temple Bar*, 'we have not been speaking of a serial story of "Reynolds's Miscellany" or the "London Journal", but of a novel, "large numbers" of which, it was advertised on its appearance, would be "taken" by the circulating libraries, where well-appointed carriages most do congregate.'[33]

Jonathan Loesberg, in 'The Ideology of Narrative Form in Sensation Fiction' (1986) focuses on the complex political implications of the sensation novel's formal arrangement. He contends that the genre's obsession with flimsy class barriers – 'a necessary aspect of the suspense that was the aim of sensation narrative' – was shaped by mid-century 'social and parliamentary' controversies.[34] Loesberg signals here not only the expansion of the British Empire but also the political assimilation of class and gender divisions through the Reform Bill and marriage property debates of the 1860s. Loesberg's essay specifies class fear not so much as a perceived threat of a proletarian uprising but acute nervousness about a world rendered chaotic and inscrutable once an individual has found his genteel social status compromised. Loesberg perceives the contradictions of Wilkie Collins's sensation fiction as a reaction to mid-Victorian discussions over class relations in his examination of the 'politically charged' framework of *The Woman in White*, which is regularly cited as a core example of the democratic impulse behind the genre. Sensation novels evoke their most typical moments of heightened response from images of fragile legal and class identity yet they structure these images of loss in narratives of 'inevitable sequence':

■ The contradiction in the structure of sensation fiction [...] is that it bases itself upon an element, the image of a loss or shift of class identity, that its thematic explanations of its plot structure, its appeals to various forms of inevitable sequence, must turn around and class as accidental. The effect of this contradiction is to unlink its most typical moments, the moments that produce sensation effects, from the thematic and structural contexts that ostensibly call them forth.[35] □

Loesberg proposes that sensation novels overturn conventional concepts of causality and motivation; in their reliance upon melodramatic, random or 'accidental' happenings and 'surprise', they exploit an associative logic that is coded as 'lower-class'. That an affluent readership should be exposed to, and even revel in, the disreputable 'nonseriousness' of thematic links is perhaps the most unsettling component of the genre. Sensation furnishes emotional indulgence and escapism because while it evokes the '*frisson* of class fear for its literary ends' it ultimately 'draws back from making any thematic claims in its use of that *frisson*.'[36]

> ■ Characterising sensation fiction as emotional evocation without thematic correlative is not merely a judgement upon it but also a virtual description of how it operates. The plot operates through various forms of transference and reversal to isolate the moments when it produces the sensation response apart from any thematic readability, insisting almost on the nonseriousness, even the illicitness, of the response it calls forth.[37] □

That 'sensational' occurrences might happen without clear, and therefore controllable causality may have been menacing, and Nancy K. Miller suggests that plots which lack the plausibility of a masculine linear logic became sidelined as the wayward 'arbitrary narrative[s]' of working-class literature, and were thus excluded from the canon on that aesthetic basis.[38]

Like Jonathan Loesberg, Graham Law's *Serialising Fiction in the Victorian Press* (2000) registers the conspicuous and wide appeal of sensationalism and how it distilled a complex of factors that together shaped a market unprecedented in the history of the English novel up to that point:

> ■ Sensation fiction transgressed accepted social boundaries [...] not only by inserting what had hitherto been seen as the proletarian themes of violence, infidelity and insanity into bourgeois settings, but also by encouraging the middle classes to participate in the proletarian mode of weekly serialisation. Braddon had succeeded in 'making the literature of the kitchen the favourite reading of the drawing room', as Fraser Rae put it in 1865.[39] □

This fiction disturbingly blurred the boundaries between the classes, between high art, low art and no art (newspapers), between the public and the private, and between the sophisticated cosmopolite and the brutalized low life. Reading such novels becomes a subversive pursuit because it brings middle and lower classes together over the same printed page. Law reveals how a threat to the seeming inviolability of class distinctions was matched by a threat to literary priorities. Closely allied with the moral objections – and imbuing most of them – are the inveterate social antagonisms, given a sharpened focus by the urban situation and increasing working-class literacy.

Deborah Wynne in *The Sensation Novel and the Victorian Family Magazine* (2001) charts the unprecedented range of new magazines appearing on the 1860s market featuring 'questionable' novels by authors who targeted their fiction at a middle-class audience.

■ Horrified Victorian reviewers complained of a 'dumbing down' of middle-class literature, although this did nothing to stop readers eagerly buying, or borrowing from circulating libraries, 'respectable' magazines [...] in order to read instalments of novels saturated with the excesses traditionally associated with working-class melodrama and 'shilling shockers.' The sensation novel became legitimate reading for the middle classes largely *because of* its magazine context, where readers were addressed as educated and domestic family members. It was this ability on the part of magazine editors to combine the 'respectable' and 'scandalous' that made the emergence of literary sensationalism in the early 1860s so controversial. [...] Reading sensation novels in book form can readily lead to the view that the invoking of titillating 'sensations' was the genre's primary function. However, an examination of sensation novels within their magazine contexts indicates an important response to the issues of the day, particularly anxieties surrounding shifting class identities, financial insecurity, the precarious social position of single women [...] and perceptions that modernity itself was undermining domestic life.[40] ☐

Wynne places more emphasis than Law on the extent to which the sensation genre and the cheap middle-class magazine emerged together as 'modern forms'; that they shared the same cultural space is not coincidental, and in order to gauge its cultural impact, the sensation novel needs to be read as 'an important signifier of social change'[41] during the mid-Victorian period. Wynne's argument also usefully modifies Patrick Brantlinger's earlier claim in *The Reading Lesson* (1998), his survey of nineteenth-century reading practices, that the sensation novel was the most controversial middle-class genre of the period because of its capacity to excite feelings of self-indulgence, producing 'sensations in readers with few if any philosophically, socially, or morally redeeming features [...] thus anticipat[ing] today's mass market thriller.'[42] Brantlinger's account does not fully reflect how the reading of sensation fiction remained a highly popular mode of diversion and its techniques soon came to be employed by journalists seeking to augment the circulation of daily newspapers. Wynne foregrounds questions about the relations between the classes, and paranoid imaginings about infiltration at a time when greater social mobility led to doubts about the sustainability of prevailing social and moral codes.

Cannon Schmitt's *Alien Nation: Nineteenth-Century Gothic Fictions and English Nationality* (1997), while elaborating these issues, proposes that the genre's interrogation of social and literary decorum, by depicting 'improper' subjects drawn from newspaper summaries of crime, is rooted in a more profoundly subversive energy that confounds generic expectations:

> ■ [Sensation] novels were not seen as diseased merely because they depicted crime; Newgate fiction had done that. Nor was the deleterious influence attributed to them due to the fictional representation of lower-class life, which by the 1860s could boast a tradition developed, in part, by well-respected authors such as Charles Dickens and Elizabeth Gaskell. Nor, finally, did the presence of victimising rather than victimised women alone identify sensation novels as a threat. Objections to and fears about sensation fiction arose in response to its discursive hybridity.[43] □

Schmitt construes the genre as not simply embracing, but advertising with an impish zeal its mixture of a plethora of conflicting ideological and literary elements within the bounds of a single opus. Indissolubly intermingled in the narrative fabric are elements from the seedy underworld and the rarefied domestic refuge, the lunatic asylum and drawing room, showing the 'overlap' of patrician and criminal trespasser. These effects, according to Schmitt, 'depend upon figurative miscegenation at all levels.'[44]

The sensation novel then infringed not only the proprieties of class difference, but also the 'proprieties of art', by exploiting a perception of lawless caprice and the unwholesome extremes of human experience. Richard Holt Hutton (1826–97), writing in 1868, declared

> ■ To heap together startling and exceptional incidents in defiance of all probability is the obvious resource of inferior artists. Such incidents do doubtless occur in modern life, nor is there any reason why they should not be introduced [...] in the novels which undertake to represent it. But our sense of the fitness of things is offended by the continual recurrence of what ought to be most sparingly employed to bring about a catastrophe or to disentangle a plot.[45] □

The sensation novel employs exaggeration and foreshortening as legitimate narrative techniques; it complicates the realist values of apparent artlessness and unobtrusive manipulation of effect. But the result, in Hutton's opinion, was an irresponsible distortion of reality, 'an entire society swarming with thieves, murderers, adulterers, and bigamists'[46] in which the freakish and the fantastic has become the norm, and the exceptional has unceremoniously ousted the rule. The eccentricity of narrative method, summed up in Charles Reade's all-purpose subtitle, 'A Matter-of-Fact Romance', raised troubling questions about how the two fictional realms of fantasy and social realism should be kept duly separated from each other. Hutton's disquiet stems from how, in literary terms, the sensationalists were relentlessly picking at the apparent seamlessness of the mainstream realist novel as well as that of the Victorian society it purported to exhibit.

This dispute about aesthetic propriety and balance reveals how form was inextricably tied to worldview, how the sensation rebellion against approved literary conventions implied equal insurgency against the moral premises those conventions sustained. G. H. Lewes averred: 'We are by no means rigorous in expecting that the story is to move along the highway of everyday life [...but] if we are to travel into fairy-land, it must be in a fairy equipage, not a Hansom's cab.'[47] For the more reactionary Victorian reviewers, the period between Sir Walter Scott (1771–1832) and the sensational 1860s was already to be perceived nostalgically as a golden age when English fiction was 'family reading' lauded throughout the novel-producing world for 'a certain sanctity [...] and cleanliness unknown to other literature of the same class.' This state of affairs was endorsed on a practical level because the novel afforded the chief amusement of youth, invalids and women.[48]

The rise of the sensation genre coincided with the height of the novelist's newly won prestige as a social and ethical force. After decades on the fringes of artistic significance, the novelist had become acknowledged as 'now our most influential writer. If he be a man of genius his power over the community he addresses is far beyond that of any other author.'[49] The novelist's legitimate office was to articulate 'good and noble thought', according to Frances Power Cobbe (1882–1904) in her essay 'The Morals of Literature' (1864); otherwise 'the art is prostituted' and human nature itself tarnished by

> ■ pictures of life which would make us all a set of crawling worms unfit to be suffered to exist, much less to be made subjects of a work of art. If men be all mean and interested and worldly-minded, then it is no more proper to make them subjects of fiction than wasps, toads, and maggots.[50] □

Wilkie Collins was acutely conscious of the fact that scurrilous rumours surrounding the sensation authors' real home lives provided fuel for opponents of the social and aesthetic indecencies located within the genre. Rhoda Broughton's *A Beginner* (1894) tells the story of a young woman who, like Broughton herself over 25 years earlier, brings disrepute onto her family by writing a sensational novel. In their 'Introduction' to *Victorian Sensations*, Kimberly Harrison and Richard Fantina observe that

> ■ [s]everal of the sensation authors lived their adult lives outside of the parameters of the Victorian nuclear family. [...] Collins's first common-law

wife, Caroline Graves, finally chose to leave him and marry another man. Collins gamely attended the wedding, then took up with another woman, Martha Rudd, who bore their three children out of wedlock. When Graves' marriage failed, Collins, apparently without a second thought, took her back and proceeded to support two households. [Charles] Reade, although employed by Magdalen College at Oxford in a position that mandated celibacy, had fathered an illegitimate son with one woman and lived unmarried with another, the actress Laura Seymour, for over two decades. Braddon, however, received the most attention for living and having children with publisher John Maxwell while he was married to another woman who was incarcerated in an insane asylum.[51] □

Collins lost no opportunity to respond to those commentators who castigated sensation novelists as mere purveyors of dangerous trash that would deaden the moral perceptions of a bourgeois readership. Nicholas Rance's class-based survey of *Wilkie Collins and Other Sensation Novelists* (1991) portrays the genre as debunking the discourse of entrepreneurial capitalism epitomized by *Self-Help, with illustrations of Character and Conduct* (1859) by Samuel Smiles (1812–1904). Collins's version of sensation fiction, Rance avers, parodies the bourgeois ideal of upward mobility by exposing those who rise as duplicitous outcasts like Magdalen Vanstone in *No Name*; this character's contravention of class barriers in turn points to a tension between two bourgeois standards, a belief in social mobility on the one hand and in a providential order of society on the other. In positioning Collins, whom he perceives as a vocal critic of Victorian class hierarchies, in relation to other sensation writers, Rance distinguishes 'radical' sensation fiction from the polemically 'conservative' version in Ellen Wood's *East Lynne*:

■ Margaret Oliphant complimented Collins on wasting 'neither wickedness nor passion' in *The Woman in White*. Wickedness, however, continued to be a prime motivator of many of the sensational plots of the 1860s. Mrs Henry Wood's *East Lynne* is an obvious and famous example. In such fiction, what is sensational is not, as in the fiction of Collins and Braddon, the suggestion of gaps and contradictions in the moral code, but the purported consequences of straying from it. In his biography of his mother, Mrs Henry Wood's son, Charles Wood, who declared of her that 'in politics she took no part, beyond being a strong Conservative', quoted the tribute to her that 'she successfully used sensational elements for moral ends', to combat a vicious tendency. If such a mission inspired *East Lynne*, Dickens's *The Mystery of Edwin Drood*, his last and unfinished novel, with its running and hostile allusion to Collins's *The Moonstone*, would seem to have been similarly inspired. There was, then, in the 1860s, a 'war of ideas' between what may be distinguished as radical and conservative sensation novels.[52] □

Such a distinction is highly problematic however; for instance, Braddon's *Lady Audley's Secret*, which Rance deems a radical narrative, has the same double impulse both to exculpate and to punish its scheming anti-heroine as Wood's supposedly conservative novel (as well as Collins's *No Name* in this respect). Rance ultimately overplays the centrality of Collins to the sensation school, making the female authors appear as rapt disciples of a male mentor rather than as gifted developers of, and innovators in, a genre in their own right. Rance's otherwise incisive analysis of the sensation genre's ideological disruptiveness tends to smother the fact that Collins's work was also a locus of studied indirection, edgy qualification and contestation of the fiery debates surrounding class unrest and social niceties.

Reinventing the middle-class clan

Literary scholars of the 1970s and early 1980s, as Chapter Two of this Guide indicates, largely valued Wilkie Collins as a 'dissident moralist',[53] a courageous explorer of forbidden territories who subjected the pieties of mid-Victorian class identity to bitterly sardonic critique. However, this packaging of literary sensationalism as a caustic interrogation of what we would term today 'family values' fosters a construction of the eminent Victorian as a bifurcated being, split between decorous social surface and insurgent secret self. Tamar Heller notes that

> ■ [s]uch a critical narrative reads those 'tales of bigamy and seduction', as Margaret Oliphant called sensation fiction, as a literary id, a doppelgänger-genre unburying all its culture's sexual and social preoccupations in tales obsessed with the others of Victorian society – deviant women, criminals, the lower classes, homosexuals, racial and cultural outsiders. [...] If we are to read [...] sensation fiction as a rebellion against some monolithic Victorian establishment, we will want to be careful in defining both the subversion and the hegemony – and perhaps avoid so crisp an antithesis.[54] □

The most accomplished recent research on sensation fiction complicates an appraisal of these narratives as in any straightforward sense countercultural. In an essay specifying the genre, Patrick Brantlinger once enquired, 'What is sensational about the sensation novel?' Nowadays scholars ask instead '*how* sensational are these narratives?', if by 'sensational' we mean 'insurrectionary' or 'debunking' in relation to concepts of social standing. In *The Power of Lies* John Kucich explains that Collins sought

■ [t]o affirm an exceptional middle-class identity, and he participated in the general Victorian strategy of defining the elite through an *upward* form of transgression, a crossing of inside/outside boundaries that testified to the acquisition of more cultural power by one subgroup than by the rest of the middle class. But instead of endorsing the genteel, largely professional upper-middle class that Trollope rendered sublime through transgression, Collins wrote about and for an entirely different middle-class elite – that of what I call 'cultural intellectuals.' Though they are surrounded by a large supporting cast of doctors and lawyers, Collins's protagonists tend to be drawing masters, writers, actresses, amateur painters and philosophers – especially in his major novels of the 1860s, when he was consolidating his literary success. In his identification with this cultural fringe, and in his attempt to produce their identity through an ambiguous antiprofessionalism, Collins's general posture of outsiderhood had a culturally specific foundation that its flamboyant individualism, as well as its flamboyant slumming, often conceals. Rather than wholly taking on an outlaw identity, Collins exploited his outsiderhood to support a particular kind of collective middle-class authority.[55] □

According to Kucich, Collins shares with Trollope the desire to distinguish an 'elite' group within bourgeois culture. This perception of Collins departs from that of critics such as U. C. Knoepflmacher and Winifred Hughes on the one hand, for whom Collins is actively engaged in deriding codes of respectability, and Nancy Armstrong and D. A. Miller on the other, who seek to disclose transgression as yet another tool of the disciplinary apparatus. Kucich attends to the symbolic tactic of Collins's public identification with 'outsider' status by comparison with Trollope's affiliation with insiders. Collins repeatedly opposes 'cultural intellectuals' to legal, medical, and other professionals in order to demonstrate that not only can intellectuals master professional standards of probity, but, by virtue of their sharper aesthetic gifts, surpass other bourgeois in their abilities to expose chicanery and uncover suppressed narratives. Collins' anti-professionalism qualifies him as a detractor of the institutional markers of legitimacy, but the transgressions of his protagonists, most notably Walter Hartright in *The Woman in White*, are not oppositional, but accomplish the justice the law cannot. Their outsider status, especially in its characteristic suspicion, enables cultural intellectuals 'to see and tell what professional "insiders" most want to know.'[56]

Ronald R. Thomas, in his essay 'Wilkie Collins and the Sensation Novel' (1994), is, like Kucich, fascinated by how the genre intimates a new class of professionals on 'the cultural fringe.' Thomas explains that the genre works directly on anxieties about class fluidity by divulging the commercial basis of personal identities and family relations – 'acts of commerce, forms of trade, commodities to be bought and sold.' While purporting to disclose transgression and punish intemperate class aspirations, sensation fiction 'subverts commercial values by revealing the essential commercialisation of the family and of the individual subjects involved in its most intimate transactions.'[57] Rather than seeking to enshrine traditional class boundaries, Collins's sensation novels show that those boundaries have already been reconfigured through financial means, with kudos and authority invested in Walter Hartright, who is pitted against 'villainous aristocratic poseurs', and *The Woman in White* depicts his remarkable rise in the social hierarchy and economic triumph over them. While beginning the narrative as an aspirational drawing teacher, Hartwright is, at the novel's end, situated within the gentry and father to the heir of Limmeridge estate.[58] In *The Dead Secret*, similarly, Collins identifies lawyers and physicians as members of the new ruling elite. Aptly, *The Woman in White* emulates a legal document and *Basil* takes the form of a medical file.

Although Thomas speaks of the subversive intensity of sensation fiction, he points out that the novels merely repackage hegemonic patriarchy as professionalism, and that Collins's lawyers and physicians arrogate the very privilege and perks they seem to chide in their enemies. As the fate of the Vanstone sisters in *No Name* implies, class identity is literally composed and executed by professional figures and is subject to their harsh monitoring and control. Thomas indicates that professional authority is gendered and imposed upon female subjects by men. Understood as a response to marriage law reform as well as class redefinition, Collins's sensation novels send a 'double message' that will be appraised further in the next chapter of this Guide. They can be seen 'as part of a growing protest surrounding the larger issue of female political empowerment' but also 'as part of a rearguard defence [...] against that protest.'[59]

John Kucich and Ronald Thomas have sought deeper historical understanding of both the Victorian reception of sensation's social messages and of the literary representation of class hierarchies. Kucich's alertness to Collins's staging of a conflict between the declining, landowning patrician elite and the encroaching power of cultural professionals through their expanding claims of expertise also illuminates Ellen Wood's *East Lynne*, which opens with the sale of property by an aristocrat to a professional, the solicitor Carlyle, and its plot hinges on the consequences of Carlyle's marriage to the aristocrat's daughter, Isabel Vane. E. Anne Kaplan's 1989 essay on the 'Maternal Melodrama' in Wood's text posits that

■ the political implications of this narrative have to do with the depiction of the aristocratic class as wasteful, decadent and sometimes immoral.

We have here a specific discourse about class: Lord Mount Severn belongs to the old noble aristocracy, but is unable to continue in a noble manner; his sister, Mrs Vane, and Francis Levison, on the other hand, represent the promiscuous, lascivious, impulsive and morally decadent wing of the dwindling aristocracy. The novel's idealisation of the middle class, whose solid families are prey to exploitation from the immoral aristocrats, has to do with the political requirement for a reshuffling of discourses about class as England was becoming more entrenched in the industrial era. Economic realities required that the aristocratic class be dislodged from its privileged status [...] and the middle class represented as the new source of morality and the Law.[60] □

If, as Kaplan expounds, the new modern citizens of the middle class such as Carlyle typify 'solid' family life in *East Lynne*, other sensational narratives, with plots based on hidden ancestries, mislaid wills and false legacies, expose deep uncertainties about women's legal status in the genteel home, the differing expectations about marriage held by men and women, and misunderstandings between marital partners which result in domestic violence and tragedy. What threatens the middle-class clan from without, such as the agents of a 'dwindling aristocracy', is often not nearly as sinister as what corrodes from within – bigamy, mistaken identity, arson, and desertion. The novelist Geraldine Jewsbury (1812–80), who as a publisher's reader had to assess many derivative bigamy novels, sarcastically mused in an *Athenaeum* review of *Lord Lynn's Wife* (1865) by John Berwick Harwood (1828–86), a novel she had recommended for rejection:

■ If, in after-times, the manners and customs of English life in 1864 were to be judged from the novels of the day, it would naturally be believed that people, in the best regulated families, were in the habit of marrying two wives, or two husbands [...] and of suppressing the one that proved inconvenient, by 'painless extinction' or by more forcible methods.[61] □

Winifred Hughes's essay 'The Sensation Novel' (2002) analyses the genre's association of the middle-class family with sites of unhomely disturbance:

■ In criminalizing the Victorian home, the sensation novels succeeded in defamiliarizing it. Characters and readers could no longer take it comfortably for granted; instead they were forced to become increasingly suspicious of whatever looked most familiar and ordinary [...] The sensation novels, like the popular press, were permeated with the sense that crime, violence and illicit sexuality were daily occurrences, the sense that there would always be more to fill the crime columns of the next morning's paper. It was the basic premise of the sensation genre that human life, even in

Victorian middle-class society, was less tame, less ordinary, less predictable than its readers may have liked or supposed.[62] □

Hughes implies that the mid-Victorian reader, by merely opening
a sensation novel, could hardly evade being implicated in its suspect
morality and apprehension of illegitimate subjects, becoming in effect
an accessory to the sensational probing of cherished institutions of
hearth, family and matrimony. In addition to the primal fear about the
nature of the home as refuge, sensation fiction articulates a range of
misgivings arising from threatened changes to the organization of the
family, and their impact on the bourgeois shibboleths of stoical self-
discipline, unflagging industry, and personal responsibility. Hughes's
account reveals how the 'sensational' operates as a bizarre debunking double to the world of domestic sentimentalists such as Anthony
Trollope and Elizabeth Gaskell, who chart, according to Wilkie
Collins, the 'miserable monotony of the lives led by a large section of
the middle classes in England.'[63] In the 'less tame', self-enclosed genre
of sensation, a supposedly genteel father can have his son confined to
a private lunatic asylum to prevent his exposing him as an embezzler,
as in Charles Reade's *Hard Cash*. Fraught relations between father and
son, as in Collins's *Basil* (1852) and *Hide and Seek* (1854) become one of
the most outlandish reactive components of the genre, as it documents
the degeneration of the mid-Victorian patriarch into a ruthless and
volatile domestic despot.

Hughes's interpretation of the irregularities which beset the
bourgeois family in sensation fiction reminds us that the institution
of marriage is a weapon to be wielded for financial gain in this 'less
ordinary' rendering of 'Victorian middle-class society.' Percival Glyde
marries Laura Fairlie in *The Woman in White* solely to dispossess her.
Magdalen in *No Name* weds Noel Vanstone to regain a stolen fortune.
Braddon describes a marriage in *Lady Audley's Secret* as 'a dull, jog-trot
bargain.'[64] In both Collins's *The Dead Secret* (1857) and Charles Reade's
A Terrible Temptation (1871), women conspire successfully to deceive
their husbands about their children's biological paternity. In Reade's
The Cloister and the Hearth and *Hard Cash* parents occasionally falsely
imprison their own children for the most venal of motives. In Collins's
Man and Wife (1870), one character attempts to kill his wife and another
has murdered her abusive husband.[65]

As Braddon's narrator explains in *Aurora Floyd*, these 'modern
tragedies' differ from the ancient variety in occurring indoors, 'in
places where we should least look for scenes of horror.' The middle-
class family, as Chapter Five of this Guide will indicate, becomes a
degraded institution if the private sphere is a source of what Braddon
calls 'jealous fury' and 'mad violence.'[66] Braddon is responding to

debates over the laws governing marriage and divorce in England in the 1850s and 1860s, a period during which readers became increasingly aware that domestic strife was endemic to their society, and that the victimization of wives by their husbands was a legally sanctioned phenomenon. Alfred Austin (1835–1913), in the 1870 *Temple Bar*, deplored how these sensational transgressions should be rendered as happening just 'round the corner', in seemingly refined communities:

> ■ When before did it ever enter the head of the writer of romance to find a field for the exercise of his more awful powers just at his own door or round the corner? With a due sense of the fitness of things, rather did he travel far afield, and seek, in remote and somewhat obscure regions, for a reasonable arena wherein to make men and women act outrageously. Outrageous their actions did not seem, happening in places where personal experience had not gone before, and set the boundaries of the probable and the improbable [...] It is on our domestic hearths that we are taught to look for the incredible. A mystery sleeps in our cradles; fearful errors lurk in our nuptial couches; fiends sit down with us at table; our innocent-looking garden walks hold the secret of treacherous murders; and our servants take £20 a year from us for the sake of having us at their mercy.[67] □

For Austin, this cavalier disregard for literary decorum undermines the author's credibility, which itself remains unquestioned as a virtue in fiction: 'One would have thought that when something exceptionally terrible and mysterious had to be made credible, the more distant and unknown the locality, the more easily would the wonder-telling author be believed'; but it is typical of the sensation novelists to 'despise that distance which not only lends enchantment to the view, but which justifies both writer and reader for accepting as likely the grossly improbable.'[68] In other words the shocking or the incredible is something that impacts upon somebody else in some other era. 'The contempt of the probable', as Austin describes it, is what distinguishes the sensation novel from its venerable predecessors in the archives of romance. The very concepts of probability and its opposite, as defined by the Victorian pundits, are inextricably linked with a particular interpretation of the transactions between civilized, middle-class family members.

Alfred Austin's review pointedly refers to the ambiguous presence of 'servants', who, as the previous chapter of this Guide demonstrates, necessarily encroach upon the bourgeois family's privacy and who may be unapologetic voyeurs, blackmailers and snoops. This notion of the 'downstairs class' infiltrating the confines of the genteel family resonates through many reactions to the genre in its 1860s heyday. As in *The Moonstone*, the chief agents of gossip, rumour and innuendo in the middle-class community are its servants, always alert to the activities of their employers. Lillian Nayder writes in ' "The Threshold of an Open Window": Transparency, Opacity, and Social Boundaries in *Aurora Floyd*' (2006): 'Hoping to witness "scenes of horror" among their masters and mistresses, Braddon's working-class spies look and listen through the windows and doors of the rooms from which they are excluded, eager to gain the knowledge that will place their social superiors in their power.'[69]

If, according to Alfred Austin, sensation fiction both articulates, and dramatises at the level of plot, a threat to bourgeois virtue, what solutions did it offer to this perceived crisis? Bruce Robbins notes in *The Servant's Hand* (1986) that surveillance in the home moved in two directions across the employer-servant relation, as the middle-class 'fear of being observed emerged together with a new burden of observing.'[70] Leonore Davidoff's *The Best Circles: Women and Society in Victorian England* (1973) explains how the servant acts as a buffer between the family and the street, helping the family to screen visitors and stall potential interlopers: 'The hall, and in larger establishments, special anterooms, were used to "hold" the caller in limbo while the servant went to find the required member of the family in the private regions of the house', thus protecting the family 'by space and time lapse from initial contacts with outsiders.'[71] Davidoff asks how sensation novels help to enforce and even produce the official separation between private and public, but how they also seize upon and exploit the symbolic ambivalence of the servant precisely in order to manage the ideological conflicts that bolster norms of middle-class seclusion. Brian W. McCuskey argues that

■ Mid-century Victorian novels like *The Moonstone* and *East Lynne* employ the figure of the servant to think through the complex dynamics of surveillance in the middle-class home because servants are highly conflicted figures who both guarantee and threaten their employers' privacy. This symbolic ambivalence allows the Victorian novel to negotiate the competing ideological imperatives of privacy and publicity in such a way as to consolidate middle-class subjective autonomy. With the help of servants [...] middle-class employers rehearse their shifting relationship to the fields of social power that both underwrite and undermine that autonomy.[72] □

McCuskey signals that if sensation fiction expressed unease about the capacity of the servant class to infiltrate the bourgeois domain, it also shows them, albeit less frequently, as a source of solace in guaranteeing privacy and protecting property: guarding valuables, sizing up strangers, escorting their employers. McCuskey's convincing analysis of 'the complex dynamics of surveillance in the middle-class home' also implies that the people who have to be watched with unstinting vigilance are not necessarily interlopers from without, but rather the 'upstairs' enclave, and especially the bourgeois wife and mother, whose role as an efficient and thrifty household manager is supposed to keep errant longings in check.

If the critical term 'sensation' operated in mid-century vernacular as a distillation of Victorian insecurities over the permeable borderline between purity and transgression, polite restraint and untrammelled ferocity, then these fraught imaginings found frequent embodiment in the ambiguous figure of the sensation heroine. For the 1865 *Westminster Review* this 'New Woman'

> ■ possesses not only the velvet, but the claws of the tiger. She is no longer the Angel, but the Devil in the House [...] Man proposes, woman disposes, is the new proverb. The Fathers, after all, were right when they said Adam was more tempted by Eve than by the Devil.[73] □

This reaction underscores how the sensation heroine, along with her counterpart women readers and writers, functioned as a device for articulating fears about the degeneration of British society, given that 'higher' and 'lower' were becoming variable and relative terms. In *The Madwoman in the Attic* (1979) Sandra Gilbert and Susan Gubar seek to extend the image of the incarcerated Bertha Rochester to apply to women in general: 'almost all nineteenth-century women were in some sense imprisoned in men's houses.'[74] That this confined wife, with 'the outward semblance of the ideal saint',[75] might actually be a passionately violent 'Devil', is a theme to which sensation fiction returns repeatedly, and constitutes the subject of my next chapter, as it traces the links between femininity, madness and maternity.

CHAPTER FOUR

Women, Gender and Feminism

Mapping the feminine

> We have grown accustomed to [...] the narrative of many thrills of feeling [...] What is held up to us as the story of the feminine soul as it really exists underneath its conventional coverings, is a very fleshy and unlovely record. Women driven wild with love for the man who leads them on to desperation before he accords that word of encouragement which carries them into the seventh heaven; women who marry their grooms in fits of sensual passion; women who pray their lovers to carry them off from husbands and homes they hate; women, at the very least of it, who give and receive burning kisses and frantic embraces, and live in a voluptuous dream, either waiting for or brooding over the inevitable lover, – such are the heroines who have been imported into modern fiction.
>
> ([Margaret Oliphant], 'Novels', *Blackwood's Edinburgh Magazine*, 102, September 1867, pp. 259, 275)[1]

So Margaret Oliphant (1828–97), one of the foremost female reviewers of the period in her 1867 essay, 'Novels', which identifies woman's intimate tie to literary sensationalism and excoriates its articulation of sexual yearning and domestic stultification. Along with Henry Mansel's 1863 review 'Sensation Novels', Oliphant's article, which strives to account for the collective psychology of the novels' immense appeal, is often construed as a definitive critical statement on the vogue by a Victorian commentator. Though not immune to employing sensational effects in her own novels – as *Salem Chapel* (1862)[2] amply testifies with its components of bigamy, hidden illegitimacy, madness and murder – Oliphant denounces new works by four exponents of the 'school' – *Rupert Godwin* (1867) by M. E. Braddon, *Cometh Up as a Flower* (1867) by Rhoda Broughton, *Played Out* (1866) and *Called to Account* (1867) by Annie Thomas (1838–1918), and *Land at Last* (1866) and *Forlorn Hope* (1867) by Edmund Hodgson Yates (1831–94). She registers how these 'shocking' novels are both an outcome of and response to a very real cultural craving that mainstream society has failed to allay, a wayward need which puts on trial and recasts mid-nineteenth-century conceptions of womanhood.[3] Oliphant saw a potential threat to the presumed stability of patriarchal culture in the emergence, in the 1860's, of the 'Women Question', with its debates and claims about female emancipation and about a woman's right to education and training, to earn and keep her own income, and as a British subject who could petition for custody of her legitimate children.

Oliphant's invective, which focuses most sharply on the 'leader' of the sensation 'school' Braddon, whose heroines in her two most popular novels *Lady Audley's Secret* and *Aurora Floyd* (1863) are both clandestine bigamists, does not simply rest on the blurred moral message offered in these works. Oliphant maintains that the 'eagerness of physical sensation' expressed 'as the natural sentiment of English girls' and 'offered to them [...] as a true representation of themselves' was not only pernicious but also psychologically incorrect. Braddon is ignorant of the respectable classes; she 'might not be aware how young women of good blood and good training feel.'[4] Indeed, 'one of the earliest results of an increased feminine influence in our literature [has been] a display of what in women is most unfeminine.'[5] If sensation novels objectify and victimize women, whose deviant otherness is both perilously proximate and uneasily seductive, then the chief perpetrators are women themselves. Why do such novels exist, and why are they so popular with a female readership? Either this avid audience envisages real life as if it were as depraved as sensation fiction claims, and they revel in this corruption; or this audience acknowledges that the pleasure of the genre resides in its grotesque falsification of lived experience. In either case, Oliphant suggests, the fundamental issue is the nature, moral wellbeing and destiny of the female consumer of fiction.

Oliphant questions sensation novelists' portrayal of women's inner natures as 'fleshy and unlovely'; she does not, however, insist that the 'feminine soul' is ideally transcendent, interior and unmediated by cultural conventions. If the term 'feminine soul' signals an essentialism critiqued by recent commentators, the idea that this 'soul' is clothed in 'conventional coverings' implies, even for the conservative Oliphant, how the 'inner self' was not always to be perceived as the uniform, coherent self that is the ostensible hallmark of bourgeois subjectivity.

Oliphant's article goes on to vilify Braddon's Lucy Audley as a cynical 'piece of imposture',[6] which reveals a complex, almost paradoxical, comprehension of feminine roles that requires women to behave 'naturally' even as they are playing a part. She views in sensation novels not new conventions but a mismatch of 'conventional coverings' and 'the natural sentiment of English girls.' As 'the inventor of the fair-haired demon of modern fiction', Braddon has, in *Lady Audley's Secret*, fashioned an ominous amalgamation of female human form and brutish appetites; a puerile, blond creature who plays a central role in the realm of private life that ostensibly requires a parade of emotional expertise – family relations, religion, childrearing, domestic taste, and aesthetics – but who then belies that appearance by enacting a brazen materialism and homicidal self-assertion. Oliphant's disquiet seems directed at the mode, not just the mere fact, of Lady Audley's pretence: that she has exposed Victorian femininity as a cold-blooded performance is bad enough; what really unnerves is the malicious relish with which the anti-heroine acts out the contradictions and perversities that validate middle-class prerogatives.

In the last twenty years critics such as Leonore Davidoff, Elizabeth Langland and Mary Poovey have extensively documented the frequently competing pressures that shaped the representations and experience of middle-class Victorian women; and those who ventured into authorship were frequently mocked as 'unfeminine', unscrupulous and even criminal.[7] Female sensation novelists were especially vulnerable to these charges, and Oliphant's construction of the category of 'fleshy and unlovely' reading underlines the ideological work of gender and genre to naturalize and safeguard social inequities. Sensation fiction's delineation of the dangerously desiring underclass heroine, 'driven wild with love', candidly opposes ideologies of bourgeois femininity that envisioned middle-class women as naturally docile and passionless – as exalted moral mistresses reigning benignantly over the domestic sphere, which in turn was imagined as privatized and insulated from economic and class imperatives.[8] By the 1860s modern woman was, according to Lyn Pykett, 'in flight from motherhood, family responsibility and domestic existence'.[9] Even before the sensation craze, *Lucretia* (1846) by Edward Bulwer-Lytton portrayed a covert 'household epidemic' of crime, in which wives were the initiators of illicit ploys and husbands the hapless victims.[10] This rebellion in the home was, in Oliphant's opinion, irrefutable evidence of the century's hazardous radicalism.

Oliphant's alarmed reaction to 'these feverish productions' exemplifies the degree to which those affiliated with the sensation school were prepared to stage an arresting 'spectacle' of femininity, whether by charting the lives of meekly submissive victims (such as Isabel Vane in *East Lynne* and Laura Fairlie in *The Woman in White*), or of the wily, designing femme fatales who exploit 'conventional' understandings of role-playing for purposes of pragmatic self-interest (Lady Audley surrounding herself with the finery of upper-crust society; Collins's Magdalen Vanstone in *No Name* or Lydia Gwilt in *Armadale*).[11] Oliphant's gravest concern is that these narratives may incite women to cultivate other priorities and commitments beyond those of acting as man's 'helpmate', which is the sacred duty extolled by Sarah Ellis

(1799–1872), whose *The Women of England* (1843) stresses that 'Woman' should not ask herself 'what shall I do to gratify myself – to be admired – or to vary the tenor of my existence' but instead she must

> ■ lay aside all her natural caprice, her love of self-indulgence, her vanity, her indolence, in short her very self – and assuming a new nature, which nothing less than watchfulness and prayer can enable her constantly to maintain, to spend her mental and moral capabilities in devising means for promoting the happiness of others, while her own derives a remote and secondary existence from theirs.[12] □

Sensation fiction persistently challenged this complacent cant by indicating, as Lynda Hart points out in her monograph *Fatal Women* (1997), that the 'trajectory of "normal" femininity and that of fallen womanhood were not two parallel lines incapable of meeting; on the contrary a slippery slope lay between the two states.'[13] Hart shows how Lady Audley enjoys the privacy that shaped middle-class women's lives but exploits that privacy for purposes of material acquisition and social climbing, rather than the self-sacrificial ends glorified by Sarah Ellis's conduct book. Oliphant construes Lady Audley's graceful manners as 'unnatural' because they so expertly camouflage her opportunism. And such violations, which destabilize strategies of perception for reading and viewing, analyzing and interpreting, generate 'thrills of feelings' (mingled exhilaration and revulsion) among the female reading clientele.

However, endeavours to defend the genre as a laudably didactic entertainment for 'young ladies' of good background were not unknown in the 1860s. The *Medical Critic*'s correspondent averred that Braddon's *Aurora Floyd* was a salutary corrective and 'admonition to young ladies not to let their early fancies run away with them':

> ■ Although a sensation novelist must step a little over the bounds of probability, although clandestine marriages with grooms are unfrequent, and although, when contracted, they usually involve a totally different chain of consequences from those imagined by Miss Braddon – still, young ladies who read newspapers will not, on the whole, learn much previously unknown evil from the romance.[14] □

These measured tones contrast all the more starkly with Oliphant's 1867 review essay, which alleges that sensation heroines have been 'imported' into 'modern fiction'. This signifies how the cultural enterprise of structuring society, which belittled a genre of popular novels for and about women, was alert to the threat of the so-called lower orders, whose boorish, exaggerated modes of entertainment might infect legitimate, sanctioned culture. Oliphant mobilizes and merges the discourses on literary genre, female sexuality and ethnography to salvage her conception of a stratified society at precisely that historical juncture when – as the previous chapter of this Guide indicates – caste and cultural boundaries were in flux.

Susan David Bernstein notes, in her essay 'Dirty Reading: Sensation Fiction, Women and Primitivism' (1994), that Oliphant's concept of a 'fleshy' sensational heroine with unappeasable appetites intersects with depictions of intellectually deficient and sexually promiscuous 'other' non-Western women from the discourses of sociology and cultural anthropology in the 1860s. For Bernstein, Oliphant's 'inscribed distinction' within British culture – 'between the higher and the lower ground in fiction' – reinforces a perceived barrier between cultures, between social groups, and especially between women of different classes and ethnicities:

> ■ If the discourse of anthropology was used to justify national imperialism at an historical moment when the sun stopped setting on the British Empire, the same idioms attempted to certify a cultural hierarchy within England [...] To maintain an established social order, these related cultural politics focus on the necessity to manage female sexual desire. Unrestrained appetites – whether for sexual pleasure or for consumer finery – characterise both sensation heroines and their largely female audience. This lust is also fuelled by the emerging consumerism of mid-century that witnessed the advent of London department stores along with the middle-class woman as a significant force in the marketplace. The anthropological figure of the primitive woman with boundless desires also underwrites these voracious heroines and readers.[15] □

Bernstein's essay argues persuasively that the 'anthropological figure of the primitive woman' informs Oliphant's critical campaign against sensation fiction's melodramatic excesses, whether in characterization, style, or reading clientele. Bernstein points out that Oliphant's rhetoric portrays sensation fiction as a disquieting instance of evolutionary upheaval, an atavistic throwback to an earlier, 'lower' narrative form. Sensation fiction reveals saintly, self-sacrificing womanhood as a tepid fatuity, merely a puppet outfitted with 'conventional coverings.' This movement, according to Oliphant, will initiate the next generation of wives and mothers into a set of values that did not appear to be constrained by hegemonic institutions such as the family or the Church of England. Nor was she alone in voicing her concerns. 'Formerly', as the *Broadway* noted,

> ■ we respected and admired our wives and sisters all the more for their innocent ignorance on certain topics, and now the most rustic maiden of sixteen, may by a diligent perusal of the works of her literary sisters,

attain an almost perfect knowledge of every vice that festers beneath the sun.[16] □

An 1863 correspondent for *Littel's Living Age* anticipates Oliphant's metaphors of cultural stratification in describing the sensation heroine. These novels behave as a cultural image for naming and containing questionable tastes associated with a narrative of evolutionary trans-mutation, not of progress as natural and logical, but of descent:

■ The heroine of this class of novel is charming because she is undisci-plined and the victim of impulse; because she has never known restraint or has cast it aside, because in all these respects she is below the thor-oughly trained and thoroughly tried woman. This lower level, this drop from the empire of reason and self-control, is to be traced throughout this class of literature, which is a consistent appeal to the animal part of our nature.[17] □

Securing this equation between the sensation heroine and the lower rungs of both the English class structure and civilizations across the 'empire' and across time, the reviewer draws attention to the bestial 'abandon' and the 'uncontrolled' carnality and cupidity which the sensational heroine has 'in common with brute nature.'[18]

Keith Reierstad, reflecting on many of these negative contemporary reviews, chronicles the rise of the ambitiously independent sensational heroine following the increase in women's authorship and tied to the expansion of a specifically middle-class readership noted in Chapter Three of this Guide.

■ One of the most significant developments which the Victorian sensa-tion novel of the 1860s, 1870s, and 1880s brought to English fiction was a resurgence of the centrality of female characters, such as had not been seen since the days of the Gothic novel, dominated by Mrs Radcliffe. While many novels of the first six decades of the century contain impor-tant and memorable women, most of them are heroines of the kind who revolve as satellites around heroes. It is only in the sensation novel that the establishment of independent women on a par of interest with men begins to be a major trend in British fiction.[19] □

Reierstad reveals that the critical discourse on sensation fiction is also a debate about cultural prestige and power at a time of expanding literacy when women and a rising middle class inundated the liter-ary marketplace. A number of influential women edited family lit-erary magazines, including Braddon who oversaw *Belgravia Magazine* for a decade, mobilizing it to uphold her type of fiction; Emily Davies (1830–1921) and Emily Faithfull (1835–95) *Victoria Magazine*, Anna

Maria Hall (1800–81) *St. James's Magazine,* and Ellen Wood (*The Argosy*). Their involvement with these periodicals and the higher rate of publications by women featured in them contributed to an atmosphere in which women writers could succeed and inflect to some degree the nation's cultural values.[20] Surveying 'Contemporary Literature' in 1879, *Blackwood's Magazine* asserted that sensational writers were 'for the most part, feminine, and their pens go dashing along with true feminine volubility.'[21] 'Feminine volubility' results in what Oliphant terms a 'flood of [...] storytelling',[22] the outcome of intermingled consumer and capitalist priorities in the 1860s.

Kate Flint's 1995 monograph *The Woman Reader 1837–1914,* like Reierstad's essay, explores how the destiny of British polite culture was monitored and deciphered through the reading diet of middle-class females. She assesses the virulence of Margaret Oliphant's 1867 attack on 'fleshy and unlovely' fiction in light of apprehension about the 'proximity of sexuality and textuality for the woman reader' of these narratives.[23] Flint argues that the primary source of anxiety about sensation novels has to do with their chiefly female audience, but registers that the female author is implicated in this equation as well: 'critical attention [...] makes no bones in showing what it was about these fictions which gave cause for alarm. Its frames of reference are drawn from familiar suppositions about women's affective susceptibility.'[24] That this genre was construed by its early opponents as stimulating female desires has resonance for several sensation novels, most famously *East Lynne* and *Lady Audley's Secret* but equally strikingly in another novel: *Love's Conflict* (1865), the debut of the once-popular Florence Marryat in which Harriet Treherne, the only daughter of an ancient family, elopes with a dancing master and is punished by having to earn a living as a Parisian prostitute before dying of an unspoken (because unprintable) disease. These novels, according to Flint 'took advantage, in other words, of an assumed innate faculty which might under certain circumstances be regarded as one of women's strengths, but which should not be exploited at the expense of her simultaneously held rational capabilities, and, above all, at the cost of the necessary exercise of self-control.'[25]

To maintain an established social order, it was a necessity to manage female cravings for the luxuries that accompany social and economic prestige. As Lynda Nead notes in *Myths of Sexuality* (1988), the construction of the separate spheres of ideology around which so much of Victorian society had been founded 'was part of a wider formation of class identity, nation and empire [...]. International leadership and the domination of foreign competition were believed to depend directly on the existence of a stable domestic base.'[26] The seemingly more adventurous representations of women's lives in this genre allowed female readers to envisage their own prospects differently. In this regard the sensation novel might also be seen to offer women the kind of 'escapist fantasy' described by Alison Light in her study of women and twentieth-century historical fiction and by Janice Radway in her book *Reading the Romance* (1984), whereby 'heroines are able to take up what would usually be seen as the masculine reins of power and sexual autonomy.'[27] These tendencies are in evidence in *Lady Audley's Secret*, which Elaine Showalter describes as 'carefully controlled female fantasy.'[28] But they are also apparent in many lesser-known texts such as Mathilda Houston's *Such Things Are* in which the heroine survives an abortion, thus permitting her to take back control of her own body from the novel's men, and in *Pardoned: A Novel* (1883), by Anne M. Hopkinson a retelling of Bertha Rochester's story in *Jane Eyre* – a woman interred in an asylum on a spurious pretext by her brother exacts revenge on her family for her lost years.

The deviant she

> It is not man's function in life to think and feel only; his inner life he must express or utter in action of some kind – in word or deed [...] everything which is displayed outwardly is contained secretly in the innermost [...] when a person is lunatic, he is lunatic to his fingers' ends.[29]

In *Body and Mind* (1871) Henry Maudsley (1835–1918), a seminal thinker in the emerging field of medical psychiatry and criminology, espouses a firmly empirical methodology grounded in a 'direct interrogation of Nature'[30] so as to disclose the 'secrets' of the 'innermost.' For Maudsley, however, interrogating 'Nature' through inductive procedures meant not only to determine the internal, somatic sources of madness (whether those sources were perceived to be in the brain, the blood, or some other organ or system) but also to construe the external symptoms of insanity, its manifestations in the lunatic's bodily mannerisms and displays. Resisting the view of mental disorder as 'incomprehensible affliction',[31] Maudsley argued that the mind is factually, physiologically, and visually accessible if only one knows what to look for, permeating the body, leaving no extremity unaffected. Given Margaret Oliphant's reaction to Lady Audley's 'act of imposture', we can see the 'sensational heroine' as a literary device that complicates Maudsley's belief in the legibility of the 'lunatic' body, by obsessively probing conceptualizations of normalcy, its enforcement, and its radical indeterminacy.[32]

What Maudsley terms 'lunacy' emerges both as a symptom or expression of femininity in sensation fiction and its negation. Collins for one tested Maudsley's claims of empirical authority, responding specifically to worries about incarceration and other scientifically sanctioned treatments for 'lunacy'. The highly speculative nature of specifying and diagnosing madness had broad cultural implications in the Victorian period, according to Elaine Showalter's *The Female Malady* (1985). The sliding boundary between sanity and insanity was crucial to reinforcing not only gender hierarchies, but also hierarchies of nation and race. Oliphant's notion of the sensation text as a 'feverish' production, assailing the female body by means of vivid delineations of agitated nerves and overmastering passion, would also affect the mind of the woman reader, Showalter contends, given that 'uncontrolled sexuality seemed the major, almost defining symptom of insanity in women':

■ Victorian psychiatry defined its task with respect to women as the preservation of brain stability in the face of almost overwhelming physical odds. First of all, this entailed the management and regulation, insofar as possible, of women's periodic physical cycles and sexuality. Secondly, it meant the enforcement in the asylum of those qualities of self-government and industriousness that would help a woman resist the stresses of her body and the weaknesses of her female nature.[33] □

As Helen Small also notes in her 1996 monograph *Love's Madness: Medicine, the Novel, and Female Insanity, 1800–1865*, which traces the literary convention of women who go mad after the loss of their lovers, feminized madness is a category that flouts the crisp contours of exact description and provokes a bewildering array of labels.[34] While the nineteenth century saw a progressive shift in attitudes towards the mentally ill marked by the construction and development of the asylum system and the emergence of medical professionals to treat the 'lunatic', specifying the essence of 'madness' remained a vexed issue despite Henry Maudsley's confidence in the rigour of his own investigative techniques.[35] Ellen Wood's novel *St Martin's Eve* (1866) implies that medical and legal authorities, by their unhealthy fixation on uncovering and defining female insane violence, aggravate the very problems they are employed to cure. The cynical sense that the asylum was a prison masquerading as a retreat becomes prominent in sensation fiction, not only in Charles Reade's *Hard Cash* (1864) but also in Joseph Sheridan Le Fanu's *The Rose and the Key* (1871), in which the heroine, Maud Vernon, thinks she is at a party at a country house when she is actually a patient in Dr Antomarchi's lunatic asylum.

In its assessment of Ellen Wood's *St Martin's Eve*, the *Saturday Review* remarked that 'madness pure and simple, as an element in sensation novels [has] become by this time rather stale'. Nevertheless, it commended Wood for the novelty she has introduced by her 'complication of disorders' through linking the heroine's mental pathology with the mysteriously complex dispensation of the St Johns of Alnwick.[36] The *Spectator*'s response to the publication of *St Martin's Eve* was a short essay that measures Wood's new novel against Braddon's *Lady Audley's Secret* and the anonymously published *The Clyffords of Clyffe* as examples of 'Madness in Novels' (1866). According to this reviewer madness was also a means of transcending the limitations of a prosaic and materialistic modern age: 'The nineteenth century believes in love and jealousy, and in a feeble way, even in hate [...] but it is aware that the mental concentrativeness out of which these passions spring is in this age rare'. The *Spectator*'s interpretation of Wood's deployment of madness reveals much about how a response to sensation fiction in the elite press sought to corral high art from the earthy incursions of the popular and middlebrow. *St Martin's Eve* shows a novelist who wants to 'paint jealousy in its extreme forms', and who, lacking the delicately nuanced artistry of Anthony Trollope for instance, has recourse to 'a strongly sensational machinery' which stretches probability to breaking point:

■ If an ordinary novelist made an ordinary woman do what Charlotte Norris does [...] we should condemn her as ignorant of the first truths of the human heart, and her story as a meaningless tissue of improbabilities. But then Charlotte Norris is mad, secretly mad, and an excess of jealousy brings out homicidal mania [...] Granted her data Mrs. Wood has worked out her story well, but then her data exclude art as much as the data of novelists who used to employ ghosts, and revengeful Italians, and secret passages, and all the rest of it, to produce impossible or exaggerated results. As a picture of a madwoman cursed with an invisible form of madness *St. Martin's Eve* is not good, as a story of crime dictated by undiscovered mania [...] it may be pronounced a good novel. It curdles the blood without exciting the feeling of contempt. [...such books are not objectionable] except when we are told that there is high art in [them].[37] □

In *St Martin's Eve* the period's medico-legal associations between female violent insanity and women's biology throw into relief Charlotte's manipulation of her sexual allure to gain a legitimate foothold in society; but now the family itself, a psychic as well as a genealogical structure, manifests and reproduces these pathological forms. Charlotte's violent paroxysms, literally the symptom of a hereditary condition, function as an intensified expression of jealous animosity in the way that the *Spectator* signifies. Her madness is also presented as both the outcome of emotional torment, and an index of her remorse for the actions that result from a failure to counteract it. She strives 'against her evil nature', at the same time as being overwhelmed by guilt for the murder of her stepson. Clashing codes of insanity both assimilate and articulate the 'secret' of Charlotte's 'nature' here, rather than being the truth consolidating the narrative's resolution.

Charlotte Norris is an example of a key female stereotype in the sensation canon: the disturbingly over-sexualized heroine 'who had been born into the world with passions unwholesome, and had not had them checked in childhood.'[38] The reader is invited to deplore the fierce actions of this proud woman whose eyes contained 'a sort of wild expression of absolute *will*'[39] while sympathizing with her struggles to overcome the morbid inheritance of an 'ill-regulated mind'.[40] Wood also uses Charlotte's psychic derangement, as does Braddon in *Lady Audley's Secret*, to complicate the issue of female criminality. Charlotte commits a murder, but she is not subjected to a police investigation or a criminal trial. Rather a male relative investigates her transgressions, and with the support of the family doctor, removes the madwoman from society by incarcerating her in a lunatic asylum, where she lives out the remainder of her days.

The need to imprison the aberrant female so as to cleanse the narrative fabric and the middle-class readership of a perceived 'infection' is treated in D. A. Miller's *The Novel and the Police*. Miller construes Collins's *The Woman in White* as not only addressing itself to the sympathetic nervous system; it also induces panic in characters and readers by staging the contagion of the male body with female nervousness – a contagion represented by adapting the familiar and homophobic nineteenth-century discourse which depicts the male homosexual as having a woman's spirit caught within a male body.

■ The drama in which the novel writes its reader turns on the disjunctions between his allegedly masculine gender and his effectively feminine gender identification (as a creature of 'nerves'): with the result that his experience of sensation must include his panic at having the experience at all, of being in the position to have it.[41] □

Resisting this contamination by female nervousness, Collins's 'antifeminist' novel, according to Miller, abandons its grotesque aberrations, reinstates the 'phallocentric system of sexual difference' and reclaims the integrity of the male body by shutting up the feminine both within and outside male bodies (including such institutional 'bodies' as matrimony and the madhouse).[42] Given that, for Miller, the hysteric provides 'the conduit of power transactions between men', he turns to *Lady Audley's Secret*, considering it a coda to *The Woman in White*. Braddon's novel is a more explicit demonstration of how incarcerating the female, whether in the lunatic asylum or in the family home, facilitates a process of self-discipline aimed ultimately not so much at the regulation of women as at specifying the power relations of men.

In a chapter on *Lady Audley's Secret* in *Fatal Women: Lesbian Sexuality and the Mark of Aggression* (1997), Lynda Hart also approaches the sensation novel's delineation of female sexuality through an analysis of Victorian masculinity, arguing that the criminal woman must be marked off as deviant in order to transform male homosexual tendencies into heterosexual desire. This reading sees the function of female sexuality as normalizing domestic ideology. Hart's argument reflects an ongoing debate about whether sensation novels, either intentionally or not, debunk Victorian gender ideologies.[43]

Jenny Bourne Taylor's book *In the Secret Theatre of Home* (1988) is fascinated by what D. A. Miller calls the 'textual and cultural mediations' of female nervousness. For Miller, however, these mediations take no institutionalized form in *The Woman in White* – that is, there is no depiction of either the structure or the therapeutic measures associated with the asylum – but are expressed only by their formidable effects on the bodies of protagonists (and readers). These effects, Miller claims, amount to an imprisonment of sensation in a tirelessly policed regime of sexual regularity. In contrast, Taylor contends that female nervousness is 'elaborated and qualified' through 'distinct forms of psychological discourse',[44] notions which enjoy the cultural kudos of institutions. Consequently, Taylor's project exposes limitations in the sort of 'carceral' reading provided by Miller. Taylor's ability to make subtle distinctions that are forsaken in Miller's more pointed analysis is anchored in a keen alertness to the theories of consciousness that 'shape the cognitive parameters of Collins's fiction', which is situated in a broader historical context. Taylor addresses the ways in which his novels assimilate, resist, and transmute 'a contradictory set of contemporary discourses [...] about consciousness and identity, about the social formation of the self, about the workings of the unconscious and the interlinking of the mind and the body, about the problematic boundaries between sanity and madness.'[45]

Consequently Collins's fictional 'use of insanity' is 'more complex than that of any of his contemporaries'. This is because 'he wrote in a context in which the fictional mediation of madness helped to shape its cultural meaning.'[46]

Miller, for example, quotes Walter Hartright asking (after his fateful encounter with the Woman in White), 'What have I done? Assisted the victim of the most horrible of all false imprisonments to escape; or cast loose on the wide world of London an unfortunate creature, whose actions it was my duty, and every man's duty, mercifully to control?' For Miller, the passage forcibly reminds us that 'Walter's protection has in fact suspended the control that it is every man's duty to exercise over the activity of the neuropathic woman.'[47] For Taylor, by contrast, the passage indicates the provisionality of the very sense of there being a duty to control, a duty associated with the specific discourse of moral management: ' "Moral management" itself [...] might promote the belief that stable, sane identity could be built up by proper training and self-regulation, yet at the same time it could also tacitly suggest the very fragility of the identity that it aimed to sustain.'[48]

In Walter's reflection, moral management is juxtaposed with another discourse inextricably allied with madness – that of false imprisonment – and as Taylor goes on to show, mid-Victorian cultural debates about the confinement of the insane involved precisely this clash. Taylor's recovery of the discursive context permits us to ascertain what is happening in Collins's novels as partaking not in some all-encompassing 'carceral problematic' as Miller would aver, but in a struggle for the authority to specify what control, if any, should be imposed upon female subjectivity.

Taylor's focus on the erratic and conflicting definitions of female madness and self-control in *The Woman in White* reveals how Collins employs the concept of moral management as a framework yet continually adjusts its meaning. In *No Name*, Taylor argues, the narrative voice 'undercuts the sources of its own ideological coherence', and reveals 'the impossibility of representing a coherent female subjectivity'[49] at the same time that it brings myriad models of subjectivity to bear on the heroine. In Taylor's view, Collins takes the sensation novel to its limits in *Armadale*, a work in which 'there are no stable oppositions between self and other, reality and imposture [...] nothing but displacement' in plots that hinge on 'a name without an identity.'[50]

Ann Cvetkovich's *Mixed Feelings*, like Taylor's book, acts as a partial corrective to Miller's thesis. She concurs with Miller that the sensation novel has to be gauged in terms of its production of bodily sensation and 'nervousness', but disputes his reading of nervousness as invariably a signifier of femininity, and also takes issue with his notion that the somatic (or bodily) experience in the sensation novel is simply a threat to be defended against at all costs. Unlike Miller she does not separate 'thematic sensation' and 'bodily sensation', but takes the view that the somatic nature of sensation has to be scrutinized in relation to its projection onto a text. Treated in this way, sensation may be construed as functioning as both a route to patriarchal power and as a screen for the class and gender politics involved in such a process.

Following Miller, Cvetkovich examines *The Woman in White* symptomatically as a narrative of the social construction of gender and sexuality. However, whereas Miller renders this as a story about queer sexuality, Cvetkovich locates a narrative that both voices and mystifies the construction of ruling class heterosexual manliness. Cvetkovich's reading incorporates Miller's, but, by foregrounding caste, moves beyond it to probe the intricate politics of heterosexual romance. In her analysis, the novel's management of heterosexual desire (like that of the wider culture) is a significant mechanism for reproducing class division.

By thematising feeling – as in *East Lynne*, where the narrative traces the heroine's mental agony – sensation fiction does provide an outlet for women's unease or 'mixed feelings' about domesticity. But, as Cvetkovich perceives it, focusing on feminine feeling does not radicalize sensation fiction so much as depoliticize it, reducing systemic problems to individual psychological crises. By portraying women as 'mysterious and compelling' the sensation novel is often not so much a slyly subversive as a diagnostic genre, whose depiction of the middle-class woman as 'feeling subject' confirms the 'importance of emotional expression' to bourgeois domesticity.[51] Cvetkovich argues that the techniques of sensationalism were appropriated by writers of high culture like George Eliot to replicate rather than ruthlessly to reappraise the structures of confinement for middle-class women. Cvetkovich illustrates the degree to which the figure of the madwoman foregrounds contradictions in Victorian conceptions of femininity that Braddon also processes through the 'beautiful fiend' Lady Audley:

■ No one but a pre-Raphaelite would have so exaggerated every attribute of that delicate face as to give a lurid brightness to the blind complexion, and a strange, sinister light to the deep blue eyes [...] It was so like, and yet so unlike. It was as if you had burned strange-coloured fires before my lady's face, and by their influence brought out new lines and new expressions never seen before. The perfection of feature, the brilliancy of colouring, were there; but I suppose the painter had copied quaint medieval monstrosities until his brain had grown bewildered, for my lady, in his portrait of her, had something of the aspect of a beautiful fiend. Her crimson dress, exaggerated like all the rest in this strange picture, hung about her in folds that looked like flames, her fair head peeping out of the lurid mass of colour as if out of a raging furnace.[52] □

The 'demonic' potency of Lady Audley's image is evident when Robert Audley and his friend George sneak into her private chambers, which have been locked in her absence. The quest culminates in the opportunity to examine the pre-Raphaelite portrait, which hangs in the antechamber. Rather than confront Lady Audley herself, they prefer the cozy certainty of a representation to palliate their curiosity about the enigmatic lady of the house. Cvetkovich furnishes an incisive account of this episode:

■ The portrait is an emblem of how sensational representations work more generally; Braddon's insistent focus on her heroine's appearance seduces the reader with both the possibility *and* the impossibility of making visible the contradictions that mark Lady Audley's identity. [...] sensationalism derives its power from rendering concrete or visible what would otherwise be hidden; the image of the beautiful and transgressive woman becomes sensational when we know that she is evil and we both see and don't see her criminality in her appearance. If Lady Audley looked as evil as she supposedly is, she would be less sensational. (Her mother's insanity, for example, is more rather than less unsettling when it turns out that she has the appearance of a golden-haired child rather than a madwoman.) The sensation of repulsion produced by Lady Audley's criminality is indistinguishable from the fascination produced by her beauty; sensationalism consists in the indistinguishability of the two feelings.[53] □

Cvetkovich proposes that the portrait shows Lady Audley as a 'beautiful fiend' not because she is 'unfeminine' (in Oliphant's terminology) or deviant, but because the marks of her femininity are wildly exaggerated. The lurid details make her frightening as well as fascinating as she becomes the object of the male viewer's unwholesome voyeurism. Once accentuated, the signs of her femininity – her blue eyes, her crimson dress, her fair hair – evince her capacity to be a 'fiend', validating male suspicions of her dangerous capabilities. By the end of the novel, Lady Audley's rebellion is diagnosed as madness and she is exiled to an institution in Belgium to die of a wasting disease, while Robert Audley re-establishes the ideal of family life in 'a dream of a fairy cottage'.[54]

Jill Matus's book *Unstable Bodies: Victorian Representations of Sexuality and Maternity* (1995), examines the matrix in which medicine, culture, and theories of the body, sex and gender intersect. Of Braddon's finale, Matus remarks that '[f]or a work that addresses itself in many ways to the question of madness, *Lady Audley's Secret* broaches the topic only as it nears its conclusion':

■ While we are asked to associate the disclosure of madness with a 'coming out' – the latent hereditary taint is made patent to explain the heroine's conduct – I want to argue that Braddon shows how the discourse of madness displaces the economic and class issues already raised in the novel and deflects their uncomfortable implications. [...] Braddon's sensation novel goes further than criticising Victorian constructions of femininity; it points the finger at work done by discourses of morality and madness in establishing and protecting class boundaries. What makes *Lady Audley's Secret* a fascinating text is that it apprehends social and medical discourses in the act of enunciating the nature of an aberrant 'other' in order to shape a healthy, middle-class self. Until madness is pulled out of the hat as a solution and the means of plot resolution, what seems primarily to be the matter with Lady Audley is that she threatens to violate class boundaries and exclusions, and to get away with appropriat-ing social power beyond her entitlement.[55] □

Matus's monograph is preoccupied with 'the medicine of sex': the discourse of morality, ethics and hygiene that sought to superintend and regulate the female body and to ensure the vitality of the body politic.[56] She posits that the male ploy of labelling the eponymous protagonist as 'mad' and consigning her to an asylum, indeed the very medical and social-scientific production and construction of lunacy itself, is a blatant and craven cover-up, allowing 'historically specific issues of class and power to be represented instead as timeless and universal matters of female biology.' Lady Audley is an interloper but a victim as well, who struggles to negotiate the tensions between marriage as an economic contract and marriage as an emotional bond. She is 'buried alive' by her husband's family because they cannot face the ignominy of a public trial. It is only by pretending that Lady Audley is mad and transporting her away from the public gaze to the more sinister and absolute privacy of the asylum – an extended version of the home – that she can really be silenced and the family's 'honourable' name salvaged. 'The novel', as Ann Cvetkovich observes, 'is obsessed with the dangers of excessive pas-sion and sexual madness, but it rewrites this dilemma as the problem of an individual woman's murderous instincts and inherited madness.'[57]

Cvetkovich's *Mixed Feelings* and Matus's *Unstable Bodies* both clarify how emphasis on the perils of unchecked 'impulse' or 'utter unrestraint',[58] exposes the link made between the unleashing of female feeling and threats to the status quo. This anxiety imbued many nega-tive reactions to the sensation genre in the 1860s. Psychic discipline becomes indispensable to maintaining moral and social equilibrium, and women in particular bear the burden of defining virtue as the strict regulation of desire. In addition to gender difference, class differ-ence is also implicitly coded in terms of the control of feeling; although the working-class woman may not be sufficiently refined to manage her impulses, the visible sign of the middle-class woman's status is her stoical self-suppression. The woman who does not behave appropriately is unthinkable, according to another contemporary reviewer, because femininity is inextricably intertwined with sexual propriety:

■ Lady Audley is at once the heroine and the monstrosity of the novel. In drawing her, the authoress may have intended to portray a female Mephistopheles; but, if so, she should have known that a woman cannot fill such a part. The nerves with which Lady Audley could meet unmoved the friend of the man she had murdered, are the nerves of a Lady Macbeth who is half unsexed, and not those of the timid, gentle, innocent creature Lady Audley is represented as being [...] All this is very exciting; but it is also very unnatural. The artistic faults of this novel are as grave as the ethical ones. Combined, they render it one of the most noxious books of modern times.[59] □

According to this account, Braddon's novel desecrates the natural relation between femininity and the emotional life; Lady Audley's crime is that she lacks the dignified and generous responses consistent with her sex, confronting her enemies ruthlessly with 'the nerves of Lady Macbeth.' Clearly uncomfortable with the gulf between Lady Audley's innocent demeanour and her deviant behaviour, the critic declares her to be, in Ann Cvetkovich's words, 'an aesthetic and ethical abomination. The claim that the sensation novel produces an "unnatural" excitement is thus grounded in assumptions about the naturalness of gender roles.'[60]

In an insightful article on the fashioning of 'gender roles' in *The Woman in White* entitled 'The Tell-Tale Surface' (1997), Elana Gomel and Stephen Weninger respond to D. A. Miller's interpretation by arguing that 'Collins's novel is as much about the clothes as about the body'. In their opinion, Collins's language of fashion complicates both Miller's conclusions about female hysteria and the quasi-biological model that underwrites it. The clothes of Collins's characters rather than their bodies serve as 'the primary site for the construction of social sexual identity':

■ Clothes function in *The Woman in White* as a locus for the instabilities and tensions that the novel explores: the frightening slippage of all identity, most especially the precariousness of gender and class. It [the novel] becomes a tool for exploring the issues of nature and artifice, of the biological body and the (im)possibility of its social reading.[61] □

In a novel that renders the body as a matter of esoteric surfaces rather than depth, and in which gender is something one 'shops' for and purchases, transvestism becomes a sign of strength and social mobility. For Miller, the character of Marian Halcombe embodies the lesbian or 'man-in-the-woman', who is eventually rehabilitated into the heterosexual angel of the house; for Gomel and Weninger (1833–1900), she is a figure who comprehends that 'the privileges of a man are the privileges of choosing a disguise' and who consciously modifies and finesses her appearance, before being forced back into a corset and crinoline by 'the exigencies of the Victorian plot.'[62]

Tamar Heller's *Dead Secrets* is preoccupied by how the 'exigencies of the Victorian plot' impinge on the representation of hysterical femininity.[63] Mid-Victorian psychiatric accounts of specific symptoms tend to expound the hysterical state as an excess of normative levels of feeling.[64] In his 1866 lecture 'On the Pathology and Treatment of Hysteria' Julius Althaus avers that

■ All symptoms of hysteria have their prototype in those vital actions by which grief, terror, disappointment, and other painful emotions and affections, are manifested under ordinary circumstances, and which become signs of hysteria as soon as they attain a certain degree of intensity. [...] Tell [a] woman suddenly that the house is on fire [...] and you may be sure to observe some or all the following symptoms. She perceives a feeling of constriction in the epigastrium, oppression on the chest, and palpitations of the heart; a lump seems to rise in her throat and gives a feeling of suffocation[65] □

Althaus's description of hysteria's impact upon middle and upper class women (the malady's main sufferers) is reminiscent of Victorian reviews that document the hazardous physiological effects of perusing sensation fiction. The 'suffocation' and 'constriction' registered by Althaus also illuminates Heller's notion that the sensation genre frequently figures hysteria as silent suffering, a strangulated incapacity to vocalize.[66] Hélène Cixous (born 1937) explains that the hysteric's initial revolt against male law is transformed into acquiescence: 'She asks the master, "What do I want?" and "What do you want me to want, so that I might want it?"'[67] Citing both Sigmund Freud (1856–1939) and Cixous on silence as the mark of hysteria, Heller locates another site of buried or smothered femininity through the delineation of Rachel Verinder's 'hysterical passion' in Collins's *The Moonstone*, which conveys 'a reductive message about gender':

■ Just as Cixous says that 'silence is the mark of hysteria', so Rachel's silence is not just her way of protecting her lover but a sign of pathology, of her difficulty in voicing her need. [...] The symptomatology of hysteria thus neutralises the power of what had seemed most threatening about women: their words and their sexuality.[68] □

According to Heller, the hysteric does not express women's subversive resistance to, or fury at, her restricted role, but actually emblematizes that role itself, and legitimates women's subjugation and confinement.[69] Clinical discourse affords the greatest help of all professional languages in charting and regulating the femininity that is perceived to be an initial threat.

Heller's insights into *The Moonstone*'s manipulation of the discourse of hysteria to invalidate women as active, desiring and eloquent subjects might seem to espouse Miller's Foucauldian judgement of Collins's novel. Yet for Heller, Miller's hypothesis of a monologic narrative implicated in the remorseless operations of surveillance and social policing is ultimately reductive. Instead, Heller advances the model of a 'double-voiced' discourse in *The Moonstone*: articulations of the ortho-dox plot trajectory are undercut by a 'deviant' subtext whose principal strategies are biting irony and canny indirection. This model becomes a means of negotiating one of the most persistent questions debated in current feminist criticism of sensation fiction: are we dealing with a group of 'dissident' novelists who engage in a radical debunking of gender norms? Or do they shirk the more far-reaching implications of their own critique, and merely buttress the prevailing law of genre by inserting the resistant female into a marriage plot that formalizes her submission to the patriarchal ordering of her desires?

The transgressive text

Let us have the satisfaction of saying at the outset that from some female writers of fiction we do get books which fully come up to our ideal of what a woman's work ought to be. The novels of 'George Eliot', for instance, [...] are not only works of high art, but books which no woman need blush to have written or to read. [...] unfortunately, the great majority of novels written by women are the very opposite of the ideal which we have pictured. They are conspicuous, not only for a laxity of moral tone and for highly-wrought descriptions of sensual passion, but in many cases for positive indecency. In saying this we are prepared for the sneer that it is unmanly to attack a woman. Our answer is that we hold it to be simply a duty to point out to the reading world the poison and the filth which is contained in so many of the gilt-lettered volumes which bear, sad to relate, women's names on the title-pages.[70]

Whereas this contributor to the 1870 journal *The Period* lambasts women's 'highly-wrought' articulation of feeling in sensation fiction, recent feminist scholarship acclaims it as a major source of the genre's iconoclastic intensity; both, however, equate this outpouring of 'sen-sual passion' with a robust reaction against stifling social conventions. But did the controversial formulations of gender and sexuality and the broader critiques of Victorian society erode mainstream values? Or is the narrative structure of sensation fiction geared towards suppressing and diluting anti-establishment rhetoric in resolutions that portray the 'moral' characters married, inheriting wealth and living contentedly? Elaine Showalter, following the lead of Dorothy L. Sayers, who in 1944 found Wilkie Collins 'genuinely feminist in his treatment of women',[71] avers that the sensation text reflects the violent passions and frustrations of women whose lives are occupied exclusively by deadening domestic rituals.

■ The sensationalists made crime and violence domestic, modern and suburban; but their secrets were not simply solutions to mysteries and crimes; they were the secrets of women's dislike of their roles as daughters, wives and mothers. These women novelists made a powerful appeal to the female audience by subverting the traditions of feminine fiction to suit their own imaginative impulses, by expressing a wide range of suppressed female emotions, and by tapping and satisfying fantasies of protest and escape.[72] □

For Showalter sensation fiction 'conveys the threat of new fantasies, new expectations, and even female insurrection.'[73] This searching and sceptical genre affords a vicarious exhilaration for female readers confined to a mundane middle-class routine; it both taps into and constructs a vibrant sense of shared values among that audience; and it crafts a series of readily recognized satirical strategies by which to ridicule social, legal and cultural codes. Moreover, these narratives frequently fashion the criminal woman as a morally ambiguous – rather than immoral – protagonist. Reacting to commentary that construed these novels as a markedly inferior and minor fictional phenomenon, either blandly conventional or largely irrelevant to cultural and literary analysis, Showalter highlights the genre's veiled interrogation of gender, race and class stereotypes. Her discussion of *Lady Audley's Secret* focuses on the eponymous protagonist as 'a new kind of heroine, one who could put her hostility towards men into violent action.'[74]

In Showalter's account the key dynamic, camouflaged by the novel's sensational apparatus, is that Lady Audley is not criminal, but acts instead out of a coolly rational self-interest to safeguard her livelihood. Abandoned by her first husband, George Talboys, she commits bigamy because marriage allows her to indulge her acquisitive love of luxurious objects. When he returns, she manages to take control of events and get rid of him; murder stands in for divorce, which was only beginning to be an imaginable solution to miserable marriages and was still very difficult to obtain. Thus, Showalter concludes that 'as every woman reader must have sensed, Lady Audley's real secret is that she is *sane* and, moreover, representative.'[75] Similarly, Winifred Hughes's *The Maniac in the Cellar* proposes that Braddon deliberately circumvents traditional moral assumptions: 'Instead of abandoning the popular conventions' she uses 'them against themselves, investing them with a new ironic significance.'[76]

Showalter's interpretation has proven seminal, though it tends to obscure the fact that while Lady Audley's crimes feed female readers' fantasies of rebellion and affective expression, her sensational appeal within the narrative is also the outcome of a masculine fantasy about women's covert capabilities. The story is largely told from the perspective of Robert Audley, the nephew who becomes a detective to investigate his aunt's seemingly inscrutable past. The narrative rarely provides access to Lady Audley's inner life or standpoint; instead, its sensationalism emerges from repeated references to the haunting beauty that belies the heroine's abnormal behaviour. Ellen Miller Casey's essay 'Other People's Prudery: Mary Elizabeth Braddon' (1984) tempers Showalter's polemic by showing that Braddon's writing expresses what U. C. Knoepflmacher calls the asocial and amoral 'counterworld' of Victorian society, indulging yet finally repudiating insurgent attitudes at variance with the codes of traditional decorum:

> ■ [Braddon] defied convention by writing of murders and bigamies committed by beautiful women who were regarded semi-sympathetically. Despite the outrage of some readers, Victorian critics recognised that Braddon's sensation novels were responding to their readers' desires rather than defying them [...] she provided a stimulus to Victorian imaginations with a wink for the knowing and a carefully proper surface for the censors.[77] □

As Casey implies, it is tempting to overstate Showalter's 'subversive' argument and the oppositional message *Lady Audley's Secret* exhibits. However, Showalter also explores Braddon's status as a failed radical, compromised by her own social conformity and by prevailing generic orthodoxies: 'By the second volume guilt has set in. In the third volume we see the heroine punished, repentant and drained of all energy [...]; the very conventions of the domestic novel opposed the heroine's development.'[78] Showalter was one of the first to politicize Braddon as a feminist author, and Collins is frequently credited with creating women characters that act in open defiance of Victorian gender norms. Catherine Peters notes that while Collins 'liked women who were intelligent and gifted and spoke their minds', he was ultimately 'not in the least interested in female emancipation.'[79] In response to such critical conversations, recent scholars underline the ideological sleight-of-hand in sensation fiction, the radically ambivalent treatment of gender norms and those who violate them. Ann Cvetkovich posits in *Mixed Feelings* that the ideological management of sensation functioned more effectually to regulate the rebellion and contention: '[A] discourse about affect serves to contain resistance, especially from women. Rather than leading to social change, the expression of feeling can become an end in itself or an individualist solution to systematic problems.'[80]

For Cvetkovich the sensation novel is a part of the apparatus that culturally produces and monitors feminine 'affect' as a construct, and becomes a site for the naturalized link between women's bodies, sensation, and gender, ultimately consolidating the domestic ideal. These novels are to Cvetkovich about the centrality of the institution of marriage for women and how they do or do not adapt to the kind of existence it entails. Complicit with the 'official' ideas for women as nurturing wives and benevolent mothers, the fictions ratify myths of patriarchal culture about the audacious heroine who must be punished for ignoring established hierarchies in her selfish bid for power, property or sex, and illustrate the necessity of female rectitude.

Lyn Pykett, in *The 'Improper' Feminine: The Women's Sensation Novel and the New Woman Writing* (1992), adopts a more cautious standpoint and urges that we treat sensation fiction 'not simply as either the transgressive or subversive field of the improper feminine, or the contained, conservative domain of the proper feminine [but rather as] a site in which the contradictions, anxieties, and opposing ideologies of Victorian culture converge.'[81]

Pykett signals that sensation novels reproduce and negotiate pervasive cultural disquiet about the nature and status of respectable femininity and the domestic ideal at a time when women and other reformers were clamouring for a widening of women's legal rights and educational and employment opportunities. They both work with and re-imagine gender stereotypes, such as the 'fast woman' and the 'angel in the house'. The designation of the proper feminine in Victorian gender ideology, Pykett argues, '*implies* the improper feminine',[82] the deviant sexual woman; one of the central paradoxes of the uproar over sensation fiction was its 'tendency to define' these narratives 'as a form both characteristically feminine, and profoundly unfeminine, or even anti-feminine.'[83]

Like Lyn Pykett, Helena Michie, in *Sororophobia: Differences among Women* (1992), focuses on the ideological slipperiness of the sensation genre, and its obsession with 'female self-replication' and fraudulence. Michie claims that this alertness to multiple feminine selves epitomizes a typically Victorian ambivalence about women's manipulation of social and public masks through carefully rehearsed artifice. Alongside the conservative fear that women are not naturally angels, there is, in plots where one woman effortlessly substitutes for another, a mordant critique of female economic and social marginality.

■ Sensation novels abound with women who disguise, transform, and replicate themselves, who diffuse their identities and scatter clues to them over the surface of their parent texts [...] In the cases of Lady Audley and Isabel Vane this duplicity, this multiplicity of identity, is explicitly marked by the text as criminal; it is the job of the reader and/or detective figure of each novel to sort through the multiple identities offered by each heroine, to work against her self-reproduction, and to close the novel with a woman confined to a single identity, a single name, and a single place – in both cases, the grave. [...] It is easy to see Lady Audley and Isabel Vane as special cases; indeed the idiom of sensation fiction is exceptionality, improbability, and excess. It would perhaps be more useful, however, to see them as somehow representative of Victorian anxieties about all women, as embodying in their many bodies cultural fears about female duplicity. In the same way, while these novels can be and have been categorised as novels about bigamy and adultery, they can also be read as novels about marriage and the changes of identity contained and displayed within marriage as an institution.[84] □

Michie construes female sexuality – whose presence threatens to disrupt domestic ideology's construction of the maternal spiritualized woman – as a crucial issue in recent analyses of sensation fiction. Braddon and Wood supply a number of contradictory possibilities for interpreting the deviant female: both writers seem convinced of the 'multiplicity' of the female self, yet they are obviously deeply conflicted about the consequences of such multiplicity as they struggle both to render their heroines sympathetically and to refine literary modes that clearly penalize and contain them.

Commentators who perceive Wilkie Collins as a formidable social critic generally foreground his recognition of gender identities as brittle social fabrications or 'inadequate categorizations',[85] that serve the ends of an inequitable patriarchal system. While she registers the 'conflicts between radicalism and orthodoxy' in his treatment of gender norms, Virginia B. Morris contends that Collins ignores 'biological explanations for women's violent behaviour' in his nuanced portraits of female criminals, and instead attributes their violence to their experience of abuse and dependence 'in male-dominated Victorian society.'[86] Donald E. Hall's *Fixing Patriarchy: Feminism and Mid-Victorian Novelists* (1996), in a chapter that he concedes is 'politically generous' in its 'reading of the cultural work performed by [Collins's] sensation novels', privileges, like Helena Michie's *Sororophobia*, the 'gender fluidity' of the characters in such novels as *The Woman in White* and *Armadale*. With their 'emphasis on role-playing as the basis for gender identity', and their recognition that 'beliefs, roles, and perceptions are [historically] specific', Collins's works divulge the 'social construction of masculinity and femininity' and 'the foolishness of those individuals who accept such roles as "reality"'.[87]

For Philip O'Neill, in *Wilkie Collins: Women, Property and Propriety* (1988), these debates about femininity and masquerade often ignore how Collins formulates the complex relation between gender stereotypes and 'the interests of property.' O'Neill indicates that Collins questions Victorian gender norms by revealing propriety to be 'an ideology with a material basis' and by representing actuality itself as a social construction that 'serves and protects the rights of property'.[88] In *The Fallen*

Leaves (1879), the novel that, in O'Neill's opinion, 'comes nearest to justifying [a] feminist label' Collins imagines 'an alternative sexual code' and uncovers 'the masculine parameters of culture, of a cultural regime which presents itself as the natural order and conceals its own specific historical formation.'[89] In *The Evil Genius* (1886), however, Collins valorizes masculinity, and his fiction sometimes attributes gender inequities to 'the functionings of chance' rather than to 'human agency'.[90] Thus while Collins goes some distance towards vouchsafing women a sense of their own subjectivity, letting them be 'free subjects rather than the objects of males', he is not, according to O'Neill, a 'feminist': 'Collins [...] is more consistent in his social and political analysis than has generally been recognized; but to see this is not to impose upon him, with retrospective hindsight, a neat form of modern political attitude or an unambivalently urged social programme'.[91]

O'Neill's investigation, especially of neglected novels such as *The Fallen Leaves*, is effective. However, his monograph tends to underestimate the ways in which Collins naturalizes social constructions and reinforces sexual stereotypes in the imaginative patterns of his fiction. O'Neill invokes a model of sexual difference that traces gender identity back to its 'natural' bodily source – the model that D. A. Miller's *The Novel and the Police* sees operating in Collins's oeuvre, to an ideologically conservative end.

Politically engaged scholars such as O'Neill, who have an investment in the sensation genre's potential to resist dominant ideologies, have to grapple with the fact that the figure of the criminal woman has just as often been mobilized to regulate femininity strictly as to undermine it. Alison Milbank makes some of the same points about Collins's relation to the Gothic in *Daughters of the House* (1992). Casting doubt on feminist appraisals of Collins, Milbank argues that he produces variations on 'the female Gothic' in *The Woman in White* and *The Moonstone*, yet abandons or discredits the plot of female escape in both texts. Milbank distinguishes Collins's 'female Gothic' from what she considers his sensation fiction – novels such as *No Name* and *Armadale*, which more closely approximate 'the male Gothic' in her view. Although these novels contain aggressive female figures who 'invade' homes (rather than attempting to escape from them, as the heroines of 'the female Gothic' do), Collins's 'errant women act only to reinforce Victorian sexual ideology'.[92] Not only do they 'collapse into passive conformity' by the novels' end; they also serve Collins's erotic aims as objects that cater to male pleasure.[93]

The Victorian sensation novel crafted by left-leaning and feminist scholarship is a profoundly contradictory text. On the one hand Wilkie Collins can be evaluated in terms of his daring deconstruction of normative class and gender identities as he champions those women who have openly broken with the family centred system (Jenny Bourne

Taylor's *In the Secret Theatre of Home*), or, on the other, he can be seen as the standard-bearer for the bourgeois, surveillance society (as portrayed by D. A. Miller). John Kucich's *The Power of Lies* (1994) intervenes to challenge what it construes as the polarization of these debates about the sensation genre. Kucich vouchsafes an instructive third way, neither dividing Victorian novelists into opposing camps of stern reactionaries and those promoting an 'anarchic and asocial' counterculture, nor eroding the distinction between the two categories and thereby revealing female 'transgression' to be a hollow gesture. Instead, Kucich posits that myriad forms of parodic assault on the values and practices of the Victorian middle-class – both in and out of fiction – were neither exactly what they professed to be, nor utterly without substance. Kucich is especially receptive to what he terms 'the political nervousness' of some recent studies of the ideological matrices of nineteenth-century fiction, which have 'hurried to demystify the oppositional postures of even the most virulent Victorian rebels.'[94] Kucich refers specifically to D. A. Miller's Foucauldian interpretation of Collins, and finds real merit in Miller's enterprise, as well as in the research of Nancy Armstrong and Mary Poovey,[95] to divulge the political naivety of endeavours by feminist historians to proclaim the ongoing critical relevance of sensation writers on the basis of their apparent subversiveness.

However, Kucich's book adroitly evades an initial act of demystification to canvass other, less polarized, methods of gauging what Lillian Nayder calls sensation's 'alternative vision in which moral codes and social norms' are 'inverted.'[96] Kucich underscores the ways in which Collins deployed the insider/outsider rhetoric of his historical moment to position himself in relation to the profession of authorship in the nineteenth century. Though this analysis bears comparison with Tamar Heller's *Dead Secrets* and Jenny Bourne Taylor's *In the Secret Theatre of Home*, Kucich's standpoint is perhaps more robust, replacing the schizoid Collins furthered by current feminist scholarship with a bullish and belligerent writer whose fiction re-imagines a middle class in which urbane cultural intellectuals like himself claim a paramount place, probing the social and political prestige of newly elevated bourgeois occupations such as the law and medicine.

Maternal melodrama

According to Marianne Hirsch, 'the nineteenth-century heroine [...] tends not only to be separated from the figure and story of her mother, but who herself tries to avoid maternity at all costs.'[97] Hirsch avers that the maternal subject makes only fleeting appearances in the Victorian novel; when she does, she functions as a critical commentary on the courtship plot and its hegemony in the classification of a woman's role. Ellen Wood's extensive scrutiny of issues surrounding the rearing of children and maternal management can be traced back to her first full-length novel *Danesbury House* (1860) and to *Mrs Halliburton's Troubles* (1862). But it is *East Lynne*, which remained a hugely popular work in stage and screen versions in both Britain and America from the 1860s to the 1930s, which has garnered judicious commentary since E. Ann Kaplan designated the novel as a 'sacrifice paradigm' of 'maternal melodrama' in 1989.[98]

Winifred Hughes, in *The Maniac in the Cellar*, addresses the degree to which Victorian melodrama, in social materials and in plot, narrowed its focus to domestic rituals and gender in the 1850s. The dramaturgy exploited an unproblematic distinction between good and evil and moved towards a reassuring finale in which honour and decency prevailed over those determined to derail the social order. While sensation fiction appears to follow this trajectory, it actually disrupts the very codes and standards in which assessments of good and evil are anchored. Deferential familial relations may be restored, but an unnerving sense of association between propriety and dissolution lingers at the close. For Kaplan, it is the mother figure who signifies this disquieting link, challenging that vision of the Victorian matriarch described in Elaine Showalter's *A Literature of Their Own* (1982) as 'a Perfect Lady [...] contentedly submissive to men, but strong in her inner purity and religiosity, queen in her own realm of the House.'[99]

Kaplan's essay 'The Political Unconscious in the Maternal Melodrama: Ellen Wood's *East Lynne*' (1989) melds psychoanalytic and Marxist criticism to situate the novel in the intertwined theoretical frameworks of mothering theory and female subjectivity. Kaplan's interest in tracing the fictional, stage and film progeny of *East Lynne* is energized by the political resonance of melodrama, given its far-reaching association with the censored, occluded and repressed voices of street theatre and working-class entertainments, though Peter Brooks has endeavoured to reclaim melodrama by stressing its influence on middle-class writing as well.[100] For Kaplan, the maternal melodrama is precisely the mode geared towards the articulation of ambivalence about female sexuality in an era when gender roles were changing, a shift which had profound implications for the disposition of 'the nuclear family':

■ East Lynne stands interestingly at the juncture of the melodramatic pattern that showed the family as threatened from the outside (by dangerous, usually male, figures, often aristocrats or men in authority abusing their power) and the later melodramas that explore the sexual dangers and problems within the nuclear family – a trend that accelerates after Freud's 'discoveries' of sexual desire between parents and children.[101] □

Kaplan is responsive to how the narrative of Carlyle's two marriages in *East Lynne* has been deciphered as a staging of the Freudian Oedipal drama by which normative female sexuality is affirmed. The marriage of Carlyle and Isabel Vane (who embody, in displaced form, the father and mother of the Freudian drama) is endangered by the rebellious daughter (Barbara Hare) who yearns for the father (Carlyle), and must repudiate, and in this case replace, Isabel. But Kaplan suggests that in the closing stages of *East Lynne*, this Oedipal drama is exposed and disturbed by another, more elliptical scenario, one that divulges what the middle-class family strenuously seeks to veil: a rival trajectory of female sexuality. Kaplan's essay indicates that this alternative story may be comprehended as a version of the Freudian drama from the mother's perspective: so Isabel as the spurned wife seeks the immediate return of the husband/father who has been enticed away by the daughter. However, *East Lynne* may sketch in a very different version of the narrative arc in Kaplan's account: Isabel's passionate longing for the child in the closing volume points to a fixation on the mother and not the father, so Oedipal drama becomes maternal melodrama.

Barbara Thaden, in *The Maternal Voice in Victorian Fiction* (1997), ponders Kaplan's psychoanalytic assessment of *East Lynne*:

■ Kaplan believes that the central problem in this novel is female passion, and that 'passion for children in the world of *East Lynne* is a "safe" location of female desire' [...] However, Barbara Hare clearly tells Isabel that passion for children is an *unsafe* place for female desire. Why? Elizabeth Gaskell's diary provides one reason; children were more likely to die than husbands, thus investing all one's emotional energies in them might lead to profound grief and despair[102] □

Thaden invokes child-care discourses of the period that negate the over-indulgent mother and privilege the more detached matriarch who demands strict obedience from her offspring. Though Thaden interrogates Kaplan's thesis, both commentators disclose that, however one may choose to interpret it, *East Lynne*'s alternative account of Isabel's function in the Oedipal drama reveals that the literal fulfilment of female desire within the nuclear family is impossible. Reconciliation with the husband/father is subject to a process of perpetual deferral, and the passion for a child can only be realized through death.

E. Ann Kaplan and Barbara Thaden are preoccupied by questions that Lyn Pykett poses in *The 'Improper' Feminine*: what constitutes a wife or mother in *East Lynne*, particularly if a husband and children do not recognize her? Who does the novel uphold as embodying the correct relation to spouse and offspring? And, most crucially, is a mother's 'part' performable by others?[103] Hearth and home, as Pykett implies, are rendered vulnerable if the maternal dignity that guarantees their sanctity and security is exposed as an elaborate stratagem. *East Lynne* 'problematizes' the concept of the 'natural' mother's superiority as a caregiver and the repeated image of 'masquerade' in the novel signals an awareness of the riddling indeterminacy of middle-class familial functions even as it seems to avow motherhood as the combination of biological fact, social role and exalted moral calling described by Sarah Ellis and other conduct book writers.

> ■ Isabel's story is a maternal melodrama or a drama of motherhood. Hers is not simply the story of a fallen woman or an erring wife, it is also, most emphatically, the story of a fallen and hence suffering mother. Isabel's maternal suffering (within the wider context of the novel's representation of mothering) foregrounds the contradictory demands made on women by the equation of true womanhood with maternal feeling. Isabel is a woman, and in particular a mother, who loves too much. Her maternal feelings, like other aspects of her emotional life, are characterised by excess. [...]
>
> Following the loss of her husband and lover, Isabel's whole identity (for both the character and the reader) is defined by her motherhood. Isabel is thus constructed as an over-invested mother, another version of the improper feminine which must be expelled from the text and replaced by the normative controlled and controlling proper femininity of Barbara Hare. However, within the text's emotional and psychological economy Isabel has quite a different function. Throughout the novel, but particularly in the final volume, the reader is repeatedly invited to identify with Isabel through the text's staging of the spectacle of her maternal suffering.[104] □

Pykett emphasizes how Wood crafts for the reader a voyeuristic window into Isabel's agonized jealousy. We are repeatedly situated as spectators watching Isabel, disguised by a disfigurement resulting from a railway accident, as she observes the joyful connubial and familial scenes enacted between her former husband Carlyle and Barbara. Winifred Hughes describes Isabel's return unrecognized to the home and children she deserted as masochistic, a 'prolonged, luxurious orgy of self-torture',[105] with Isabel maintaining a sacrificial and expiatory silence about her erotic history. Pykett explains that the so-called masochism of the novel becomes a major facet of its 'pleasures' for the 'middle-class woman reader.'[106] Our witnessing of Isabel's unbearable maternal deprivation functions didactically to enforce the novel's moral message, warning of the perils of intemperate longing and female marital indiscretion. *East Lynne* was published four years after the 1857 Divorce Act, a law which many believed would shift the balance of power within the home and prompt women to forsake their families. Wood's novel allays the cultural misgivings roused by the 1857 Act, by showing a penitent woman who returns to the home of her own volition and then dies for her wrongdoing. However, Pykett contends that we are also encouraged to 'identify' with the errant Isabel and her desperate effort to retain a connection to the children whom she abandoned. Indeed she becomes 'the repository of the text's and the reader's emotional ambivalence and resistance.'[107]

Pykett's argument about *East Lynne*'s portrayal of the masochism of the maternal melodrama is important because it pinpoints 'the potential subversiveness' of a novel whose resolution 'tends to leave its readers, like its sacrificial heroine, feeling powerless to change the situation.'[108] The reader's emotional investment in Isabel creates a vantage point from which to scrutinize the smug piety of the novel's 'official' morality, in which Isabel, the wayward wife, is punished while Barbara Hare's unassuming, homely and steadfast virtues are generously rewarded. As my previous subchapter indicates, some recent Marxist-feminist criticism is wary of scholarship that celebrates sensation fiction's oppositional debunking of the heterosexual nuclear family as the cornerstone of bourgeois culture. However, Pykett shows it is equally rash to dismiss *East Lynne* as an ideologically complicit text that reproduces and reinforces the reactionary power dynamics of the period. Pykett posits instead a complexly conservative novel torn between empathy for the frank expression of female, and especially maternal, passion, and a mistrust of the socially disruptive consequences of such emancipation. For Pykett, the subtext of *East Lynne* is rooted in the way it prompts readers to think 'two otherwise contradictory things at once; in other words [...] its dialogism.'[109] By manipulating perspective, *East Lynne* seems to require its readers to demonize a 'fallen woman' whose sense of severe dislocation, claustrophobia and maternal anguish awakens our sympathetic identification. As Ann Cvetkovich claims in *Mixed Feelings*, this kind of ambivalence imbues a genre unsure whether to classify the prodigal woman as a 'transgressive adulteress' or as a victim consumed by 'psychic pain and repressed feelings.'[110] It was precisely this ability to goad the reader into illicit sympathy with a 'Magdalen' and her 'fiery ordeal' that so disconcerted Margaret Oliphant in her 1862 review.[111]

The formulation of maternal torment in *East Lynne* is a concern for Laurie Langbauer in her 1989 essay 'Women in White, Men in Feminism':

■ *East Lynne* explicitly refers the hysteric, as it refers all else, back to the mother, exposing in the process the fantasies of power involved in that collapse. [...] this novel makes clear that [...] hysteria is natural to women [...] because it is a direct function of woman's most natural role, her maternity:

[...] women's nervous afflictions appear to come from their motherhood. Isabel has inherited her nervous oversensitiveness from her own mother [...] another important mother in this book, Mrs. Hare, has become an hysterical invalid explicitly because she is a mother, separated from her only son.[112] □

Wood's novel evaluates the degree to which hysteria, far from being a non gender-specific disorder, is effectively tied to cultural definitions of the maternal role. 'Mother' is, as Langbauer reminds us, an 'archaic synonym' for the hysteric, and both figures are 'confined' for their own safety and indeed for the wellbeing of bourgeois society in general.[113] A 'fallen' mother's licentious proclivities could be genetically bequeathed to her daughter. Langbauer treats *East Lynne* as 'the premier example of humble propitiation by the mother, of what Julia Kristeva might call her ultimate abjection', given the nature of the disfigured Isabel Vane's return as a governess and servant of her own family. *East Lynne*, Langbauer proposes, is not concerned with the daughter's responses to her mother or how the knowledge of her mother's temperament and fate shapes her own sense of self; she is simply determined by her mother's disposition. As Lynda Nead demonstrates in *Myths of Sexuality* (1988), the hereditary madness passed from mother to bigamous daughter in a novel like *Lady Audley's Secret* encrypts the Victorian medical discourses that 'defined infidelity in woman in terms of a congenital disease that could be inherited by the female offspring.'[114] The heroine's struggle to avoid her maternal legacy in *Lady Audley's Secret* is, for Langbauer, the key to her actions, and the novel depicts maternal insanity as a metaphor for the daughter's social and psychic inheritance, rather than using it to signify her biological instability.

Jill Matus in her chapter on 'Maternal Deviance' in *Unstable Bodies* also reflects on the melodrama of *Lady Audley's Secret* as a challenge to medico-scientific representations of the mother that underwrote cultural conceptions of woman as specifically framed for reproduction and equipped with 'high' maternal instinct. Matus elaborates one of the core ideas imbuing Laurie Langbauer's fascination with the novel: Braddon's rendering of the discourse of madness provocatively prompts the reader to consider maternal inheritance not solely as a matter of biological organization and bodily functioning, but also in terms of economic and legal disenfranchisement.[115]

■ Medico-legal representations of maternal insanity are concerned with how to draw the fine line between badness and madness [...] Maternal insanity is itself a slippery term that signifies both madness occasioned by becoming a mother (puerperal insanity) as well as madness inherited from the mother (insanity transmitted through the maternal line). This discourse of insanity allows matters of class, economic and social position to be represented as the instability of the female body, and its propensity to pass on such instability to its female issue. [...] In Lady Audley's maternal history, women go mad at the point that they become mothers. [...] On becoming a mother herself, she confronts exactly what she sought to avoid – drudgery and dependency and want – and she experiences fits of madness which cease when she takes action to make a new and better life for herself.[116] ☐

According to Matus, Braddon exploits the vexed distinction between vice and psychosis, drawing on her readers' familiarity with the controversial insanity plea, less to hint that crime may masquerade as insanity than to point out that her society would rather accept an inadequate explanation of madness than confront the grave implications of a mother's transgressions. Matus shows that the discourse of maternal instinct and its perversions serves to inscribe class differences among women, and to naturalize the distinctions between middle-class mothers and deviant others in *Sorrow on the Sea* (1868) by Lady Emma Caroline Wood (1802–79). In this novel the vulnerability of a young mother attempting to save her child from the clutches of a midwife employed by her evil brother-in-law provides occasion for sensational and melodramatic treatment. While the heroine, Cora Noble, is a paragon of virtuous and instinctive motherhood, the callous midwife contradicts any notion of natural and intrinsic mother love. She loathes and exploits her own son, who resembles Caliban in the play *The Tempest* (1611) by William Shakespeare (1564–1616).

Andrew Mangham's essay ' "Murdered at the Breast": Maternal Violence and the Self-Made Man in Popular Victorian Culture' (2004) weighs the question of how Victorian discourses of motherhood react to or accommodate obvious departures from the bourgeois ideal in sensation fiction. Mangham posits that the representations of demonic and pathological maternity in Braddon's early fiction contrast with characterizations of masculine social positions and professions as rational and productive in 'On Liberty' (1859) by John Stuart Mill (1806–73) and Samuel Smiles's *Self-Help*. Mangham contends that motherhood, for the Victorians, was perceived not just as an organic phase of womanhood, but a solemn undertaking that required a constant system of behavioural actions or inactions to make it a success rather than a hazard. Mangham highlights how the biological apotheosis of maternity and childbirth could also result in women murdering their babies, given that Victorian medical treatises suggested that motherhood was never far removed from 'sanguinary impulses':

■ Braddon's fictional work of the early 1860s [...] reveals a thematic interest in the social and personal ramifications of aggressive and unhealthy
forms of motherhood. For example, in *The Trail of the Serpent*, Braddon's
first, unsuccessful, novel, which predated her best-seller *Lady Audley's
Secret* (1862) by a year, the novelist appropriates her era's concerns with
child murder to outline the tragic history and nefarious present of the
text's villain. Jabez North, the demonic half of a twin duo, is cast, as a
baby, into a river because his slum-living mother can only afford to raise
one of her illegitimate offspring. He is providentially rescued by a fisher-
man [...] His twin brother, Jim Lomax, is meanwhile raised to the best of
his mother's abilities. As Jim becomes a poor, honest labourer, and Jabez
turns out to be a wicked social climber, the didactic message of the novel
seems to be that motherly love, regardless of its social status, is an indispensable part of creating healthy subsequent generations.[117] □

Notions of 'motherly love' are also central to Shirley Jones's essay,
'Motherhood and Melodrama: *Salem Chapel* and Sensation Fiction'
(1999), which appraises Margaret Oliphant's aesthetic and moral
critique of a genre whose stock effects she nevertheless both exploits
and modifies in her own most popular novel.[118] Jones demonstrates
that through *Salem Chapel* (1863), Oliphant endeavours to counteract
the harmful influence of the equivocal sensational heroine – attacked
in her reviews for *Blackwood's Magazine* between 1862 and 1867 – by
offering instead a range of female characters by which to reassert a
decorous strength and duty overlooked by the sensation vogue. The
central figure in this valorization of 'proper' womanhood in *Salem
Chapel* is Mrs Vincent, an ardent model of maternity:

■ The analysis of maternal experience is a vital and challenging aspect of
Oliphant's writing [...] In her own sensation novel Oliphant writes out sexual desire as the prime focus of female 'sensual passion' and replaces
it with maternal passion. Maternal passion as it is represented in *Salem
Chapel* is as extreme in its emotion and physicality as sexual passion
[...] The plot of Oliphant's novel articulates the kind of maternal anxieties
and concern for young womanhood that her criticism of the sensational
voices. Oliphant seeks to expose the dangers of romantic fantasy and to
re-emphasise the importance of fiction as a moral guide.[119] □

While 'maternal passion' is as vehement as 'sensual passion' in Jones's
thesis, the former, as reflected in Mrs Vincent's wholesome and protec-
tive maternity, works for the defence of precious family bonds, while
the latter epitomizes an egocentric betrayal of the pieties of domestic
life. As Jones signifies, Oliphant strives to show that women writers,
like mothers, should exert a benign and considerate influence on their
impressionable women readers, fostering a community of responsible

and measured femininity. But in their excessive 'craving' for sexual adventure and fulfilment, sensation heroines reject such a community in a fictional mode that persuades its practitioners to distort reality and diminish the humanity of its subjects.

Oliphant's insistence on the role of fiction as 'a moral guide' returns us to her 1867 *Blackwood's* article that began this chapter. Her review fashions female sensation writers such as Braddon and Rhoda Broughton as heedless purveyors of 'fleshy' and 'unlovely' chronicles that should be banished to the fringes of polite discourse. Oliphant is particularly exercised by the notion that these 'unlovely' stories delineate the dynamics of intemperate female passion within the 'home', a site that should ordinarily vouchsafe a harmonious retreat from the upheaval of the public sphere. Alison Milbank notes in *Daughters of the House* that the 'last twenty years have witnessed intense scrutiny of the Victorian woman, whose association with domesticity' has attained 'an emblematic significance, encapsulating for the modern reader the sexual ideology of a whole culture.'[120] Milbank's methodology raises a key question: if 'the Victorian woman' is no longer a byword for bourgeois propriety, then how can she uphold the continuing vigour of 'Englishness' as an exportable commodity in an age of imperialist expansion? In an 1866 article for the *Cornhill* entitled 'Criminal Women', Mrs M. E. Owen asked

■ How is it that we have a class of women amongst us who poison the springs of their home life – who bring forth children to follow in their steps – whose influence helps so largely to degrade our streets, to fill our gaols, and whose cost, consequently, to the country is considerable? □

For Owen, the degraded female body is 'one of the sores of the body politic.'[121] Sensation fiction frequently signifies an enfeebled 'body politic' that is fast losing sight of what John Ruskin calls, in the next chapter of this Guide, 'the true nature of home'.[122] The genre's preoccupation with tainted domesticity also operates as a scathing critique of a modern 'homeland' acutely vulnerable to 'foreign' incursion.

CHAPTER FIVE

Domesticity, Modernity and Race(ism)

Wild yet domestic

> This is the true nature of home – it is the place of Peace; the shelter, not only from all injury, but from all terror, doubt, division. In so far as it is not this, it is not home: so far as the anxieties of the outer life penetrate into it, and the inconsistently minded, unknown, unloved, or hostile society of the outer world is allowed by either husband or wife to cross the threshold, it ceases to be home; it is then only a part of that outer world which you have roofed over, and lighted [a] fire in. But so far as it is a sacred place, a vestal temple, a temple of the hearth watched over by Household Gods, before whose faces none may come but those they can receive with love [...] so far it vindicates the name, and fulfils the praise, of Home.
>
> (John Ruskin, 'Of Queens' Gardens', *Sesame and Lilies* (1865), New York: Chelsea House, 1987, p. 85)

Like the 1851 census report which paid lavish tribute to the English house as a 'shrine' of 'joys and meditations',[1] John Ruskin's paean to domesticity in his 1864 lecture 'Of Queens' Gardens' delineates the home as secularized holy ground. Ruskin's 'temple of the hearth' is a spatial as well as a social unit, whose achievement of balance and security of enclosure approximates to peace of mind: physically indistinguishable from 'a part of that outer world which you have roofed over', the home is only valid if it can minister to psychological solace, amity and concord.[2] Ruskin seems to complicate this stance by suggesting that the female custodian is guilty of dereliction of duty if she turns her back on the workaday tumult outside:

■ there is a little wall around her place of peace: and yet she knows, in her heart, if she would only look for its knowledge, that outside of that little rose-covered wall, the wild grass, to the horizon, is torn up by the agony of men, and beat level by the drift of their life-blood. □

119

That the 'hearth' might become a locus of resistance, refusal and disturbance if it ignores responsibility to the surging outer world and to public welfare points to contradictions in the domestic ideology that sensation fiction takes up with boisterous verve. The sweet domestic enchantress, fulfilling her holy duty to preserve the secrets of home, may be construed as a dangerous figure harbouring values contrary to those of established pieties.[3] Sensation fiction's unrelenting focus on the despoliation of 'hearth' was perceived by Ruskin and others as a full-scale assault on the domestic credo, whose cultivation was the special moral mission of the bourgeoisie, which embodied at mid century, according to John Burnett, the most 'family-conscious and home-centred' social group in English history.[4] For Braddon in *Lady Audley's Secret*, the possibility that violence might erupt into a recognizable quotidian reality is always lurking:

■ What do we know of the mysteries that may hang about the houses we enter? Foul deeds have been done under the most hospitable roofs; terrible crimes have been committed amid the fairest scenes, and have left no trace upon the spot where they were done. I do not believe in mandrake, or in bloodstains that no time can efface. I believe rather that we may walk unconsciously in an atmosphere of crime, and breathe none the less freely. I believe that we may look into the smiling face of a murderer, and admire its tranquil beauty.[5] □

The sensation genre not only debunks the outward semblance of the domestic idyll, the well-established English home with its beckoning promise of repose (such as Rose Maylie's cottage in Dickens's *Oliver Twist*), but also criminalizes it by showing 'foul deeds' to emanate from seemingly 'hospitable' interiors. Henry James noted this in his 1865 review of Braddon's *Aurora Floyd*, underscoring 'those most mysterious of mysteries, the mysteries which are at our own doors':

■ This innovation gave a new impetus to the literature of horrors. It was fatal to the authority of Mrs. Radcliffe and her everlasting castle in the Apennines. What are the Apennines to us, or we to the Apennines? Instead of the terrors of 'Udolpho', we were treated to the terrors of the cheerful country-house and the busy London lodgings. And there is no doubt that these were infinitely the more terrible.[6] □

James's reference to 'the terrors of Udolpho', casts ironic light on Ruskin's conception of home as a magical interior, 'shelter' from all 'terror', while also making explicit the relationship between Victorian sensation fiction and earlier Gothic romances by Ann Radcliffe (1764–1823), author of *The Mysteries of Udolpho* (1794), and Matthew

'Monk' Lewis (1775–1818). The rendering of aberrant or unsanctioned impulses, despotic brutality and supernatural threat, which the earlier Gothic romance had situated in a Catholic southern Europe of crumbling medieval fortresses and deserted mansions, is relocated to the humdrum domestic hearth as a place of enduring physical and emotional peril.[7] 'Society is a vast magazine of crime and suffering, of enormities, mysteries, and miseries of every description, of incidents, in a word' was James's core sense of these 'dark' sensation novels, a more topical literature of terror that uncovers alcoholism, financial fraud and the sexual double-standard, among other abuses of authority. He pinpoints how Braddon's sensation narratives deviate from their Gothic forerunners by using an outlandish fusion of the mundane and the marvellous, the diurnal and the fantastic. This becomes the characteristic form for articulating the supra-rational in a materialistic, secular epoch, far removed historically from Radcliffe's fictional site of feudal politics and papal deception. James's sometimes jaunty tone in this account belies, as Chapter Three of this Guide shows, the cultural disquiet created by this image of a social class that by the mid-Victorian era had become the principal holder of political and economic power, and whose freshly starched curtains and well-scrubbed Bloomsbury doorsteps might conceal unlawful intent, as in Braddon's double sensation novel *Birds of Prey* (1867) and *Charlotte's Inheritance* (1868).

Tamara Wagner elaborates these ideas in her trenchant analysis of Collins's overlooked novel *The Two Destinies* (1876):

■ A new interest in deviance induced writers to take up aspects of the Gothic and to transpose them into the domestic realm precisely to expose mid-Victorian ideologies of domesticity as premised on the strategic definition and containment of the abnormal [...] this transposition facilitated critiques of society that voiced concerns about privacy and social control.[8] □

However, Pamela Gilbert's *Disease, Desire, and the Body in Victorian Women's Popular Novels* (1997) signals that the capacity of popular sensation to bring 'the terrifying' into a locale synonymous with the snug domestic ideal may be overrated:

■ Far from bringing the terrifying into the midst of the middle-class neighbourhood, as [Winifred] Hughes asserts, the sensation novel's purpose was to remove it and frame it, so that it might be perused safely and at some distance. A novel about a bigamist or a child-murder in a fictional middle-class neighbourhood is far less immediate than a newspaper which places such events a block and a day away. Also, whereas news items appear without prior warning, with limited explanation and often, without resolution, the novel provides all of these, bounding the uncanny within the conventional structures of plot development and denouement, in which conventional values are, at least nominally, upheld. Yet perhaps this is the real outrage to which the critics were reacting. It may very well be subversive to suggest that there can be order and reason within such 'pathological' social dysfunctions.[9] □

Gilbert responds to Thomas Boyle's assessment of the genre as an extension of existing news journalism by arguing that its objective was to 'shape and provide coherence for that barrage of information.'[10] Gilbert proposes that in the very act of affording a framework and structure within which madness and jealous rage are naturalized and dissected, the sensationalists furnished a searing indictment of a society whose medico-scientific experts glibly assigned motive and legibility to these actions, as if they could be traced back to a discernible source or explained away, leaving the 'hearth' cleansed of 'foreign' contamination.

Pamela Gilbert's research prompts us to consider how the 'uncanny' elements of sensation fiction are tied to a portrait of mid-Victorian Britain in which the quality and speed of life disconcerts readers, as it were, in their own homes; the fiction evokes more sinister possibilities of perception through a decentring and destabilizing of the domestic assumptions outlined by Ruskin. My next subchapter indicates that commentators have always been attuned to the psychic unease implicit in a sensational rendering of modernity, of a radically altered world in which even the present seems to be passing away under the tides of the new. In the sensation genre a tale of our own times frequently conveys a haunting sense that legibility cannot be imposed on a populace and a landscape subject to the hectic rhythms of decay and replacement, ruin and reconstruction.

Shock of the new

> Sensationalism had [...] a fairly definite meaning and a long literary tradition. It was romance of the present consciously adapted to new conditions and to a new public; and found [...] material in records of crime and villainy [...] if a scandal of more than usual piquancy occurs in high life, or a crime of extraordinary horror figures among our *causes célèbres*, the sensationalist is immediately at hand to weave the incident into a thrilling tale with names and circumstances slightly disguised, so as at once to exercise the ingenuity of the reader in guessing the riddle.[11]

Walter Phillips's 1919 book on *Dickens, Reade, and Collins: Sensation Novelists,* is among the first full-length studies of the genre to ponder Henry James's concept of Braddon's pioneering update of Gothic paraphernalia. Phillips's interest in 'romance of the present' suggests that a nervous reaction to industrial and metropolitan modernity becomes one of the genre's chief concerns, a reading borne out by Collins's *Basil* (1852), in which the eponymous hero describes with appalled fascination the sterile clutter in the home of bourgeois arriviste, Sherwin:

> ■ Everything was oppressively new. The brilliantly-varnished door cracked with a report like a pistol when it was opened; the paper on the walls, with its gaudy pattern of birds, trellis-work, and flowers, in gold, red, and green on a white ground, looked hardly dry yet; the showy window-curtains of white and sky-blue, and the still showier carpet of red and yellow, seemed as if they had come out of the shop yesterday; the round rosewood table was in a painfully high state of polish; the morocco-bound picture books that lay on it, looked as if they had never been moved or opened since they had been bought; not one leaf even of the music on the piano was dog-eared or worn. Never was a richly-furnished room more thoroughly comfortless than this – the eye ached at looking round it.[12] □

Here domesticity is impelled towards an act of exposure and display of material plenitude. *Basil* transposes the 'terrors' of confinement associated with Ann Radcliffe's 'castle in the Appenines' into the stifling claustrophobia of the suburban villa, where crass emulation passes for genteel refinement. Lillian Nayder refers to this type of literary sensationalism as 'domestic Gothic'[13] in her book *Wilkie Collins* (1997) and Nicholas Rance affirms how the 'sensation novel recurrently alludes to Gothic fiction, the preceding literary sensationalism, to mark a distinction. [...] If ghosts in Gothic fiction signified a past as liable to erupt into an enlightened present, Collins substituted the present for the past as a source of dread.'[14] Collins's specific use of the words *A Story of Modern Life* in his subtitle, 18 months before it gained wide currency to designate a new art of the modern life problem picture, such as *Past and Present* (1858) by Augustus Egg (1816–63), is suggestive. Collins was alert to a vibrant critical conversation about the representation of contemporary culture circulating in progressive artistic circles around 1850. The sculptor John Tupper (1824–79) argued in the Pre-Raphaelite journal *The Germ*:

> ■ If, as every poet, every painter, every sculptor will acknowledge, his best and most original ideas are derived from his own time: if his great lessonings to piety, truth, charity, love, honour, honesty, gallantry, generosity, courage, are derived from the same source; why transfer them to distant periods, and make them *'not things of to-day'*?[15] □

Tupper proposes that the 'things of to-day' supply unique opportunities for art's 'great lessonings': its fundamentally moral function to concentrate on the idea of a society in which material prosperity and social climbing have usurped spiritual aspiration. It is the solemn duty of any conscientious 'literary man', Collins declares in *Basil*, to chronicle the multiple pressures of a modernity that beckons us towards the unpredictable. The fantastic coincidences of romance – the 'extraordinary accidents and events which happen to few' – are part of that life and are therefore legitimate subjects for his fiction.

Collins claims that he is attempting an original kind of serious fiction in *Basil*, yet as Tim Dolin and Lucy Dougan suggest in their essay '*Basil*, Art and the Origins of Sensation Fiction' (2003), 'the novel that follows evinces an undeniable disgust for the new petty-bourgeois' classes that are 'the very source of its self-proclaimed avant-gardism.'[16] When he had written to Richard Bentley (1794–1871) in November 1849 negotiating terms for *Antonina*, his first published novel (about the fifth-century siege of Rome by the Goths), Collins had pleaded its worth by claiming to appeal to 'other sympathies' than 'the modern taste for present times and the horrible', which had 'been somewhat surfeited of late.'[17] He abandoned the historical mode for a 'story of modern life' in his very next novel, however: *Antonina* secured only modest success[18] and because in the two intervening years the historical novel had lost ground to the domestic novel, and the Great Exhibition had lent what Martin Meisel calls a 'glamour to contemporaneity'.[19] Collins quickly decided that he should appeal, as he put it in the Letter of Dedication prefacing the 1852 first edition of *Basil*, 'to the readiest sympathies and the largest number of readers, by writing a story of our own times.'

H. L. Mansel, in his review over a decade after the publication of Collins's *Basil*, noted with dismay the sensation genre's brash vulgarity as it sought to distil the essence of the *zeitgeist* (the spirit of the age) through its tabloid fascination with details of Victorian law, medicine, science and psychology – anything that contributed to the feeling of a frantic modernity:

> ■ The sensation novel, be it trash or something worse, is usually a tale of our own times. Proximity is, indeed, one great element of sensation. It is necessary to be near a mine to be blown up by its explosion; and a tale which aims at electrifying the nerves of the reader is never thoroughly effective unless the scene be laid in our own days and among the people we are in the habit of meeting [...] The man who shook our hand with a hearty English grasp half an hour ago – the woman whose beauty and grace were the charm of last night [...] – how exciting to think that under these pleasing outsides may be concealed some demon in human shape, a Count Fosco or a Lady Audley![20] □

Jenny Bourne Taylor's *In the Secret Theatre of Home* proposes that Mansel's account, like many of the early vituperative or alarmist reviews, employed 'sensation' as a mode of cultural-critical shorthand: 'When critics self-consciously referred to the 1860s as an "age of sensation", they meant [...] that the word encapsulated the experience of modernity itself – the sense of continuous and rapid change, of shocks, thrills, intensity, excitement.'[21] In discussing the interpretive conflicts and the 'countervailing [...] paradigms' of Collins's sensation fiction, Taylor presents a portrait of a ' "modern" (even post-modern)' Collins who values 'play, doubling, and duplicity', who constructs 'dialogic and self-reflexive' narratives, and who 'breaks down stable boundaries between wildness and domesticity, self and other, masculinity and femininity, "black" and "white." '[22]

Taylor focuses on the extent to which the plain view of daily surfaces crumbles under the new order of sensation fiction, with its unsettling distortions and abrupt juxtapositions of material drawn from the context of 1860s life. As Christopher Kent notes of Collins's texts, we should resist the temptation 'to dismiss the sensation novel as unreal.' Examining Collins's concern with the *nature* of reality, Kent argues that Collins depicts his tangible surroundings as an intensely subjective phenomenon, and as 'a construct undergoing significant change' in his day, 'a change which entailed a redefinition of the boundaries of probability and possibility' in response to the science of statistics, intricate theories of determinism, accounts of spiritual phenomena and the turn to the sensational in the popular press. Although Collins's fiction 'affronted [everyday] reality' with its focus on the deviant, we should remember that 'Victorian novelists and their critics assumed that the novels of their day would be read by posterity as social history.'[23]

As the sensation genre shows in its engagement with 'the thrills and intensity of modern life [...] to keep its readers off balance',[24] the impact of the new is registered as an assault on the nervous system. Mansel's phrase 'preaching to the nerves' not only captures sensationalism's secularizing of religious rhetorical modes, but also underlines to what extent the genre physicalizes ideology, signifying narrative's intimate dependence upon the reader's somatic response. In reviews of the novels themselves, divisions between individual readers' bodies and what Susan Bernstein calls 'a conglomerate social body',[25] were frequently erased. Tim Dolin's essay on 'Collins's Career and the Visual Arts' (2006) argues that seismic social convulsions have become internalized, rendered imperceptible through the Byzantine complexities of the law, the silent movements of money, the petty cruelties camouflaged by modern matrimony, and 'the shattering of the nerves'[26] as a result of industrial and technological advance:

■ [Collins] recognised that in England in the 1850s and 1860s, modernity was experienced not as Dickens had imagined it in the more restive 1830s and 1840s, as a tumult of productive and destructive energy and change, but rather as an insidious, compulsory ordinariness.

To offer a definition of modernity – 'the social and cultural upheavals caused by rapid capitalist economic development and corresponding new modes of perception and experience of time and space as transitory, fleeting, fortuitous or arbitrary' – is to miss the subtle and crucial differences between the decades of *Oliver Twist* (1838) to *Dombey and Son* (1846–8) and that of *The Woman in White* (1859–60) [...] But in Collins the experience of modernity itself does not misshape the entire novelistic world as it does Dickens's world. [...]

In Collins [...] what is visible on the surface is an eerily incomplete and sometimes apparently motionless landscape, where signs of change are omnipresent but the *processes* of change are subterranean and mysterious. The modern world looks unfinished – especially the houses and streets – and unused: in a permanently suspended state of transition from the old to the new.[27] □

It is precisely this 'unfinished', inchoate quality to the urban terrain that, in Dolin's interpretation, sets the nerves on edge, generating psychic disquiet as human consciousness struggles to determine the source of all these baffling, carefully concealed 'processes of change.' Sensation fiction's intimation of subterranean plots and covert conspiracies mirrors to some degree Dolin's thesis that technological innovations tend to spread just beneath the crust of quotidian existence at mid-century. In stark contrast to the extension of the vast network of railways crisscrossing the English shires some decades earlier, the 1860s saw the installation of underwater telegraph cables between Britain and North America, and underground transportation and sewage systems in London.

Like Dolin, D. A. Miller's account of sensation in *The Novel and the Police* retains the original view of the genre as 'preaching to the nerves' but explicates the 'sermon' of industrial modernity rather differently. Instead of conceiving *The Woman in White* as releasing a flow of pernicious energy, Miller historicizes the repercussions of modernity, and its impact on sensory experience in terms of the disciplinary function of the novel, specifically in terms of its promulgation of a stable model of domestic existence through the simultaneous entertainment and violent disavowal of same-sex desire. For Miller, these modern nerves are coded as feminine and feminizing. The novel's underlying aim then is to employ this modern nervous condition to transmute Walter Hartright's misgivings – and by extension the reader's – into heterosexual desire, thus clinching by the end of *The Woman in White* the unchallenged superiority of the nuclear family, with its own delicate equipoise between heterosexual and homosocial tendencies. For

Miller, the 'positive personal shocks' and paranoid plotting of *The Woman in White* epitomize a novelistic disciplinary tool, with which to forge a peculiar form of modern subjectivity that keeps the reader in check.[28]

Nicholas Daly's 2004 monograph *Literature, Technology and Modernity, 1860–2000* also recognizes to what extent the shock of modernity sets 'nerves [...] everywhere aquiver' in *The Woman in White*.[29] However, while he concedes that Miller is 'correct' in proposing that 'nervousness is pandemic in *The Woman in White*,' Daly contends that Miller 'overestimates the part that Anne Catherick, the Woman in White herself, plays in circulating this affect.'[30] To understand these 'nerves-without-a-cause', and their readerly attractions, Daly counsels that we look beyond Miller's terms of homosexual panic to the experience of automatism and involuntary motion,[31] associated with a vertiginous sense of social and economic acceleration. This sense went against the prevailing Victorian ideal of progressive mastery and dominion in both politics and culture:

> ■ the specifically modern nervousness which Miller identifies in the sensation novel is bound up with that modernisation of the senses effected by the technological revolutions of the nineteenth century. The defensive gait of the city dweller, the mechanical movements of the factory worker, the compulsive dice-throwing of the gambler – for Walter Benjamin these are the somatic indices of a new experience of space and time. And it is such bodies we find in the sensation novel, bodies 'feminised', but also galvanised.[32] □

Of these 'technological revolutions' Daly privileges the recently speeded up world of railway travel, its literal and metaphorical impact on the human body and on conventional temporal systems. The passenger's experience of a train journey is, in Daly's discerning account, reminiscent of the mid-Victorian reader's reaction to a sensation novel: in both instances the consumer is reduced to the level of a blankly passive subject, yet is simultaneously over-excited and discomposed by the experience – uneasy, tense, even frightened. Whereas for Tim Dolin the modern moment articulated by Collins's oeuvre is one of shapeless and unfinished uniformity, Daly interprets the genre as an endeavour to register and assimilate the dizzying blur and incessant din of the railway age through the staging of nervous debility in characters and readers.[33] Daly construes the popular fiction of the 1860s as evolving an appropriate subject for this experiential domain by preaching to and buffeting the fragile nervous system. Mrs. Merridew remarks in Collins's *The Moonstone* that 'Railway travelling always makes [her] nervous';[34] the protagonists in Braddon's *Lady Audley's Secret* and

Collins's *No Name* lose their parents in offstage railway accidents; *East Lynne*'s Isabel Vane is maimed in a railway mishap in which her illegitimate child is killed.[35] All these examples, according to Daly, show how in the second half of the nineteenth century Britain seemed to express its mutability with extraordinary intensity. Mechanized modernity becomes a hazardous potency with which the subject has to grapple as a new form of discipline. It is a discipline from which Lady Dunstane could benefit in George Meredith's *Diana of the Crossways* (1885):

> ■ Those railways! [...] When would there be peace in the land? Where one single nook of shelter and escape from them! And the English, blunt as their senses are to noise and hubbub, would be revelling in hisses, shrieks, puffings and screeches, so that travelling would become an intolerable affliction.[36] □

But in sensation fiction, by contrast, machine culture, rather than seeming 'an intolerable affliction,' becomes a potential fund of multiplied consciousness, and even available for aesthetic consumption. The genre is in effect a complex contrivance for generating a suspense that bestows upon its recipients a revitalized subjectivity, in order to process the dissonances and disjunctions associated with railway travel. We are, according to this view, educated by sensation fiction; it helps us apprehend both the physiological and cognitive aspects of strong emotional experience. These narratives grant us then a measure of protection from surprises and divest particular impressions of their novelty, thus neutralizing their shock potential. Daly's concept of a genre that provides 'a species of temporal training'[37] illuminates critic Stephen Knight's sense of how the social and physical mobility of a modernizing society are essential ingredients of detective and sensation stories from the 1820s on, where '[t]he recurrent mechanism [...] is travel to resolve mysterious crimes: up the road to York, out to the towns of the Thames valley, in and around the swelling villages that were rapidly becoming London'.[38] Like the detective thriller, in which a Bradshaw's railway schedule and a watch become indispensable to the principal characters, the resolution of a sensation plot can hinge upon faultless time-keeping and unwavering attention to the calendar, to the patterns of external, objective time.[39]

Daly's appraisal of the 'nervous affections' explored in and triggered off by sensation fiction prompts us to revise our conception of literary history. In general accounts of the modern movement, nervousness tends to be related to early twentieth-century notations of violent disruption and physical upheaval rather than to the 1860s: some commentators take the 'alignment of modernism and nervousness as axiomatic.'[40] The history of shock as a discursive formation of modernity, epitomized by Freud's analysis in 1920 of the mechanisms of traumatic neurosis, imbues ideas of modernization itself as pathogenic. But Daly skilfully foregrounds the seminal arguments of Walter Benjamin, who regards hyper-stimulation of the nerves as a core facet of historical modernization, becoming a feature of everyday life in the great Victorian cities of Manchester, Glasgow and London before it makes itself available as a favourite theme of the modernist avant-garde.[41] In his essay 'On Some Motifs in Baudelaire' (1939) Benjamin points to the accommodatory function of modern nervousness as the defining experience of metropolitan existence in the nineteenth century, whether it be the discomfort felt by a commuter jostled by hordes of shoppers, or the jolts registered by industrial workers on a factory floor.[42]

Benjamin's reference to a nervous condition that is allied with the volatile rhythms of modern city life is telling and trenchant. Sensation writers are preoccupied with charting not only aberrant identities but also the tangible localities from which they emerge. As Collins shows in *Basil*, the metropolis offers to the cursory glance an astounding revelation of reckless dynamism and technological prowess; yet the more intrepid wayfarer can glimpse a sharply contrasting picture of London as an aggregation of rundown hinterlands, lonely enclaves and in-between suburban sites that elude precise classification. My next subchapter surveys recent research into the elaborate geographies delineated by the sensation genre. Commentators have enquired whether sensation writing depicts speculative building in the suburbs and the feverish activity of imperial conquest as one issue spreading from the borders inwards. If this is the case, imperialism and housing are then effectively synthesized into a single issue: London epitomizes the British Empire in miniature. The genre's employment of space, place and 'native land' raises questions about contested ideologies of Englishness and the cognitive and aesthetic mapping of urban modernity, as well as the debilitating effects (and furtive pleasures) of a labyrinthine metropolis, that domain to which crime and scandal are literally and symbolically connected.

Safeguarding a green and pleasant land?

Alfred Austin, in the June 1870 *Temple Bar*, identifies the most striking components of 'the novels of the time which are called sensational':

> ■ The scene is invariably laid in our own country. [...] Our sensation novelists [...] stick to their native land; and as a very large proportion of

subscribers to the circulating libraries live in London or its vicinity, they usually restrict themselves to the metropolis for their town-life, and to the home-counties for their rural life. In London itself, they find it difficult to make the *mise en scène* [the setting] of rich and fashionable existence gloomy and suggestive of horrors; so there they devote themselves to contrast, and place a female murderess [...] amid light and joyous surroundings. But when they get into the country, they can more easily prepare the reader for shocking disclosures. Fish-ponds, dry moats, and ruinous walls covered with dark moss, surround a house surmounted by chimneys broken down by age and long service, and which would topple down but for the ivy which supports them.[43] □

Austin's description sheds light on Linda Dryden's thesis in *The Modern Gothic and Literary Doubles* (2003) that the fractured selfhoods dominating sensation novels are closely tied to 'the social, geographical and architectural schisms' of the mid-Victorian city.[44] Judith Walkowitz's monograph *City of Dreadful Delight* (1994) probes the historical referents of sensation narrative, given the insistent contextualizing at the basis of much recent scholarship. Walkowitz maps the spatial geographies that structured Victorian gender and class ideology and that divided men and women, bourgeoisie and proletariat, into properly partitioned insides and outsides – a division disrupted by such trends as the growth of an urban working class, immigration, and the movement of women from private to public space:

■ The literary construct of the metropolis as a dark, powerful, and seductive labyrinth held a powerful sway over the social imagination of educated readers. It remained the dominant representation of London in the 1880s, conveyed to many reading publics through high and low literary forms, from Charles Booth's surveys of London poverty, to the fictional stories of [Robert Louis Stevenson (1850–94), George Gissing (1857–1903)] and James, to the sensational newspaper exposes by W. T. Stead [1849–1912] and G. R. Sims (1847–1922). These late-Victorian writers built on an earlier tradition of Victorian urban exploration, adding some new perspectives of their own. Some rigidified the hierarchical divisions of London into a geographic separation, organised around the opposition of East and West. Others stressed the growing complexity and differentiation of the world of London, moving beyond the opposition of rich and poor, palace and hovels, to investigate the many class cultures in between. Still others among them repudiated a fixed, totalistic interpretive image altogether, and emphasised instead a fragmented, disunified, atomistic social universe that was not easily decipherable.[45] □

Walkowitz's examination of social history shows which groups were disempowered or elevated by late-Victorian constructions of sexuality.

Indeed, Walkowitz's study is notable for its finely tuned concept of ideological construction, or fictionality, which affords a stimulus for charting how Victorian sensation writers employed melodramatic conventions to interpret and naturalize their experience. In analyzing these conventions, Walkowitz is herself influenced by their structure, employing London as a disputed terrain or 'stage set' in which 'social actors' finesse 'new stories of the city that competed, intersected with, appropriated, and revised' the key imaginative topographies of London.[46] This structure infuses the sensation genre's scrutiny of social identities rehearsed and performed through mannered artifice. Walkowitz's concept of the liberating vitality and capaciousness of the metropolis, its historical centrality within the mechanics of a system, as well as the imprisoning marginality of one's existence within it or on its fringes, underscores the plight of stifled suburbanites in Collins's *Basil*. In Braddon's defence of the sensation genre, 'a neglected suburban garden upon the 21st of July 1852' is already parodied as an established sensational site, 'underlining' the prominence 'of suburbia in sensation fiction, and vice versa, of sensationalism in the reshaping of this new literary imaginary.'[47]

W. J. McCormack asserts, in *Sheridan Le Fanu and Victorian Ireland* (1981), that the sensation genre springs 'from the anxious imagination of suburbia'.[48] This reminds us that in a metropolis which expands and contracts according to the economic cycles of boom and bust, countless victims of 'bad nerves' might be found. Dr Downward, a suspect medical practitioner in Collins's *Armadale*, sets up a sanatorium to treat 'shattered nerves', shrewdly locating his asylum in a half-built suburb south of Hampstead and, sending out invitations to the local inhabitants on open days, presuming that the surrounding villas will provide him with a steady stream of neurasthenic unfortunates. Deborah Wynne, in *The Sensation Novel and the Victorian Family Magazine*, signifies how

■ The newly-developed suburbs housed a considerable body of readers for the sensation novel: the leisured middle-class wives and daughters at home, along with the husbands, fathers and brothers who may have whiled away their daily journeys to work by reading sensational magazines or 'railway novels.' As *Armadale* indicates, the expansion of urban centres and suburbs during the mid-Victorian period, along with their associated problems of anonymity and alienation, created a new landscape for representation, where crime and mysteries tested the already frayed nerves of the inhabitants.[49] □

Rather than supplying a panorama of recuperative potential, the suburbs are 'a dingy brick labyrinth of streets' in Collins's *The Law and the*

Lady (1875)[50] – a cramped, joyless no-place where ceaseless flux fails to mask capitalism's predatory and parasitic appetites. Tamara Wagner's essay 'Sensationalizing Victorian Suburbia' (2006) documents how Collins's early fiction fashions this sensational environment:

> ■ [S]uburban Gothic played a crucial part in the sensation novel's development. Wilkie Collins's first venture into the genre, *Basil: A Story of Modern Life*, is symptomatically set in motion when the upper-class hero, driven partly by boredom, partly by a fascination with the everyday, the mundane, randomly boards an omnibus. But if his casual habit of embarking on such voyages of social tourism aligns him with the figure of the flâneur [the idler or wanderer], it ultimately propels him across the permeable boundaries of voyeurism into fatal entanglements. In that his attempt at a cross-class alliance fails utterly, and sensationally, the novel invests in a new interest in social strata generally, but suburbs, as a developing literary space, specifically invite a sensational treatment as unfamiliar wastelands and rapidly denigrated epitomes of bourgeois respectability.[51] □

Like Lynne Hapgood's 2005 monograph *Margins of Desire: The Suburbs in Fiction and Culture 1880–1925*, Wagner's essay reveals how Collins approached the task of defining the enigma of a patchwork suburban Empire which aped social progress by the sheer force of its directionless spread. In *The Heart of the Empire* (1901), the liberal politician C. F. G. Masterman (1874–1927) viewed with trepidation the moment when the 'two arms' of suburban growth would 'snap together like a vice', and 'completely encircle the Imperial City.'[52] For Masterman, as for Collins in *Basil*, the suburbs possess an unsettling and boundless inscrutability, whose essence can be apprehended only through a synthesis of a multiplicity of perceptions. Wagner succinctly demonstrates that the latent and un-discerned literary possibilities of this locale, with its mixture of the homely and the foreign, the mediocre and the mysterious, generated original themes in the contemporary novel.

Collins's *Basil* chronicles how London's outskirts were being redrawn as new migrant communities colonized them, reinventing what was peripheral as integral. Though as historian J. R. Seeley (1834–95) warned in *The Expansion of England* (1884): 'when the State extends beyond the limits of nationality, its power becomes precarious. [...] The subject or rival nationalities cannot be perfectly assimilated', and remain 'as a permanent cause of weakness or danger.'[53] The sensation genre's portrayal of these 'subject or rival nationalities' has attracted detailed scrutiny since the 1980s.[54] These novels offer, as my next subchapter illustrates, a complex reaction to the manifold pressures of a modernity that determines both imperial centre and colonial outpost. Moreover, the sophistication that typifies current research into the genre's conception of the foreign trespasser is mirrored in the attention scholars gives to myriad forms of hybridity – of race, gender, ideology, class and even aesthetic merit.

Fears of the foreign

> Try as I might to resist it, my mind drew a dreadful picture of the Hindoo, as a kind of monster in human form [...] The instant I felt him approaching, my darkness was peopled with brown demons. He took my hand. I tried hard to control myself – but I really could not help shuddering and starting back when he touched me. To make matters worse, he sat next to me at dinner. In five minutes I had long, lean, black-eyed beings all round me; perpetually growing in numbers, and pressing closer and closer on me as they grew. It ended in my being obliged to leave the table. When the guests were all gone, my aunt was furious. I admitted my conduct was unreasonable in the last degree.[55]

Set in 1858, the second and final year of the Indian Mutiny, Wilkie Collins's novel *Poor Miss Finch* (1872) persistently refers to British India without naming the uprising itself. Collins describes Lucilla Finch's hysterical reaction to a foreign guest at her aunt's London home as one common among the blind, while also signifying the 'blindness' of a virulent British prejudice that fashions 'brown demons' out of affable 'Hindoos.' The suggestion here that racial identity may be socially constructed rather than inborn, has been taken up by commentators to calibrate Collins's attitude to imperial politics.[56] Sensation fiction itself was perhaps the ideal vehicle for interrogating versions of the atavistic 'Other' – whether it was the imperial subject in a distant colonial station, the tarnished inhabitant of the inner-city slum or the newly denigrated criminal underclass. Braddon's novels were identified with alien and lower cultural forms – 'Her principles appear to us to resemble very strikingly those by which the Thugs [an organisation of robbers and assassins in India] used to regulate their lives'[57] – and the genre as a whole was coded by its earliest opponents as

> ■ a plant of foreign growth. It comes to us from France, and it can only be imported in a mutilated condition. Without entering on the relative morality or immorality of French and English novelists, one may say generally that, with us, novels turn upon the vicissitudes of legitimate love and decorous affection; while in France they are based upon the working of those loves and passions which are not in accordance with our rules of respectability. Now, unlawful passions are inevitably replete with a variety of sensational situations, of which authorised love, however, fervent, is devoid.[58] □

Jenny Bourne Taylor notes how the appeal of literary sensationalism was connected to 'anxiety about imminent cultural decline' by evoking 'an image of an explicitly "feminine" body that was at once its product and metonymic model',[59] marked by the neurotic susceptibility to excitement that was specifically a reaction to industrial modernity.

However, this 'body' was not simply feminized, but racialized as foreign, fevered and passive. Thomas Boyle's *Black Swine in the Sewers of Hampstead* (1989) identifies

■ a racial undercurrent near the surface of many of the discussions of sensationalism throughout the 1860s. Images of disease, bestiality, and sex occur and recur in the context of 'blackness' [...Boyle quotes from an 1866 *Westminster Review* article:] 'as those diseases always occurred in seasons of death and poverty, so does the Sensational Mania in Literature burst out only in times of mental poverty and afflict only the most poverty-stricken minds.' Now the mania for Sensation seems to have changed from 'epidemic' to 'endemic.'[60] □

That Boyle traces a connection between race, 'epidemic' and 'endemic' in early reviews of sensational narratives is highly significant, according to Pamela Gilbert:

■ The [1860s] saw a determined, even a desperate attempt to control the ravages of cholera which had repeatedly decimated urban England. Cholera was particularly associated with impoverished immigrant workers [...] and was considered by most medical experts to be not native to Britain. In 1867, the *Quarterly Review* published an article on 'The Cholera Conference', which principally concerned itself with tracing the progress of the disease from various other localities, most notably India and the Mediterranean, to 'the present year [in which] it has overrun the whole of the continent, and has attacked England.'[61] □

Gilbert indicates how the sensation genre was likened to an overseas epidemic that might take root in the 'pure' English soil and become endemic – part of the unwholesome detritus of an industrial empire, with British India as its focal point.

Given that 'no episode in British imperial history raised public excitement to a higher pitch'[62] than the Indian Mutiny, according to Patrick Brantlinger, it is unsurprising that the sensation genre should be haunted by the uprising and its aftermath. Florence Marryat's *Love's Conflict* (1865) plays out against the 'Mutiny' which 'had just commenced in India at that time, and every mail brought home fresh accounts of barbarities practised on our unfortunate country-people – accounts which had curdled the blood of [...] all who possessed hearts to feel.'[63]

Braddon's *Lady Audley's Secret* uses, according to Lillian Nayder's essay 'Rebellious Sepoys and Bigamous Wives' (2000),

> ■ the imagery of the Indian Mutiny and the racism it generated to defend the social status quo. Suggesting that mutinous wives and daughters, like rebellious sepoys, are 'unnatural' and ungrateful creatures who should be punished for their transgression and returned to their 'proper place', Braddon responds to those seeking to gain legal and political rights for Englishwomen in a notably reactionary way. Her use of the Mutiny in *Lady Audley's Secret* calls into question her status as a feminist writer, and lends force to those critics who feel that her subversive qualities are, at best, heavily qualified and contained.[64] □

Nayder, in *Wilkie Collins* (1997) and elsewhere, has also explicated Collins's response, both direct and covert, to imperial programs in his fiction, journalism and melodramas, especially with regard to the grounds and significance of racial identity and difference. Nayder argues that Collins, given his capacity to connect imperial brutality to a scalding critique of male privilege and enforced powerlessness among women in such narratives as *Armadale* and *The Frozen Deep* (1856), was one of the best placed among the sensation novelists to dissect the growth and riddling ambiguities of empire.

> ■ In a career spanning nearly fifty years, Collins bore witness to many of the events that made 'Rule, Britannia' a catchphrase of the Victorian era; but he also perceived how so-called 'subject races' and rival European powers threatened British hegemony. During Collins's lifetime the British abolished slavery in their possessions (1834); they defeated the Chinese in the Opium Wars (1840–2, 1860) and annexed the Punjab (1848–9); they brutally suppressed the Indian Mutiny (1857–8) and the Jamaica Insurrection (1865); they designated Victoria 'Empress of India' (1876); and they saw General Charles Gordon [1853–85] 'martyred' in the Sudan (1885).[65] □

Nayder portrays an author who was absorbed by the presumed differences between savage and civilized societies from his 1860s heyday to his final published work *Blind Love* (1889), which depicts English perceptions of an unruly and primordial Irish population.[66] *Iolani, or Tahiti as it was*, Collins's first novel, was written in 1844 and centres on life in Tahiti when the island 'was yet undiscovered'.[67] Recalling this novel in 1870, Collins disparaged it as a tale in which his 'youthful imagination ran riot among the noble savages, in scenes which caused the respectable British publisher to declare that it was impossible to put his name on the title page.'[68] But the novel, in Nayder's view, foreshadows Collins's later, successful stories about savagery and empire, despite its focus on an aboriginal culture before the arrival of Europeans – a subject unique among Collins's work. Thus in *The Moonstone* Rachel Verinder comes to resemble the Hindus in her angry sense of violation, while a headstrong Lydia Gwilt is horsewhipped like a slave by her husband in *Armadale*.

Patrick Brantlinger indicates that in the 1830s and 1840s, Tahiti provided English writers with a site on which to imagine a Christian triumph over barbarism or to preach the civilizing gospel of free trade.[69] Collins proves even more apprehensive about the 'barbarism of women' in *Antonina* (1850), his first published novel, which again links imperial themes with gender politics. Collins continued to interconnect forms of domination in his more topical representations of empire in the 1850s, when public attention focused on the loss of the Franklin expedition and the Indian Mutiny, and he began to collaborate with Charles Dickens in response.[70] While the press virtually ignored the Indian Mutiny at its outset, coverage gained momentum after alleged firsthand reports of atrocities inflicted upon the women and children taken prisoner at Cawnpore began to filter back to Britain.

Jenny Sharpe proposes that 'long before the British army regained control over its Indian territories, the tales of terror were discredited as having little or no historical basis.'[71] Christopher Hilbert, in his extensive study of the narrative accounts of the Indian Mutiny, concurs with Sharpe that 'most of the appalling crimes rumoured to have happened, and reported as facts in letters to England, bore scant relation to the truth.'[72] Collins alludes to the staying power of such misinformation in *The Moonstone*, which was published on the tenth anniversary of the Indian Mutiny in 1868. Ezra Jennings refers to unnamed slander that had dogged him throughout his time in England. 'Evil report', he says 'with time and chance to help it, travels patiently and travels far' (*MS* 447).[73] The public encountered these lurid stories, according to Vicki Corkran Willey, 'at a time when it was not only unaccustomed to questioning the veracity of what appeared in the papers [...] but also when [...] it was developing a taste for sensation fiction.'[74]

Collins's *The Moonstone* was reviewed by Geraldine Jewsbury in the July 1868 *Athenaeum*. She noted how Collins brought his readers to tears as the novel ended – not by uniting the English hero and heroine but by dividing three South Asian men. These men are Hindu priests who have together travelled to England and back, infringing caste restrictions to restore a sacred Hindu diamond to its shrine in remote Kattiawar:

> ■ Few will read of the final destiny of *The Moonstone* without feeling the tears rise in their eyes as they catch the last glimpse of the three men, who have sacrificed their cast[e] in the service of their God, when the vast

crowd of worshippers opens for them, as they embrace each other and separate to begin their lonely and never-ending pilgrimage of expiation. The deepest emotion is certainly reserved to the last.[75] □

Though Jewsbury implies that Collins uses sentimentality in *The Moonstone* as a politically evasive tactic, the novel is in fact politically charged. Indeed, the representation of racial difference and imperial transgression in *The Moonstone* has been a subject central to Collins criticism since the 1973 publication of John R. Reed's essay on 'English Imperialism and the Unacknowledged Crime in *The Moonstone*'. Reed was one of the first scholars to appraise Collins's account of imperialism in this novel at any length. Reed points out that Collins's opening gambit evokes the bloody military victory in Seringapatam (1799) that gave the British their foothold in India, and sets its main action in 1848–49, the years in which the British forcibly annexed the Punjab, arguing that Collins uses the theft of the Hindu diamond to expose 'England's imperial depredations'. Britain's exploitation of its 'jewel', India, symbolized by Colonel Herncastle's greedy plunder of the Hindu diamond, is the main target in Collins's indictment of an 'oppressive society'. Basing his thesis on the 'appeal' of the unconventional characters in *The Moonstone*, Reed proposes that 'the Indian priests' are 'heroic' figures, while the 'representatives of Western Culture are plunderers.'[76]

Reed's approach inaugurated a lively debate over the imperial politics of sensation fiction generally and his reading remains a seminal one. His view that *The Moonstone* tears 'the mask of respectability' from the British Empire has been echoed by numerous scholars during the past 20 years. For example, Patricia Miller Frick contends that *The Moonstone* reveals the Indians 'to be morally superior to the English characters'; in her assessment, as in Reed's, the novel contrasts the sincerity, fierce loyalty and probity of the Hindus with the 'doubt and disorder' of their 'hypocritical English counterparts.'[77] Collins signals, according to Frick, the existence of a culture-wide xenophobia that actively promotes divisiveness between the conqueror and the conquered. In comparing *The Moonstone* to Conan Doyle's *The Sign of Four* (1890), similarly, Arthur Liebman and David H. Galerstein measure the racist portrait of Tonga against Collins's heroic portrait of the Indian priests – 'the most noble characters in the book, far superior in morality and ethical values [to] almost all the English characters.'[78]

More frequently, however, commentators have sought to contest and problematize, if not entirely disavow, Reed's argument about *The Moonstone*. Just as Collins's status as a social reformer has been called into question by D. A. Miller and others, so, too, has Collins's reputation as an incisive critic of empire. Ashish Roy's essay 'The Fabulous

Imperialist Semiotic of Wilkie Collins's *The Moonstone*' (1993) is most clearly opposed to Reed's, and perceives Collins's novel as a fiction-alization and justification of imperialist rule in India, figuring it as an 'instrument' of 'surveillance of the other.'[79] Roy offers an intricate analysis of the text's narrative economy and its complex 'semiotic rep-ertoire', both of which romance away the possibility of a fierce critique. Similarly, Robert Crooks asserts that *The Moonstone*, like detective fic-tion generally, 'articulates a fantasy of mastering otherness.'[80]

Deirdre David, in *Rule Britannia: Women, Empire, and Victorian Writing* (1995), reinforces these readings and dismisses the political significance of Collins's Prologue, which she calls 'a fable of individual brutality erased by a subsequent and coherent sequence of individual stories gathered in the cause of a common good.' This polemical stance allows her to suggest that Collins's plot validates the reductive and sabre-rattling outlook of primary narrator Gabriel Betteredge, an English steward whose fondness for *Robinson Crusoe* (1719) by Daniel Defoe (1660–1731) – 'that core work of territorial conquest which returns the rebellious individual from foreign risk to domestic security' – counters the treatment of the subject in the frame narrative.[81]

■ From [Betteredge's] xenophobic perspective, Britons never will be slaves, and it is always nasty foreigners who must threaten a domestic social order founded on upstairs benevolence and downstairs loyalty. By his lights, those inquisitive, loitering Indians [...] can only be in search of the family silver. In terms of his suspicion of anything beyond Yorkshire, to say nothing of what lurks across the English Channel, however, it is significant that the plot of *The Moonstone* proves him correct. It *is* foreign Indians [...] who disrupt the social system so dear to Betteredge's impe-rial heart, who fracture the domestic social harmony secured by half a century of British colonial conquest.[82] □

In David's opinion, Collins limits his critique of British imperialism to what she identifies as its outmoded form of military subjugation, already replaced in the 1860s by the 'hegemonic' model that, David claims, Collins tacitly commends. Thus she construes Ezra Jennings as the product of an empire that rules its colonized peoples by the more subtle coercion of discipline and education: 'Jennings's work' reveals him 'as a colonized figure so trusted by his masters, so purged of the native savagery that flourished at the time of the thuggee gangs, that he can be assigned the labour of cleansing the centre of empire itself of its own corruption.'[83] What sets David's analysis of *The Moonstone* apart from others, and also renders its claims peculiarly problematic, is her notion that Collins represents imperial rule maintained by means of strict surveillance and acquiescence rather than by violent military intervention, and that the military domination of India was, by the late 1860s, a thing of the past. On the contrary as several critics have pointed out, Collins's novel was inspired, at least in part, by the particularly savage and none-too-distant episode of the Indian Mutiny of 1857–58.

Ian Duncan, in his essay '*The Moonstone*, the Victorian Novel, and Imperialist Panic' (1994), supplies one of the most sophisticated responses to the imperial question in Collins's oeuvre. Duncan shows that *The Moonstone* 'is the sole mid-Victorian novel of the first rank to make India the centre of its business.'[84] Although Collins avoids explicit mention of the Indian Mutiny itself, he situates the main action of the novel in 1848, another period distinguished by insurrections both of a personal and a political nature. Personally, the year marked Collins's first publication, a biography of his father, *Memoirs of the Life of William Collins*. As Duncan explains, this was a period of democratic ferment, especially in the Austrian Empire, Italy, France and Germany; and in India, of a final defeat of the Sikhs which permitted annexation of the Punjab territory in the following year. By setting *The Moonstone* primarily in this profoundly unsettled era, Collins utilizes the historical moment to insinuate implications of insurgency into his narrative. Duncan explicates how Collins prompts his readers to stop seeing India through the gloomy English lens of the Mutiny and to survey it instead irradiated by the Moonstone's light.

> ■ The positive alterity of India, its victory over English police skill, complicates recent accounts that make *The Moonstone* perform a double gesture of ideological totalisation and ideological closure in the name of an omniscient detection. The mystery novel is supposed to cure a crisis of representation with a hermeneutic virtuosity that regulates the relation between world and subject. D. A. Miller argues that Collins's narrative subjects a familiar social world to the alienating surveillance of an interloping detective, then localises guilt in a scapegoat and disperses the function of detection throughout the register of the realistic representations. [...] Miller's account of a 'thoroughly monological' narrative that 'promotes a single perception of power' remains strategically blind to the novel's most conspicuous signifier of historical power [...] Despite the sack of Seringapatam that opens the novel, with the British taking the place of previous, Muslim invaders, *The Moonstone* apprehends an India that exceeds and outlasts British dominion and knowledge.[85] □

India calls into question the Western linear history that posits the expansion of the British Empire as reasonable, natural and inevitable. In Duncan's opinion *The Moonstone* is neither an ideologically closed justification nor a scathing denunciation of imperialist avarice. The novel supplies instead a nightmare glimpse of the 'world economy of modernity', where the British themselves turn out to be the colonized subjects of empire, embittered and alienated from their own past and dominions. Rejecting John R. Reed's overly 'sentimental' reading of *The Moonstone* and its sympathy for the Indians as well as Ashish Roy's blunt indictment of the novel as a reactionary text, Duncan argues that Collins 'harnesses the imperialist panic' produced by the Indian Mutiny 'to depict another world triumphant in its darkness' and to prophesy 'the public, democratic, history-making vastnesses of a world economy.'[86] This new world order destabilizes the English outlook, a process conveyed through the effects of opium, the imperial commodity that enchains the subject to an unfamiliar Asiatic identity.

Duncan's thesis, like Lillian Nayder's 1991 essay 'Robinson Crusoe and Friday in Victorian Britain' furnishes a compelling and rigorous riposte to D. A. Miller's stress on the 'monologic' nature of Collins's multi-voiced narratives. Distinguishing himself from this Foucauldian standpoint that tends to reverse the terms of sensation fiction as dissident assault, Duncan's intervention encourages us not to scrutinize Collins as merely a mouthpiece of imperial hegemony but rather to examine more fastidiously the cultural mediation in his oeuvre.

Timothy L. Carens's book *Outlandish English Subjects in the Victorian Domestic Novel* (2005) registers that, while Collins does not necessarily debunk prevailing notions of 'the Indian personality' in *The Moonstone*, he does ponder the extent to which 'Englishness' deviates from its supposedly ungovernable and atavistic colonial counterpart.

■ Collins wrote *The Moonstone* during a period in which few Victorians questioned the legitimacy or necessity of imperial rule in India. It was widely believed that Indians were instinctual, impulsive, and fanatic, that they lacked the mechanisms of self-control that guaranteed sound government at the level of self and society alike. The 1857 rebellion [...] seemed to confirm the passionate volatility of Indians and their general antipathy to law and order.[87] □

Carens argues that Collins appropriates ethnographic commonplaces about Indian subjectivity and social mores, projecting them onto the English domestic milieu. Thus the supposedly cultivated characters in *The Moonstone* are 'overmastered by their own "dark" and irrational obsessions, inordinate desires, unruly aggressions, and fanatical idolatries.'[88] Moreover, the contrast between the half-caste but honourable Ezra Jennings and the handsome but dishonest Godfrey Ablewhite, an English hypocrite whose own racial purity is subsumed by a complete lack of decency, stands out in high relief.

Frances M. Mannsaker contends that the majority of Indian Mutiny fiction portrays 'half-castes' as 'tak[ing] only the worst qualities of each parent race – the stubbornness and pride of the English, without their courage and principle; the deviousness of the Indians, without their cultivation and dignity.'[89] However, Carens reveals that of all the characters in *The Moonstone*, only the injured Eurasian Jennings – slighted by a hidebound, humourless and bigoted society – is imbued with the intelligence and courage that allow him to succeed where others have so signally failed. The depiction of Jennings bears comparison with Collins's earlier racial hybrid, Ozias Midwinter, in *Armadale*. In this novel and in *The Moonstone*, Collins depends upon mixed-race figures to complicate his readers' assumption of British national superiority. Most important, Carens implies, may be the ability of this amorphous individual to connect to something deep within the nature of the English themselves. Carens's interpretation of *The Moonstone* is also sensitive to Collins's qualifying of his political critiques, muting their subversive impact so that Jennings can be perceived as a figure both for Collins's sympathy with the subjugated and voiceless of Victorian culture, and his tentativeness about his own identification with them. Lillian Nayder, in her chapter on 'Reverse Colonization and Imperial Guilt' from her book *Wilkie Collins* (1997), points out that

■ [i]n *The Moonstone*, as in virtually all of his novels, Collins reinscribes the very ideals he criticises. [...] As is to justify imperial rule, he highlights the devotion Blake receives from Jennings, a 'half-caste' born in the colonies. The product of an exploitative relationship between an Englishman and a native woman, Jennings is continually subject to prejudice and persecution. But rather than expressing resentment towards the English, Jennings identifies with and serves them. [...]

Yet Collins questions this idealised colonial relationship at the same time that he invokes it, using Gabriel Betteredge, and the parallel between imperial and class relations, to reveal the pitfalls of identifying with one's masters.[90] □

Ezra Jennings not only embodies the Other but also British hegemony itself through his father, an Englishman, which anticipates the concept of hybridity, defined as 'what is new, neither the one nor the other,' developed by the postcolonial theorist Homi K. Bhabha (born 1949)[91] '[A]t one place', Jennings's 'white hair ran up into the black; at another, the black hair ran down into the white'.[92] Postcolonial theorists read the startling placement of black hair next to white, in addition to the total absence of grey, as the metaphorical concomitance of two cultures – one imperial, one colonial – which must learn to coexist before any successful mixing can occur.[93] Jennings personifies the inevitable result of the British colonial project – his hair emblematic of the white minority invading and dividing the darker-skinned majority, and his skin the ineluctable consequence of miscegenation. While Jennings's hair may symbolize separateness, his blood – his essence – does not. But the rendering of Jennings also implies the pressures placed on Collins by publishers and readers anxious to uphold the social status quo, and ready to repress imperial guilt. Although the 1996 BBC adaptation of *The Moonstone* tended to downplay Jennings's complex racial heritage, it is difficult to imagine future commentary on the sensation genre doing the same.

Many conservative commentators in the 1860s forecasted that the sensation genre would not have any 'future' beyond 1870. However, in 1882, the *Athenaeum* lambasted what it described as 'our lady novelists [...] who try to attract their public by describing what they imagine to be "life" [...] dwelling on sins they presumably know only at second hand [...and] select brainless ruffians and shameless harlots as their ideals of manhood and womanhood.'[94] Such sensational depictions were still an intrinsic part of the scene of fiction and still possessed the power to disconcert and infuriate middlebrow reviewers. These novels comprised a sizeable number, so much so that in 1885 the *Athenaeum* was prompted to observe that '[t]he tales of mystery and murder which went out of fashion as soon as art came in are beginning to captivate once more, and the novel of furniture is giving way to the raw tones of the romance of crime.'[95]

Surveying sensation fiction, the critic Jonathan Loesberg perceives a genre 'whose life span is so short as to be historically specifiable, and whose definition is as much a matter of literary reception as of intrinsic features'.[96] This supplies an energizing opportunity to trace how commentators have documented the genre's evolution beyond its 1860s heyday. Sheridan Le Fanu opens the following final chapter of this Guide, on 'The Mutation of Sensation'. Chronologically contemporaneous with sensation novelists, Le Fanu was actually born in the same year as Ellen Wood; yet his macabre supernatural stories lay the foundations for *fin de siècle* Gothic horror. During his final years the notoriously elusive and reclusive Le Fanu was allegedly referred to around Dublin as the 'Invisible Prince.' Such a sobriquet implies that this Protestant Anglo-Irish writer might have preferred to remain invisible to literary historians after his death, and it seems, he very nearly did so. Victor Sage observes that while Wilkie Collins 'who for years was Le Fanu's twin "sensationalist", and was in a similar state of semi-oblivion, has been put back into contention as a leading Victorian novelist', Le Fanu languished among the canonical minority because scholarly misprision failed to register the subtlety of his hybrid narrative forms.

The final chapter of this Guide shows that the figures chiefly responsible for developing sensationalism beyond 1870 should not be restricted to women writers whose plots foreground the intrigue of bigamy, incest, adultery and madness, such as M. E. Braddon, Rhoda Broughton and Ouida. Initially these authors had secured a profitable market for serialized fiction in the primarily female readership of the circulating libraries of the 1860s, and they continued to publish successfully up to the first decades of the twentieth century. This chapter also addresses an intricate genealogy of generic indebtedness on the part of canonical novelists such as George Meredith (1828–1909), Henry James, Thomas Hardy and even Joseph Conrad to a popular and 'feminine' narrative tradition. Conrad is an especially striking example, given the extent to which he drew on, as well as distanced himself from, his sensational literary precursors. Moreover, it is difficult, as Judith Mitchell and others have pointed out, to imagine George Moore (1852–1933) writing his novels *A Modern Lover* (1883) and *A Mummer's Wife* (1885) without his more sensational contemporaries.[97] The genre permeates not only the three-volume novel, but also the pages of provincial newspapers and cheap magazines, and blends into the cultural phenomenon of the 'New Woman' as well as the rise of 'naturalism' as a literary mode.

CHAPTER SIX

The Mutation of Sensation

Sheridan Le Fanu: a gruesome hybrid?

> May [the author] be permitted a few words [...] of remonstrance against
> the promiscuous application of the term 'sensation' to that large school
> of fiction which transgresses no one of those canons of construction
> and morality which, in producing the unapproachable 'Waverley Novels',
> their great author imposed upon himself? No one, it is assumed, would
> describe Sir Walter Scott's romances as 'sensation novels'; yet in that
> marvellous series there is not a single tale in which death, crime, and
> in some form, mystery, have not a place.
>
> (Joseph Sheridan Le Fanu, 'A Preliminary Word',
> *Uncle Silas: A Tale of Bartram-Haugh*, ed. Victor Sage,
> Harmondsworth, Middlesex: Penguin, 2000, p. 3)

Although Hilary Pyle calls Joseph Sheridan Le Fanu 'master of a sensational fiction that is still attractive and readable a century after his death',[1] Le Fanu's writings, with the exception of *Uncle Silas* (1864), were relegated until the 1980s to the margins of a literary history more enraptured by 'great traditions.' That commentators nowadays applaud Le Fanu's signal contribution to the sensation novel is ironic since the author himself, whom Victorian reviewers christened 'the Irish Wilkie Collins', testily denied both that he himself was a sensation novelist and more radically, that there was any such category as a 'sensation school' of the 1860s. In 'A Preliminary Word' to *Uncle Silas*, Le Fanu pleads for critics to consider his novel as 'part of the legitimate school of English romance' in line with Walter Scott's canonical oeuvre.[2] For Le Fanu, perhaps, the term 'sensation school' implied an overly neat thematic coherence, as well as a network of formal and ideological correspondences that simply did not exist between the works and authors themselves. Despite attempting, however, to distance his narrative from the associations of a genre that thrived on making a vulgar appeal to readers' nerves, Le Fanu's *Uncle Silas* contains ample plot details to merit the charge of following the sensation school assiduously.[3]

144

But the initial critical reaction to *Uncle Silas* also registers Le Fanu's manipulation of earlier supernatural stock-in-trade; leading Gothic away from its stress on external sources of terror and towards a focus on the psychological effects of fear, loneliness and dread. Recent scholarship has paid much attention to the curious and persistent appeal of the Gothic to mid-Victorian authors of varying class backgrounds, aesthetic orientations, and political identifications. However, Le Fanu is unusual in the degree to which he refurbished the tradition; his vampire story *Carmilla* (1872) is a complex anticipation of *fin de siècle* horror narratives such as *The Great God Pan* (1894) by Arthur Machen (1863–1947), *Dracula* (1897) by Bram Stoker (1847–1912), and *The Beetle* (1897), published only weeks after Stoker's novel, by Richard Marsh (1857–1915). Machen's conception of Helen Vaughan, the demonic harbinger of dissidence in *The Great God Pan*, recalls not only Le Fanu's rendering of sexual menace beneath ostensibly demure exteriors, but also the destructive mid-Victorian sensation heroines Lady Audley and Lydia Gwilt.

Lady Caroline Norton (1808–77), Le Fanu's second cousin, reviewed *Uncle Silas* positively for *The Times*, calling it a perfect sensation novel because 'nothing is related which might not have happened, and the most absolute consistency is maintained in the different characters described.'[4] Sensation fiction was, for Norton, a credible and gripping mode of contemporary realism. The debate over realism versus romance also absorbed the *Saturday Review*'s correspondent, who perceived a line of unbroken continuity stretching from *The Castle of Otranto* (1764) by Horace Walpole (1717–97) to Le Fanu's writing of the 1860s, which was his most prolific period in an extensive and discontinuous career:

> ■ There are no intervals of repose in the story. Mr Le Fanu interposes none of those quiet grey and green tints which Sir Walter Scott employs as a background or foil to his most striking situations. [...] He is feverishly intent on producing a set of Rembrandt effects. He is always darkening the stage and turning on the lime light. Seen through this ghostly medium, all the characters, from the principals to the merest supernumerary, appear more or less weird and unearthly. Mr Le Fanu depicts a state utterly at variance with the prosaic experience of everyday life. The English country-house becomes a veritable Castle of Otranto. □

The *Saturday Review*'s construction of Le Fanu as 'feverishly intent' evokes Margaret Oliphant's polemical attack on sensation novels as 'feverish productions' in *Blackwood's*, explored at the outset of Chapter Four of this Guide. However, this correspondent permits Le Fanu to escape the category of 'sensation', but not because he is construed as a belated acolyte of Scott. In the *Saturday Review*'s account, *The Antiquary*

(1816) signifies Scott's status as an adroit practitioner of realism, while *Uncle Silas*, appearing exactly 70 years after Ann Radcliffe's *The Mysteries of Udolpho*, manifests a profound alterity that typifies the 'purest form of sensation writing' – the Gothic novel and its preoccupation with paranoia, barbarism and taboo. Silas Ruthyn's sepulchral Great House on his Derbyshire estate is the equivalent of Radcliffe's haunted castle, with the plot device of secret passageways evolving into the convention of the locked-room mystery, which Oscar Wilde (1854–1900) will go on to exploit in *The Picture of Dorian Gray* (1891).

> ■ We do not object to the term, but the true type of the tragic romance, in our opinion, is not the *Antiquary*, but the *Mysteries of Udolpho*. Mr Le Fanu has much more in common with Mrs Radcliffe than with Sir Walter Scott. His descriptions of scenery read like passages from that once-favoured author-ess. The melancholy corridors are just the place she would have selected for some thrilling adventure. Both revel in the same nightmare effects; both are intent on making their subject matter yield the maximum amount of vague horror; and this we take to be the purest form of sensation writing.[5] □

The *Saturday Review* goes on to suggest that the ability to conjure an ambience of 'vague horror' shared by Radcliffe and Le Fanu is based on their vivid portrayal of fearful inheritance in time as well as a clammy sense of entrapment in space ('the melancholy corridors'). This backhanded tribute signifies that Le Fanu is more extreme, more committed to elaborating the traditional Gothic sources of the sensation genre than Collins, Ellen Wood and M. E. Braddon, whose 'nightmare effects' are by contrast anchored in the impedimenta of Victorian domesticity, 'the prosaic experience of everyday life' outlined in my previous chapter. According to Nicholas Rance, in *Wilkie Collins and Other Sensation Novelists* (1991) Le Fanu's London publisher, Richard Bentley, encouraged the author to bring his peculiar brand of 'Gothic romance' up to date, by fashioning *Uncle Silas* into a distinctively 'English' (rather than Irish) narrative, set exclusively in 'modern' times to harmonize with the popular novels written by Collins, Braddon and Charles Reade, and thus explicitly marketable as sensation fiction to a British readership.[6]

The *Saturday Review*'s 1865 reaction to *Uncle Silas* raises questions that resonate as powerfully in today's criticism, as feminist scholarship, historicist intervention, a return to the politicized readings of the Gothic, and the contextualization of Le Fanu in relation to Irish studies have all staked their claim on the territory of his oeuvre.[7] Is Le Fanu really a cultural embalmer, preserving the exotic relics of a venerable Gothic mode epitomized by 'Mrs. Radcliffe [...] that once-favoured authoress'? Or does his fiction articulate the most multifaceted sensationalism, whose aesthetic moves across generic boundaries with beguiling ease? Whatever their theoretical affiliations, most commentators concur with Patrick Brantlinger, whose 1982 essay 'What is "Sensational" about the "Sensation Novel"?' asserts that '[m]any of Le Fanu's stories of terror and the occult should perhaps be categorized as Gothic rather than sensation fictions, if only because of the dominance of supernatural over realistic elements.'[8] Brantlinger goes on to explain that Le Fanu's 1860s fiction sets out the motifs and preoccupations that will become central to *fin-de-siècle* authors such as Stoker.[9]

Elizabeth Bowen (1899–1973), in her preface to a new edition of *Uncle Silas* for Cresset Press in 1947, was one of the first to suggest that Le Fanu was actually concerned with mapping Irish history rather than the more 'sensational' topography of modern England favoured by Richard Bentley.[10] Bowen, an Anglo-Irish Protestant of the same class as Le Fanu, similarly obsessed with images of destructive isolation as she watched the land of her birth alter from metropolitan colony to semi-independent nation-state, construed *Uncle Silas* as 'an Irish story transposed to an English setting'.[11] Bowen's intuitions have been borne out and elaborated by W. J. McCormack's *Sheridan Le Fanu and Victorian Ireland,* and its critical and reflective counterpart *Dissolute Characters* (1983), which refines the relation between the Irish subtext of *Uncle Silas* and its context. McCormack proposes that the voice of the narrator, the impressionable *ingénue* Maud Ruthyn, whose frightened guilt and unease speaks of and for Victorian Ireland, is Le Fanu's cadence in feminine disguise. Bowen's concept of Le Fanu as springing from 'a race of hybrids' is translated by McCormack into a richly detailed sense of *Uncle Silas* as a hybrid narrative form, whose superficial adherence to the 'Wilkie Collins school' (for instance equating the enclosure of woman in the house with live interment) belies a uniquely nervous and highly charged literary style:

■ Le Fanu's best fiction – *Uncle Silas* and *In a Glass Darkly* – is amenable to formal and stylistic criticism to a degree surprising in sensationalism. The characteristic Le Fanu plot conforms roughly to the rules of the Wilkie Collins school: there is murder, suicide, attempted bigamy, a little detection, a great deal of sentiment, sleep-walking, lunatic asylums, shipwrecks, and debtors' prisons. A synopsis of any of these tales is strangely pointless, for the real significance of the plot lies elsewhere, in recurrent imagery, in symmetrical patterns, in the use of female narrators. As far as the sensational narratives are concerned, the most important feature is perhaps the suggestion which Le Fanu generally creates that his hero or heroine stands at one extremity of a process which began in the past. [...] These narratives do not simply expose past crimes and guilty consciences; they show us the historical past acted out in the present, sometimes in ironical mimicry, sometimes with a metaphysical *frisson*.[12] □

Le Fanu is an intriguing cultural hybrid in the Victorian sensation canon, writing from the peripheries of Anglo-Irish Dublin, whose radical ambivalence towards the sensation tag, with the roots of the term affixed to metropolitan London, evinces a formulation of character in his fiction as a process of dissolving, a collapse into social and psychological disunity or disjointedness. Le Fanu's conflicted political and cultural identity is dramatized as an Anglo-Irish oscillation between the 'English' embrace of cool rationality, the technological, a future of progressive advance, and an 'Irish' susceptibility to anachrony, the atavistic and a superstitious past. Though Le Fanu set most of his stories and novels in England (and as his names announced both Gaelic and French Huguenot origins), even his identity as 'English' sensationalist becomes questionable. Le Fanu's hybrid voice articulates its most primal fears through a fixation on the subject of the house, which for his novels, if not for his short stories, meant the venerable 'country-house' of Gothic romance noted by the 1865 *Saturday Review* and later by Elizabeth Bowen in her preface to *Uncle Silas*. As a Protestant, a member of the Anglo-Irish ascendancy whose authority was increasingly eroded by moves for national self-determination, his fiction concentrates on the threats to the mansion's security from invasion, destitution and decay, both actual and metaphysical.[13]

Alison Milbank, in both *Daughters of the House: Modes of the Gothic in Victorian Fiction* (1992) and her 2002 essay 'Victorian Gothic in English Novels and Stories, 1830–1880',[14] investigates these ideas first of all by showing how Le Fanu and Dickens both sensationalize the domestic space and the mansion as a crypt, as part of a restless quest for personal, political and religious significance. Like Wilkie Collins, Le Fanu shares, according to Milbank, a concern with the formal divisions of the house: its function as an obstacle, its separation of outside from inside, the encroachment by alien forces, and its fragility under assault. However at that point, the similarity ends, for the incursion that obsesses Le Fanu, even when it takes the form of a conspiring governess, is supernatural:

■ Whereas the narratives of his full-length novels are versions of classic 'female' Gothic, with heiresses trying to escape from romantic ivy-clad mansions, his short stories involve illicit entry into the house. His housebreakers, however, are not sensation adventuresses but supernatural visitants. [...] the ghost not only invades the house but also the body of its victim, to demolish the false front he offers to the world. The detective element in the haunting is made plain in the cry of the unmasked villain in Le

Fanu's *The House by the Churchyard*: 'Another gloss on my text! Why invade me like housebreakers?' In the doom-laden and often suicidal heroes of his longer tales and novels, and in his febrile, self-consciously Radcliffean heroines, Le Fanu provides the most extreme examples of the development of the 'male' and 'female' Gothic forms of the previous century.[15] □

Helen Stoddart's 1991 essay ' "The Precautions of Nervous People Are Infectious": Sheridan Le Fanu's Symptomatic Gothic', shares Milbank's fascination with the domestic and political agendas of Le Fanu's idiosyncratic brand of sensationalism. However, Stoddart is more preoccupied by the instances of homosexuality and aristocratic corruption in Le Fanu's supernatural tales 'Green Tea' and *Carmilla*. One tendency of Stoddart's research is to move away from the strict emphasis on female Gothic characteristic of earlier feminist scholarship towards a rigorous re-theorizing of male Gothic that confronts the genre's relation to Victorian masculinities – the intricate and changing definitions of gender and sexual identity for men during the latter half of the nineteenth century. Stoddart shows how late-Victorian Gothic is a crucial site for this scholarly enterprise, since during the 1890s the genre becomes at once more aggressively masculinized and medicalized – more securely the domain of male writers such as Bram Stoker and Arthur Conan Doyle, and also marked by the professional language of scientific discourses about homosexuality, eugenics and female hysteria.[16]

Victor Sage's monograph *Le Fanu's Gothic: The Rhetoric of Darkness* (2004), while it registers the bold contribution of Stoddart and others, also notes the tendency of these Gothic studies to play down Le Fanu's indebtedness to the 'sensation school', as well as to reduce *Uncle Silas* to an ideological cipher, the mere outcome of abstract political, and social forces that determine the very possibilities of literary production. For Sage, *Uncle Silas* takes the Gothic of the 'classic' phase (1764–1820) in a different direction by reinventing it not so much as a genre but rather as a flexible repertoire of rhetorical manoeuvres, one of whose functions is to suggest the presence of a traditional supernatural world while exposing it to the dispassionate and curious judgement of an impartial investigator. In contextualizing and thereby disclosing the numerous formal and aesthetic traces of *Uncle Silas*, as these come to be encrypted within, and focused through, the principal protagonist Maud, Sage indicates Le Fanu's textual apparatus as historically grounded.

Earlier readings of *Uncle Silas* have implied there is little distance between Maud and a Radcliffe heroine, permitting us to maintain a position of authority over the character, and therefore the textual world. Sage avers by contrast that 'there are levels beyond the speaker, Maud, perpetually present';[17] but far from permitting any transcendent readerly perspective, 'the device of the first-person *ingénue* narrator' ensnares 'the reader in the folds of the text like a butterfly' because 'Maud is ventriloquized, a composite.'[18] This is how Le Fanu creates his own 'new Gothic rhetoric' out of 'a traditional set of moral oppositions between hypocrisy and candour.'[19] And it is this marking of the narrative by conflicting textual and historical signs that problematizes its reception and interpretation.[20] Sage shows Le Fanu carefully repackaging the sensational to accommodate a milieu in which the ideal of total understanding is repeatedly undercut, and where readers – as well as characters – are poised between suffocating rationality on one side and sinister superstition on the other.[21] By making this feeling of entrapment a centrepiece of his imaginative repertoire, Le Fanu offers us a foretaste of the dark obsessions infusing *fin de siècle* literature.

Beyond the 'sensation school'

Peter Keating's *The Haunted Study* (1989) notes that while generic boundaries remained fluid, giving writers licence to range between them, the tangled elements of the sensation novel tended to separate into discrete strands of popular fiction as the literary terrain became increasingly disjointed during the last third of the nineteenth century.[22] Detective tales would address the innovations of forensic science; while Robert Louis Stevenson, Bram Stoker, Grant Allen, Oscar Wilde and H. G. Wells (1866–1946) would augment Le Fanu's sensational and uncanny modes, employing scientific discoveries to inspect the dissolution (and distortion) of the human body, the malleability of identity and the forbidding contours of a dystopian future.[23] Wilkie Collins's post-1870s fiction obliquely reflects this phase: his later novels span a remarkably wide generic spectrum, from the Gothic flourishes of *Jezebel's Daughter* (1880) to the domestic melodrama *Poor Miss Finch* (1872). Many highlight particular social, clinical and legal dilemmas – the helplessness of working-class married women in *Man and Wife* (1870); the rehabilitation of 'fallen' women in *The New Magdalen* (1873) and *The Fallen Leaves* (1879); neurology and its philosophical ramifications in *The Two Destinies* (1876); divorce and child-custody in *The Evil Genius* (1886); and vivisection in *Heart and Science* (1883).

Patrick Brantlinger proposes that the rightful legatees of the sensation novel are the popular genres of the twentieth century – 'modern mystery, detective and suspense fictions and films.'[24] However, Philip Davis argues in his 2002 survey of *The Victorians 1830–1880*, that the impact of sensationalism was much more profound than this model permits:

■ [T]he existence of the sensationalist sub-genre and its modification in other contexts acted as a testing ground for the development of fundamental novelistic techniques, such as the balance between character and story, demanding a more creative awareness of the beliefs about reality that were implicit within them. [...]

Yet [...] to confine sensationalism to being simply a sub-genre is to limit the life of its significance. It bursts into the reality of the realist novel itself whenever realism's secure boundaries are threatened, transforming everything.[25] □

Like Davis, Lyn Pykett's concept of 'The Sensation Legacy' signifies that the genre should not be cordoned off or isolated as what Richard D. Altick calls 'a craze that lasted an entire decade.'[26]

■ [j]ust as the phenomenon of sensationalism existed before the term entered general usage, sensation conventions and plots continued their existence long after the term went out of fashion. [...] The tentacles of sensationalism spread widely and deeply into many different kinds of fiction in the mid-Victorian period, and stretched out their reach as far as Hardy and his contemporaries at the end of the century [...]

All novelists of the 1850s, 1860s (and beyond), whether or not they were labelled as sensationalists, worked with complex multiple plots, and engaged in the process of defining, reworking and redefining realism. However extreme their plots and their rhetoric, sensation fiction was concerned with many of the same issues as the so-called mainstream Victorian novel: class, sex, money, family, morals, manners, marriage and social change. Similarly, sensation types, sensation plots and sensation machinery were integral parts of the storehouse of conventions upon which all Victorian novelists drew.[27] □

Pykett's delineation of 'The Sensation Legacy' furnishes a means of reappraising a number of canonical Victorian novelists for whom the genre may have seemed little more than a regrettable and frivolous literary fad. Though George Meredith, who has been called one of the first 'highbrow novelists',[28] deprecated the far-fetched characterization and gimmicky melodramatic storylines in Le Fanu's and Collins's literary output,[29] he did not scruple to employ such contrivances, albeit in modified form. In *Evan Harrington* (1860) Meredith 'effected', according to Benjamin Fisher, 'some deft inversions of Collins's materials in *The Dead Secret* to serve his own idea of greater depths in psychological portraiture. [...] Meredith could not wholly eschew popular fiction substance as a means to financial gain. So in part he emulated Collins's sensationalism.'[30] Fisher's argument is persuasive, and allows us to inspect one of Meredith's most sparsely and unfavourably reviewed novels *Rhoda Fleming* (1865), published five years after Meredith had become a reader for Chapman and Hall, as partly inspired by, and seriously reflective upon, the countless sensational manuscripts that had landed on his desk. Indeed, Meredith's plot machinery of intercepted correspondence, misappropriated funds and family intrigue would not have been out of place in a Le Fanu novel of the same period.

Anthony Trollope felt that the sensation genre's excesses invited elaborate parody, and his *melange* of political novel, ironic romance and detective thriller, *The Eustace Diamonds* (1873) rewrites *The Moonstone* in his own more realistic idiom to address themes of power, property and patrimony. He fashions the plot around a socially ambitious young woman who filches her own gems, as Cuff had mistakenly suspected Wilkie Collins's Rachel Verinder of doing.[31] However, given that Trollope proposed that an effectual novel should be 'at the same time realistic and sensational',[32] it is hardly surprising that he adopts the basic sensation ingredients of crime and sexual intrigue more straightforwardly, as in *Orley Farm* (1861–62), with its portrayal of confusions over wills and codicils, and its exploration of a patrician lady whose seemingly unblemished moral reputation conceals a dark secret in her past.[33]

Pykett's investigation into 'The Sensation Legacy' also reveals that George Eliot's lofty disavowal of those 'silly lady novelists' whose immense popularity coincided with the early years of her own literary career veils a dependency on the very sensational conventions that she decried in novels by M. E. Braddon. The imperious Mrs Transome in *Felix Holt the Radical* (1866), published in the middle of the sensation boom, whose literary tastes extend to 'dangerous French authors', is also a woman harbouring a secret, which involves an adulterous affair and its continuing results. Mrs Transome's secret is a variation of those illicit details which are uncovered in sensation fiction: a cross-class sexual liaison which erodes the dignity of the patrician elite, leaving them exposed to their wily social inferiors, and destroying the harmony and continuity of the family and its property. Eliot's reliance on sensational stock-in-trade was noted by the 1867 *Contemporary Review*, which depicted 'Lady Audley and Mrs Transome [...as] true twin sisters of fiction', and accused Eliot of joining hands with Braddon in reversing 'the grand old idea of [...] heroic behaviour, by cunningly eliciting our sympathy for individuals placed in doubtful circumstances, who fall into falsely tragical positions because of their weakness.'[34]

Braddon's ability to condition not only George Eliot's imaginative vision but also Henry James's has been explored by Adeline R. Tintner, whose perspicacious reading of the James short story 'Georgina's Reasons' (1884) underscores the complexity of this author's fastidious construction of himself as a 'man of letters', given his 1865 review of Braddon's career and the keen awareness of mass popularity that this discloses.[35] James's later admission to Charles Eliot Norton (1827–1908) of his 'intellectual exhaustion' after having 'popped up faint praise for a succession of vapid novels'[36] camouflages a readiness to exploit sensational tactics in order to consolidate a niche in the crowded and highly competitive literary marketplace.

In 1911 James actually wrote to Braddon, calling her 'a magnificent benefactress to the literary estate' and recalling how 'I used to follow you ardently, and track you close, taking from your hands deep draughts of the happiest of anodynes.'[37] As Tintner and others have signified, plentiful evidence for this 'close tracking' of Braddon's career can be found in James's *Watch and Ward* (1871), a story of sexual obsession, suicide and despair, and *The American* (1877), James's tale of an innocent abroad, entangled in the baleful machinations of an aristocratic French clan. *The American* evinces not only the international dimension to sensation fiction but also James's own deeply vexed attitude to the commercial drives of literature, which Michael Anesko has described in *'Friction with the Market': Henry James and the Business of Authorship* (1986) as: 'the "mysterious" links between works of literature and its potential audience, between the sanctity of culture (the library) and the vulgar street [...and] the marketplace (the office), a business-like domain where values are filtered through a sole medium of exchange: windows papered in bank-note green.'[38]

Anesko's fascinating account signals how the sensational might rehabilitate our view of more canonical authors and the popular components of their work. For instance, both James's *What Maisie Knew* (1908) and *The Awkward Age* (1899) revise the basic plot mechanics of Wood's *East Lynne* to illustrate the damage done to family by maternal sexuality.[39] James performs this revision in *What Maisie Knew* by shifting the perspective to a vulnerable and isolated child, which stifles any sympathy we might feel for the adulterous or socially marginal mother as in the 'maternal melodrama' of *East Lynne*. Anesko is alert to how a popular feminine narrative of sensation fiction afforded major challenges for writers such as James, who had to sell literature as well as elevate its status as art.[40] This need to balance a zealous commitment to serious craft with a hard-headed notion of its commercial appeal complicates those orthodox histories of Victorian fiction that tend to enforce an artificially imposed 'high' and 'low' divide which segregates works of consummate literary skill from what James himself reviled as 'trash triumphant.'

The examples of Meredith, Trollope, Eliot and James underline Lyn Pykett's contention that in order to register the sheer variety of 'sensationalism', as well as the cultural and historical developments of the form itself, it is crucial to gauge its impact on Victorian literature more generally. This cuts against many of the Victorian middlebrow periodicals that confidently predicted the dwindling of the genre after its 'brief' heyday. In its 1869 review of *Hester's History*, the *Spectator* claimed that younger writers were turning away from the hackneyed motifs of literary sensationalism,[41] and by 1873 it was detecting in one new novel by Sir Francis Vincent (1803–1880) a marked resistance to the genre's dependence on melodrama: 'Sir Francis Vincent's last novel, if we remember it aright, was full of incident. Possibly some critic told him that it was too sensational, and now, with the docility characteristic of authors, he has been attempting to correct the fault.'[42]

The *Spectator's* glib prediction of the sensation school's demise did not in the least discourage Thomas Hardy, whose engagement with the genre in his debut novel *Desperate Remedies* (1871) and in his Wessex Novels as a whole has generated a vital body of criticism since the publication of Lawrence A. Jones's 1965 article '*Desperate Remedies* and the Victorian Sensation Novel' as well as Paul Ward's '*Desperate Remedies* and the Victorian Thriller' (1973–74).[43] For Jones, Hardy's sensational antecedents can be seen in his incendiary handling of the 'deadly war waged between flesh and spirit', and his persistent focus on the problematic nature of the institution of marriage:

■ On the surface, at least, Hardy did write in *Desperate Remedies* a conventional sensation novel. However, he could not totally suppress his personal mode of regard. [...] There is definitely a tension in the novel between Hardy's natural impulse, and the opposing demands of the conventional genre, between the tragic pattern implicit in his 'mode of regard' and the ultimately comic pattern demanded by the sensation novel.[44] □

These early commentators on Hardy's decision to offer what the *Life* calls 'the eminently "sensational" plot of *Desperate Remedies*'[45] have generally agreed that, in Robert Gittings' words, it is a 'mixture' of disparate elements that 'do not combine.'[46] Its doubleness has also been perceived as an initial and 'unsuccessful resolution' of difficulties that would resurface later in Hardy's career.[47] However, since the publication of Elaine Showalter's 1976 essay '*Desperate Remedies*: Sensation Novels of the 1860s'[48] and Walter M. Kendrick's 'The Sensationalism of Thomas Hardy' (1980), scholars have situated *Desperate Remedies* more confidently in its contemporary critical context, assessing the bizarre incongruity of its components in terms of the rich generic possibilities of the sensation genre. Showalter and Kendrick variously indicate that although Hardy was later to disown the sensationalism of his early work as quite against his natural artistic bent, sensational and melodramatic concerns and modes of representation continued to be a vitalizing part of his fictional repertoire, particularly in his portrayal of wilful female protagonists – for example the Braddonesque 'Queen of the Night' passage on Eustacia Vye from *The Return of the Native* (1876).

Walter Kendrick's 1980 essay on *Desperate Remedies* probes how sensationalism is manifested in Hardy's frequent use of coincidence, and in the way in which his plots are moulded by the shameful secrets of the past habitually returning to blight the present and future lives of his characters. Yet Kendrick contends that to evaluate *Desperate Remedies* as a realistic narrative clumsily paired with a sensational one, as previous commentators had done, is seriously to miss the point of Hardy's artistic enterprise. The novel

■ reflects a thorough familiarity with the sensation novel of the previous decade [and] an equal familiarity with comments on sensation. Not only did Hardy know his predecessors, he also knew his predecessors' critics. And he took them both into account [...] The proliferation of sensation parodies in the late 1860s and early 70s also suggests that to write a sensation novel when Hardy wrote his could not have been the precritical gesture it might have been a few years earlier. By 1871 the genre was well defined [...] Its characteristics had been exhaustively enumerated by critics, and any newcomer in the field would easily be able to construct an orthodox sensation novel without having read a single one.

Indeed, the most striking feature of *Desperate Remedies* is its extreme orthodoxy, verging on the parodic.[49] □

Kendrick declares that the true subject of *Desperate Remedies* is neither its tormented protagonists nor its typically tortuous plotting but the stylistic mannerisms and quirks of sensationalism itself. However, Kendrick overplays Hardy's unthinking fidelity to these rhetorical tics in the cause of garnering public attention. *Desperate Remedies* challenges and overturns one of the definitional facets of the genre: its tendency to exorcize the feeling of helplessness so crucial to the earlier Gothic romance's widespread appeal by ascribing evil to the machinations of a single malefactor. As Sally Mitchell remarks in *The Fallen Angel: Chastity, Class and Women's Reading 1835–1880* (1981):

■ At first reading, Hardy's use of the sensation materials appears simply bungled. The changes of identity and secrets of the past are obvious [...] In comparison to Collins, Hardy seems plodding and self-conscious in dropping the clues [...] Yet the method itself – arriving at a rational explanation for every detail [...] – comes, in Hardy's hands, to imply cosmic interdependence. The characters' fortunes do not depend on individual efforts, or virtue, or villainy, [...] but on half-chance events that arise from the intersection with other lives. One story's hero, the author muses, is a walk-on in the story of another life.[50] □

In *Desperate Remedies*, as Mitchell asserts, trains are delayed not by 'spectacular accidents' but because it is Christmas and 'everyone is travelling'; concealments arise from motives no more sinister than embarrassment.[51] So the ultimate effect enunciates the very sense of helplessness that literary sensationalism tried to eradicate. In his later Wessex Novels, this helplessness assumes a weightier philosophical dimension, informed by the findings of Karl Marx (1818–83) and Charles Darwin (1809–82).

According to Mitchell, Hardy shared with many 1860s commentators a sense that the phenomenon of literary sensationalism marked a provocative point of transition from the socially responsible mimesis of mid-Victorian realism to the artistically self-sufficient novels of the 1890s and beyond. Hardy's rendering of a drably deterministic Darwinian cosmos, in which the typical experiences are existential emptiness and frustrated passion, continues the revision of the conventions and moral vision of popular melodrama that was inaugurated by the sensation novelists. For Hardy, the abstract struggle between moral absolutes which was staged in the popular melodrama became a much more historically and socially specific set of discordances. These were played out in a fragmented milieu in which the boundaries between moral categories were increasingly blurred and aggressively relativized.

While Hardy cleverly manipulated sensational devices in *Desperate Remedies*, the generic and sentimental expectations of sensation writing were being reworked in the 1870s as a predominantly female mode. The extremely long careers of Braddon, Ellen Wood and Rhoda Broughton took them well beyond the sensation decade and into different fictional territory.[52] Later works by Ouida, Broughton, Braddon and Wood, are also scrutinized in terms of how they foresee the political concerns typical of 'New Woman' novels.[53] Lyn Pykett delineates the fertile continuities between the women's sensation novel of the 1860s and the 'New Woman' writing of the 1890s in *The 'Improper' Feminine* (1992):

■ At first sight nothing could appear more dissimilar than the popular sensation novel of the 1860s, with its bigamous or adulterous heroines and complicated plots of crime and intrigue, and the 'modern women's books of the introspective type' [...] on the wrongs of women and the evils of men and marriage which appeared in the 1880s and 1890s. Many twentieth-century readers have readily identified the progressive social views and proto-feminism of some of the New Woman writers. Few (if any) of the female sensationalists could be regarded as either feminist or progressive. However [...] the women sensationalists and the New Woman writers both worked with forms which have usually been regarded as predominantly feminine, even when they have been used by male writers.[54] □

Pykett's approach shows how the women's sensation novel, in melding and reworking the dominant female forms of the early nineteenth century – female Gothic, melodrama and domestic realism – foreshadowed the stylistic and generic hybridity of the 'New Woman' novels to highlight the contradictions of contemporary marriage and the domestic ideal. Both genres were produced by, and were vigorous interventions in, the changing debate about woman's prescribed social and familial roles, and both generated critical controversies that became a focus for broader cultural ambivalences and anxieties about gender.

Pykett's judicious discussion of Braddon's attitude towards, and influence on, the 'New Woman' writing raises questions about her considerable body of work after the 1860s, which evinces an ability to range widely beyond the sensational mode she helped create. In his biography of Braddon, Robert Lee Wolff reveals that she successfully experimented with other genres; however her work is still, almost a hundred years after her death, organized by the brief phrase 'by the author of *Lady's Audley's Secret*' homogenizing her prolific and experimental oeuvre: 'Even today, when she is remembered at all, she is still associated with her artless and somewhat trashy first great success.'[55] This reductive assessment tends to overlook the achievement of novels published in the 1870s such as *Joshua Haggard's Daughter* (1876) and *Vixen* (1879), both of which complicate the conventions of the genre. As Albert C. Sears argues of the latter novel in his essay 'Mary Elizabeth Braddon and the "Combinational Novel"' (2006):

■ Filled with references to other sensation novels, *Vixen* challenges readers to transgress their sensational reading patterns. One of the text's telling sensation novel citations is when the reader learns that Violet 'Vixen' Tempest, the heroine, is a reader of the sensation novel *Foul Play* (1868) by Charles Reade and Dion Boucicault [1820–90]. *Foul Play* provides Violet with moments of escape during an unsensational banishment to a spinster's house in Jersey. Most significant, her stay on the island is her fantasy of being *Foul Play*'s heroine, Helen Rolleston, who becomes shipwrecked on a tropical island, alone with a man who desperately loves her. Even though Helen is chaste and conventionally feminine, her improper circumstance, living unmarried with a man in an exotic locale, enables Violent to fantasise about her desire for Roderick Vawdrey, her love interest in *Vixen*.[56] □

As Sears points out, even though there has been a renewed focus on Braddon as 'Queen of the Circulating Library' who sustained her popularity until late in her life, critical interest in *Vixen* has been minimal. In its few interpretations, the work has been explicated both as a sensation novel and a repudiation of the mode she helped establish. Wolff reads it apart from Braddon's sensation novels, suggesting that it is 'a vehicle for vigorous radical social satire'.[57] Gillian Beer scrutinizes the novel as sensational alongside the works of Rhoda Broughton.[58] For Sears, these various twentieth-century responses might be attributed to the way Braddon both evokes and undermines sensation genre techniques in the 'combination novel form'. *Vixen* is reflexive of Victorian popular print culture and examines the production and consumption of texts while it complicates its own status as a sensation text. This shows how Braddon intervened in the nineteenth-century reception of her fiction and of other sensation writers. In discussing similar allusions in her appraisal of Braddon's earlier novel *Joshua Haggard's Daughter*, Pamela K. Gilbert notes that 'Braddon uses [...] references to popular literature [...] to critique attitudes towards popular literature and reading itself.'[59]

The emergence, in the 1870s and 1880s, of a second generation of women novelists – Rhoda Broughton, Ouida, Florence Marryat, Helen Mathers (1853–1920) and Lady Emma Caroline Wood – certainly added to this sense of the sensation novel as something which was, far from waning, actually reinventing itself and adapting cannily to evolving literary tastes. The review columns of magazines such as the *Athenaeum* furnish a valuable insight into the literary landscape of this period and the estimated 60,000 works of fiction published between 1855 and 1890. There is little doubt that the sensation novel continued to flourish, led – so the magazine pundits believed – by a 'phalanx' of women writers.[60]

Among this 'phalanx' was Rhoda Broughton, who produced 27 novels between the years 1867 and 1920. Her work sold widely, and well, though she receives no mention in either Winifred Hughes's *The Maniac in the Cellar* or Thomas Boyle's *Black Swine in the Sewers of Hampstead*. Initially perceived as a sensation novelist when her first, extremely popular novels came out in the 1860s, such as *Not Wisely But Too Well* (1867) and *Cometh Up As A Flower* (1867), she was later classified as a writer of love stories, long after romantic entanglements had ceased to be even the principal theme of her fiction.[61] Along with Sally Mitchell's *The Fallen Angel* and Kate Flint's *The Woman Reader, 1837–1914*, Helen Debenham's 1996 essay on intertextuality in *Not Wisely But Too Well* registers the difficulty of categorizing Broughton's early works as sensationalist:

■ Modern criticism which [...] reads Broughton's early novels simply as sensation fiction, or rather through definitions of sensationalism derived principally from the narrative practices of Wilkie Collins, Mary Braddon and Ellen Wood, can do little except praise the assertive sexuality and deplore the conventional moralising. Even Lyn Pykett, whose 1992 study of the 'improper' feminine could provide a strong argument for reading Broughton as sensationalist, adds little to Elaine Showalter's dismissive verdict in *A Literature of Their Own*.[62] □

Debenham's essay privileges the way in which Broughton's early novels offer a subversive and often puckish blend of discourses and genres, appropriating and repackaging (often masculine) 'high' cultural references. For Debenham, this artistic strategy supplies insights into the young female writer as a reader, reacting to her culture's definitions of her as a woman, and 'negotiating her right of entry to and her difference from the literary establishment that shaped those definitions'.[63]

Unlike Broughton, whose almost entirely female group of protagonists focus on pursuing love and defining meaningful labour such as writing and philanthropy, or Braddon, whose protagonists are women committed to carving out and maintaining a social identity, Ouida's central characters are just as likely to be men as women. Ouida's fiction is a reflection of the generic transition of sensation fiction in the 1870s, fusing sex, romance, mystery and political chicanery, and presages what we refer to today as society novels, by Danielle Steele (born 1947), Harold Robbins (1916–97) and others. For Vincent E. H. Murray in 1873, Ouida's novels are pernicious because they

■ throw an evil light on the social corruption of which they are an exhalation [...] Precisely as certain diseased conditions of the body give rise to a craving after unnatural food, so do certain morbid conditions of the mind produce an appetite for literary food which a sound mental organisation would reject [...] we believe further that the society which reads and encourages such literature is a 'whited sepulchre' which, if it be not speedily cleansed by the joint effort of pure men and women, will breed a pestilence so foul as to poison the very life-blood of our nation.[64] □

Murray's vituperative attack on Ouida in terms of her efforts to gratify 'unnatural' appetites is reminiscent of H. L. Mansel's anti-sensation invective in the early 1860s. By shifting from the image of contaminated food to the parallel threat of the diseased cadaver, Murray identifies Ouida's readers as subhuman, and a threat to an entire nation of 'pure' men and women who must be unceasingly watchful so as to prevent the poisoning of their homeland by degenerates. In an 1879 review of 'Contemporary Literature' in *Blackwood's*, Ouida's works are referred to both as 'sensational' and as 'novels of society that are as frivolous [as sensation] though less harmless.' A distinction is being made between the two genres, but they actually overlap:

■ The mischief they must answer for is likely to survive the unnatural excitement and the extreme absurdity which were their redeeming virtues [...] Stories written for the gratification of the ordinary subscribers to Mr. Mudie, are passed on in due course to be devoured by the milliners' apprentices and lawyers' clerks. [...] These stories are circulated or imitated in the columns of the 'penny dreadfuls' [and are dangerous like] the demagogues who get a living by stirring strife between classes.[65] □

The 'unnatural excitement' of Ouida's fiction is perceived as corroding social stability and class hierarchies, goading the lower orders to commit sexual and other transgressions, in a clear echo of the more paranoid denunciations of the sensation genre two decades earlier. But as Pamela Gilbert writes in *Disease, Desire and the Body in Victorian Women's Popular Novels*:

■ Ouida's work is quite different from Braddon's or Broughton's, in that the setting is displaced from the middle-class urban or suburban domesticity characteristic of the latter two authors. Perhaps because of this, Ouida had no trouble gaining entry to the circulating library market, despite her characters' explicit improprieties.

If the sensation novel may be seen as a structuring container for anxieties focused on the domestic, perhaps the novel of high life was [...] a sort of adventure story for women, in which the reader could vicariously experience the joys of being, in a couple of senses, an adventuress, while comfortable in the knowledge that it was acceptable to enjoy this sort of behaviour.[66] □

Gilbert indicates that Ouida's stories, unlike those of the sensation school, furnish a methodically regulated and self-contained fantasy of 'high life'. Ouida's adulteress figures, as opposed to their sensational counterparts, escape punishment in a fictional scheme that does not rely upon Braddon's edgier conception of a more violent and turbulent side to middle-class domesticity.

While Pamela Gilbert has brought a welcome and trenchant focus to Ouida's neglected oeuvre, the novels of Dora Russell, with *Beneath the Wave* (1878) notable among them, warrant more diligent scrutiny. Russell's fiction is best comprehended, according to Graham Law's 2004 'Introduction' to the reissue of *Beneath the Wave*, as 'newspaper fiction': 'leading examples of a type of women's sensation narrative prevalent in Britain from the earlier 1870s.' Though 'Newspaper Novel' was another name for the sensation genre, because of its close connection to the world of journalism and the public disclosure of domestic secrets, bigamies and sexual wrongdoing relished by the popular press, Russell's writing complicates this term:

■ 'newspaper fiction' is [... derived] from, but by no means narrowly limited to, the print context in which stories like Russell's initially appeared – syndicates of cheap provincial weekly news miscellanies. In spite of their number and variety, these venues provide specific indications of the cultural identities of the communities of readers who constituted Russell's principal audience – identities which can be charted in terms of regional, social, religious and political affiliations, as well as by gender. At the same time, the format of the local weekly paper must be seen as having an impact on the narrative form and content of the fiction appearing in its pages. [...] publication in newspaper columns alongside the latest reports, editorial comments and subscribers' responses encouraged an especially intimate engagement with the events and issues of the day [...] Yet these events were by no means restricted to vice and crime [...] Instances with powerful contemporary resonances range from the opening of railway stations and tramlines, through outbreaks of scarlet fever and typhoid, to new developments in the printing and publishing trades or visits to the latest pantomime and concert venue.[67] □

Law's examination of Russell's 'newspaper fiction' is a timely contribution to the process of recuperation of her work, given that she is omitted from both the original and the new edition of the *Dictionary of National Biography*. And among the nearly 900 novelists recorded in John Sutherland's *Companion to Victorian Fiction* (1990) Russell is not seen to justify an entry. Law proposes that there is obviously scope for investigating some of the processes by which this happened and some of the ways in which in the literary climate of the 1860s and 1870s, women, in particular, developed confidence in presenting themselves as public figures. As pundits both then and now have noted, it is not difficult to imagine busy magazine readers engaging with lots of different fictional and non-fictional narratives at the same time, the prolonged juxtaposition of which had the potential to shape and intensify their understandings of the events and characters of the novels in particular ideological ways.[68]

Law's account encourages us to think about the diverse audiences for sensation fiction and the ways in which novelists refined their art to cater to numerous reading communities. For example, in a recent analysis of the changes to form and publication which modified sensation fiction in the 1870s, Mark Knight explains how some novelists 'adapted sensational narratives to a more restrained style' permitting them to sell to more obviously respectable magazines with a strongly religious bent such as *The Quiver* '*Designed for the Defence of Biblical Truth and the Advancement of Religion in the Homes of People*', *Good Words*, which spoke to a sizeable Evangelical readership, and the *Family Herald: A Domestic Magazine of Useful Information and Amusement*, a cheap weekly periodical launched in 1842.[69] The domesticated, religious and conservative accents of these magazines with their emphasis on utility and edification are not ones that we immediately associate with the sensation genre. Yet there were several novelists, such as Mary Cecil Hay, author of *Among the Ruins* (1882), *Bid Me Discourse* (1883) and *Lester's Secret* (1885), who were marketed as offering a less abrasive and disputatious type of sensationalism than many of their contemporaries; mixing the saintly and the secular for didactic ends. Although another novelist, Charlotte Elizabeth Riddell (1832–1906), accused Ellen Wood of being 'simply a brute; she throws in bits of religion to slip her fodder down the public throat'[70] – the synthesis of the sacred and the profane incorporated in these magazines caused less controversy than might have been expected.

Conrad and fictions of empire

> Indeed, we have been, since the Romans, the only truly imperial people. We have embraced the globe with the arms of our ambition; we have scoured every sea; we have colonised every sphere. But the insularity with which we were once unfairly rebuked is at last becoming [...] our characteristic and opprobrium [...] We are determinedly insular, and we find even the island too big [...] 'our neighbourhood' is the most delightful and absorbing thing in life [...] It is this quality of narrow curiosity which is the paralysis of all wide and noble interest, which the novel stimulates and feeds [...] these are the main concerns of a once imperial people.[71]

In an 1874 review of 'The Novels of Miss Broughton', *Temple Bar* reflected ruefully on Rhoda Broughton's fiction, which was seen to typify the sensation genre's tendency to reduce its readers' enthusiasms to a narrow and petty provincialism. A 'truly imperial people' should celebrate extrovert virility, crusading verve and panoramic vistas, but these narratives have manufactured, and continue to feed, a passive audience that is feminized, infantilized and meekly colonial. *Temple Bar*'s construction of popular literature as eroding a once proud 'imperial' nation underestimates the complexity with which literary sensationalism depicts 'Englishness' in an age of expansionist foreign policies and increasing emigration, with men seeking to make their fortunes abroad before returning home rich.[72] Braddon's *Lady Audley's Secret* exploits this device, as do more canonical texts such as Emily Brontë's *Wuthering Heights* (1848) and Elizabeth Gaskell's *Sylvia's Lovers* (1860). Collins's late novella *The Guilty River*

(1886) centres upon the return from Germany of the young heir to an English estate Gerald Roylake, who looks 'more like a foreigner than an Englishman', a 'stranger among [his] own people'.[73] Moreover, the typical sensation plot's delineation of dynamic characters and criminality would seem to align the genre with the more 'masculine' escapades of imperial romance in *Plain Tales from the Hills* (1888) by Rudyard Kipling (1865–1936), Allan Quartermain in the narratives of H. Rider Haggard (1856–1925) and Robert Louis Stevenson's *South Sea Tales* (1893) in which colonial outposts are transformed into 'sensational' sites that mirror an emerging awareness of, even sympathy for, the subjectivity of the colonial Other.[74] Anindyo Roy argues that Anglo-Indian romances owe a particular debt to the sensation genre:

■ As the many forms of popular imperialism proliferated in the last two decades of the nineteenth century, these romances found immediate popularity with the reading public looking for new sources to feed its curiosity. The audience's familiarity with the 'sensational novels' of the 1860s had helped generate and sustain an appetite for these romances. As products of a rapidly expanding commodity culture in the 1860s and 1870s, the 'sensation' novels of Mary Elizabeth Braddon and Wilkie Collins had exploited the demand for an immensely marketable sensationalism to produce stories about women who had transgressed the norms of Victorian Britain's social and moral order. [...] The Anglo-Indian romances continued on the track that had already been laid out by the sensation novels of the 1860s. By establishing British India as the new site for dramatising the fantasies of a colonial culture, they articulated questions of power, racial identity, and sexuality that had been taboo for mainstream metropolitan Victorian culture.[75] □

Roy's thesis illuminates Joseph Conrad's imaginative investigation into 'the fantasies of a colonial culture.' The sensation genre might seem an unlikely model of inspiration for Conrad, given that he spoke witheringly in 1898 of popular contemporary women writers, such as Marie Corelli, the best-selling sensationalist, 'whose thought is commonplace, the style without any distinction.'[76] While Conrad may have been scornful of the genre, his own writing benefited from this tradition and commented on it, according to Ellen Burton Harrington and Susan Jones, who remind us that the female novel of sensation has never been associated with Conrad's oeuvre. Ford Madox Ford (1873–1939) recollected that Conrad read voraciously outside as well as inside the canon of his day. Ford's account offers a fruitful alternative to the orthodox view promoted by Conrad's biographers of an uncompromising and austere man of letters. Ford clearly feels the exposure to sensation fiction was an advantage for Conrad during his years at sea.

■ It was Conrad's good luck to be spared the usual literature that attends the upbringing of the British writer. He read such dog-eared books as are found in the professional quarters of ships' crews. He read Mrs. Henry Wood, Miss Braddon – above all Miss Braddon! [...] She wrote very good, very sound English; machined her plots inoffensively and well; was absolutely workman-like, her best novels being the later and less-known ones.[77] □

This passage is remarkable for its suggestion that Conrad may have learned as much about writing from popular female authors of the period as he did from the great names usually linked with his work. In addition, the major influence of Charles Dickens on Conrad is well documented; Frederick Karl calls *The Secret Agent* (1910) 'in its view of London at least, Conrad's *Bleak House*'.[78] As Karl and others have noted, *Bleak House* itself bears a significant connection to the sensa-tion genre, anticipating and inspiring fiction of the 1860s in the use of the male detective Bucket investigating dangerous females, one a murderess, the other an out-of-wedlock mother. Ellen Harrington's essay 'The Anarchist's Wife' (2004) demonstrates to what extent the sensation genre furnished a crucial model in *The Secret Agent*, whose plot dynamics invite detailed comparison with *The Woman in White* and *Lady Audley's Secret*. The common thread running through all these narratives is the frustrated struggles of women with the domestic pact and the potential for bitter division in the home. In his reading of *The Woman in White*, D. A. Miller observes the generally prevalent narrative technique of 'enclosing and secluding the woman in male "bodies", that is, using institutions like marriage or the asylum as a form of mastery over women'.[79] The murderous fury inspired by feminine dissatisfaction with the institution of marriage, so disquieting in sensation novels of the 1860s, has become, according to Harrington's analysis, the province of a supposedly emancipated young woman, Conrad's Winne Verloc, who is stymied by a desperate faith in bourgeois culture's consoling myths of law and order, myths *The Secret Agent* cannot endorse.

■ *The Secret Agent* should be read in terms of [...] the Victorian sensa-tion novel. [...] Conrad's characterization of Winnie's downfall through a series of roles that range from obedient to brazen to bereft, draws on the range of stereotyped, sensational roles for women, ultimately offering little hope for a 'free woman' within Victorian social constraints [...] Ending the novel with the disintegration of the domestic sphere, Conrad makes an ironic commentary on gender roles and women's liberation, effectively referencing and re-envisioning the popular sen-sation novel and its themes of feminine frustration, the desire for lib-eration, and the dangers of degeneracy.[80] □

Harrington declares that Winnie's secret is not, like Lady Audley's, a terrified apprehension of hereditary madness, but the mercenary bargain of her marriage. Edward Garnett (1868–1937), a contemporary critic and friend of Conrad, refers to the sensation novel *The Woman in White* in his unsigned 1907 review of *The Secret Agent* in the *Nation*, lavishly praising Conrad and emphasizing the political rather than the sensational plot:

> ■ By *The Secret Agent* [Mr. Conrad] has added to the score of our indebtedness [to him], and he has brought clearly into our ken the subterranean world of that foreign London which, since the death of Count Fosco, has served in fiction only the crude purpose of our sensational writers.[81] □

Fosco, the corpulent villain of *The Woman in White*, still provides a vivid frame of reference nearly half a century after the novel's initial publication. Though Garnett's review elevates Conrad above the level of these sensation novelists, he notes the correspondence with that 'subterranean world' of corruption and chicanery also evident in Collins's oeuvre, a portrayal that makes even familiar London seem shrouded, ominous and 'foreign'. This notion highlights, in Harrington's opinion, the shared concerns of *The Secret Agent* and sensation fiction: both dissect the grievous failings of traditional female roles while also being profoundly troubled by the political and social repercussions of greater rights and autonomy for women.

Susan Jones's essay 'Stepping out of the narrow frame' (1998) also charts the mature complexity of Joseph Conrad's encounter with the female sensation novel, focusing on the posthumously published *Suspense: A Napoleonic Novel* (1925). Jones proposes that Conrad's later, neglected texts are aim to reach a female readership of popular fiction. His final novels are frequently drawn to the genre's patterns of representation, particularly exploiting their use of visual and dramatic tropes, their suggestions of sexual ambivalence and exploration of covert identities:

> ■ *Suspense* integrates various elements of sensation fiction in its attention to suppressed female identity: the Gothic device of enclosure in the domestic scene; the suggestion of sexual deviance in the incest plot; the use of an animated painting of the heroine to generate terror; and the affirmation of male bonding in the final remaining chapter. The case of *Suspense* shows that right up to the end of his career Conrad was, contrary to our traditional assumptions, exploring the representation of female identity and responding to the popular genres which have both questioned and propagated conventional roles for women.[82] □

Jones reveals that Conrad reproduces the iconographic traditions and melodramatic style of the sensation novel while treating its less than radical strategies with sarcastic irony. *Chance* (1913) alludes to the genre in the portrait of the 'criminal' governess (Lady Audley, for example, starts out as a governess), and in the unearthing of the de Barral secret. In *The Arrow of Gold* (1919), Therese irrationally fears that the house in the Avenue of the Consuls would provide a suitable location for murder. Her appearance resembles that of the spectre-nun from Charlotte Brontë's *Villette* (1853), a Gothic figure with lighted candle, transfixed in silent poses on landings and in doorways, fleetingly appearing and disappearing from sight into the darkened recesses of the house. The histrionic rendering of Mrs Travers's extra-marital relationship in *The Rescue* (1920) supplies a snide comment on the tired plotting of sensationalism, and in *The Rover* (1923), Arlette's Gothic figure epitomizes a further continuity in Conrad's largely barbed references to the genre. For Jones all of these examples evidence Conrad's recalibration of sensation towards the end of his literary career. Indeed, his depiction of the deaths of Winnie Verloc in *The Secret Agent* and of Lena in *Victory* (1915) evinces that women's roles have been further circumscribed rather than unshackled by the conventions of a genre which relegates the venturesome heroine to the hackneyed and hidebound status of femme fatale.

In contrast to Jones, who suggests that Conrad evokes the popular only to exorcize it, Kelly A. Marsh's 1995 essay 'The Neo-Sensation Novel: A Contemporary Genre in the Victorian Tradition' claims that much may be gained by the recreation of the conceptual as well as formal components of an ostensibly 'low' cultural mode.[83] If what Marsh designates as the 'neo-sensation novel' seems at first glance a reactionary or regressive phenomenon, this illusion is quickly dispelled by its robust challenge to conventional definitions of morality, ethics and responsibility. Like their Victorian predecessors, the neo-sensation writers are preoccupied with crafting provocative stories of today that compel us to interrogate prevailing ideologies. In contemporary fiction such as *The Radiant Way* (1987) and *A Natural Curiosity* (1989) by Margaret Drabble (born 1939), *Possession: A Romance* (1990) by A. S. Byatt (born 1936), *Waterland* (1983) by Graham Swift (born 1949) and *The Gold Bug Variations* (1991) by Richard Powers (born 1957), Marsh identifies a self-conscious return to Victorian vocabularies of loss, mourning and memory to affirm the abiding value of historical recollection. All these novels variously illustrate how the fabric of family threatens to unravel, and the defect is traceable to secrets, crimes and misdemeanours from the past. However, Marsh's claim that *Waterland* can be treated as a descendant of *Lady Audley's*

Secret because it focuses on aberrant psychology, is problematic given that numerous genres also deal with the origins and results of mental imbalance.

Marsh's most incisive arguments spring from her exploration of Byatt's *Possession* as a text which acclaims, promulgates and gives voice to a continuing desire for cultural memory in an era marked by loss of faith in historical pattern or design. Byatt is fascinated by imaginative archaeology: excavating the secret histories that persist and flourish in written records, journals and letters. Byatt's distinctive use of this convention strongly recalls Collins's narrative strategies in *The Woman in White*, *Armadale* and *The Moonstone*. *Possession* indicates, according to Marsh, the inherence of the Victorian past in contemporary culture, not as unbroken continuity, but as a series of repetitions and ghostly echoes that underline the estranging otherness of this legacy, while also, paradoxically, generating a frisson of recognition.[84] Recently published novels that employ Victorian visual technologies such as *Afterimage* (2001) by Helen Humphreys (born 1961) and *Sixty Lights* (2004) by Gail Jones (born 1955), signify that the Victorian past exists not only in its textual traces, but also as a rich repertoire of shared cultural images.

The publication of Marsh's essay on the neo-sensation school coincides with one of the most surprising developments in recent fiction: the emergence of the Victorian novel in a post-modern frame, whose critical and commercial success implicates it in what is often misconstrued as contemporary nostalgia for a distant epoch.[85] In some instances Victorian plots are appraised from new standpoints or are given sequels or prequels which emulate or debunk nineteenth-century fictional forms or moral and political assumptions. This extraordinary flowering of literary activity reveals, among other things, why sensation is such a tenaciously resilient genre: it supplies an imaginative 'lens' through which to inspect our own culture's prurient curiosities, embracing celebrity, consumerism, the melodramatic and the macabre. That the appetite for sensation fiction seems undiminished in the twenty-first century prompts us to enquire about the future for research into these narratives. To such a question my conclusion now turns.

Conclusion

In an age recognizing the powers of public opinion and the double-edged resources of journalism, our age as well as that of the Victorians, culture plays out a rhythm of predictability and astonishment, familiarity and monstrosity. [...] [W]hen the conventional transforms into the sensational, we remain guided by the belief that these stormy episodes are not mere exceptions or wild anomalies. Hectic and overwrought they may be, but they remain part of the social field, sometimes as revealing symptoms, sometimes as keen diagnoses, but always tied to the daily life they challenge.

> (Karen Chase and Michael Levenson, *The Spectacle of Intimacy: A Public Life for the Victorian Family*, Princeton: Princeton University Press, 2000, p. 16)

Sensation fiction, and the authors associated with it, supplies a bracing and transitional constellation of texts that disclose core Victorian obsessions – metropolitan modernity, the grievous constraints of bourgeois domesticity, imperialism and its discontents, the dangers for women of romantic fantasy, and the emergence of novel criticism as a form. Recent approaches to the literary canon exhort us to cultivate an adventurous independence of mind in the mapping of a Victorian genre which now constitutes formidable textual terrain. By seeking out putatively 'marginal' cultural documents, we can dismantle a hierarchical perception of nineteenth-century literature. Consequently, this grants increased access to those sensation texts which exemplify Victorian popular literary tastes and offer spiky commentary on the culture they represent and helped fashion.

In an astute discussion of fiction and the marketplace, Valerie Sanders notes how writers that 'we now regard as "canonical" struggled for recognition, whilst those since relegated to minor status seem to have exploited the marketplace on a scale that relatively few novelists achieve even today.'[1] One of the purposes of this Guide has been to situate these writers 'relegated to minor status' – male and female – in the history of the sensation novel, so that like other 'Victorian things' according to Asa Briggs (born 1921), we get answers which are 'different', based on texts which openly parade radical discontinuities and strategic contradictions, 'parody as well as derivation, escape as well as exploration, individual fantasy as well as imitation.'[2] This perception is certainly valid for the women sensation novelists who amplified the imaginative resources of the genre in their 1870s and 1880s fiction. Pamela Gilbert has demonstrated how these novels stubbornly resist any critical tendency to reduce them 'to mere exempla of generic formulae created to describe and contain them, formulae which were never identical with any of these texts', and which were 'invoked, subtly mocked, and opportunistically disregarded by turns by authors and readers seeking to define themselves against or within the market (or both).'³ This belated but nevertheless welcome recognition means that those investigating the sensation genre can transcend the potentially crude examination of what Lyn Pykett terms 'the conservative/radical dilemma' to think about sensation writers on their own merits, rather than as lax and haphazard disciples of Dickens.⁴

However, because the overwhelming majority of literary historians still target *The Woman in White*, *East Lynne* and *Lady Audley's Secret*, a further refinement in thinking is required. As a result of the continuing popularity of the two novels he wrote relatively early in his career, *The Woman in White* and *The Moonstone*, many readers still recognize in Collins 'only a figure instrumental in the development and growth of English detective, mystery, and sensation fiction.'⁵ Indeed, Philip O'Neill's book *Wilkie Collins: Women, Property and Propriety* (1988), begins by regretting that Collins's 'large and varied output' in the 1870s and 1880s 'has been allowed to slip into oblivion.'⁶ Collins was himself touchy about the role his most acclaimed novels would play in future analyses of his literary career. As early as 1869, he lamented to a publisher: '[D]on't let us encourage the public [...] in its one everlasting cry to me: "Ah, he may write what he pleases! He will never do anything again like *The Woman in White*!" '⁷ Collins wrote more novels in the last 20 years of his life than he had written in the first 45, most of them popular successes at the time. One of his final novels, *The Evil Genius* (1886), earned him greater financial rewards than any of his other works. Anticipating the direction popular and scholarly evaluation of his oeuvre would take, he gave instructions that his gravestone in Kensal Green cemetery should be inscribed thus, 'In Memory of Wilkie Collins, Author of *The Woman in White* and Other Works of Fiction.' Commentators have only recently registered the social range and intellectual breadth of these 'other works of fiction.'

A search of contemporary articles indicates that Victorian readers and reviewers, working in a complex literary landscape, could not restrict sensation fiction to a few bestsellers of the 1860s. Re-evaluation of literary sensationalism and late-Victorian Gothic too often results in the construction of a discouraging alternative canon, with rigidly defined ghettoes for *Lady Audley's Secret*, *Moonstone*, *East Lynne* and

Dracula studies. Stoker's novel, partially inspired by Le Fanu's *Carmilla*,[8] elaborates the sensational enterprise of bringing horror home to an English milieu, uncovering anxieties about the institution of the family itself and portraying the nation as an 'open' body menaced by tainted external threats which efface clear distinctions between race, caste and gender. The sheer bulk of research on Stoker's vampire narrative and how it is 'haunted' by 'the traces of influential male writers'[9] such as Le Fanu, may be in danger of overshadowing Le Fanu's other stories.

It is salutary to be reminded then, by Andrew Maunder and Graham Law among others, of M. E. Braddon's bold experimentation with an array of genres, modes and publishing initiatives in a lengthy and prolific literary career that stretched from the eve of the American Civil War to the outbreak of World War I in Europe.[10] This versatility was even acknowledged by one of Braddon's most implacable opponents, Margaret Oliphant: 'Miss Braddon [...] is perhaps the most complete story-teller [among the sensationalists] [...] and has not confined herself to that or any other type of character, but has ranged widely over all English scenes and subjects'.[11] Unfortunately, some twenty-first-century commentators are just as committed to fixing Braddon's fiction within the discourse of sensationalism as were those sententious mid-Victorian pundits whose critical terminology they have so sedulously probed. A strict scholarly focus on the peculiarities of the genre tends to segregate Braddon's narratives from the so-called mainstream realist tradition, and thus perpetuates the undervaluing of her craft initiated by 1860s reviewers such as W. Fraser Rae, who saw her as 'a slave [...] to the style which she created. "Sensation" is her Frankenstein'.[12]

These issues have been raised by historians of the periodical press such as Peter Sinnema in *Dynamics of the Pictured Page* (1998) and Jennifer Phegley in *Educating the Proper Woman Reader* (2004).[13] Phegley's detailed alertness to Victorian family literary magazines poses questions about reading communities of various religious and political persuasions and classes rarely canvassed in accounts of sensation fiction. Did the novels produced for sizeable provincial audiences in Sheffield, Newcastle and Glasgow significantly differ from their metropolitan counterparts in terms of form and content?[14] Moreover, the overwhelming abundance of inexpensive magazines in the 1860s meant that sensation novels could be presented as exhilarating serials, often with lavish illustrations. 'Intricacy' and 'artfulness', terms frequently deployed in surveys of the genre to signify narrative trajectory or verbal texture, have been extended to include the methods perfected by canny publishers to advertise these titles in an industry dominated by elaborate promotional strategies.[15]

This research, which ponders the sensation novel's evolution beyond the salubrious and cosy confines of the middle-class reading room – the locus that exercised mainstream Victorian reviewers – into other spaces typifies a vibrant new direction for studies of the genre. Sensation fiction, according to Andrew Maunder, often transmits a convoluted, even 'contradictory' message; and 'as our knowledge of how it was written, published, received and consumed increases, so our sense of what it encompasses will continue to fracture.'[16] Yet it is also true that, as Karen Chase and Michael Levenson imply in the extract which heads this conclusion, the 'stormy episodes' at the heart of the genre are an inextricable part of our 'social field'. Indeed, the frequency with which these novels appear on university syllabi and book club reading lists evinces that we are not so post-Victorian as we sometimes like to pretend.

Notes

INTRODUCTION

1. [Anon.], 'Novels Past and Present', *Saturday Review* (14 April 1866), pp. 438–39.
2. Around 1860 a spate of miscellany periodicals, including *All the Year Round*, *The Cornhill*, and *Temple Bar*, made their debuts on the print scene of London. Over a thousand British periodicals were ushered into print in the course of the nineteenth century; 115 appeared in 1859 and 170 additional magazines during the 1860s. These magazines all carried serial fiction, frequently with two novels running simultaneously in the same issue. See Linda Hughes and Michael Lund, *The Victorian Serial* (Charlottesville: University of Virginia Press, 1991), pp. 5–7.
3. See Richard Fantina and Kimberly Harrison, 'Introduction' to *Victorian Sensations: Essays on a Scandalous Genre*, eds Harrison and Fantina (Ohio: Ohio State University Press, 2006), p. ix.
4. Quoted in Winifred Hughes, *The Maniac in the Cellar: Sensation Novels of the 1860s* (Princeton, NJ: Princeton University Press, 1980), p. 5.
5. Quoted in Hughes (1980), p. 5.
6. M. E. Braddon, *The Doctor's Wife* (London: John and Robert Maxwell, n.d.), p. 40.
7. See W. J. B. Owen and Jane Worthington Smyser ed., *The Prose Works of William Wordsworth* (Oxford: Oxford University Press, 1974), I, pp. 128–30.
8. Quoted in Norman Page, *Wilkie Collins: The Critical Heritage* (London: Routledge & Kegan Paul, 1974), p. 169.
9. David Skilton, 'Introduction', *Lady Audley's Secret* (Oxford: Oxford University Press, 1987), p. vii.
10. Ann Cvetkovich, *Mixed Feelings: Feminism, Mass Culture and Victorian Sensationalism* (New Brunswick: Rutgers University Press, 1992), p. 14.
11. Lyn Pykett, 'Collins and the Sensation Novel', in Jenny Bourne Taylor ed., *The Cambridge Companion to Wilkie Collins* (Cambridge: Cambridge University Press, 2006), p. 50.
12. See Catherine Peters, *The King of Inventors: a Life of Wilkie Collins* (Princeton, NJ: Princeton University Press, 1991), pp. 227–45 on the impressive sales figures for the novel and Collins's earnings from it.
13. See Nicholas Rance, *Wilkie Collins and Other Sensation Novelists: Walking the Moral Hospital* (London: Macmillan/Rutherford, NJ: Fairleigh Dickinson University Press, 1990), p. 1.
14. In that famous portrait, Wilkie Collins is depicted as a small man with tiny hands and feet wearing a dark coat and striped trousers, hunched anxiously on the edge of his seat, his expression obscured by his gigantic whiskers and clouded spectacles. 'Just as his physical features are distorted in this illustration, so too has his literary legacy been misrepresented for over one hundred years.' See Maria K. Bachman and Don Richard Cox, 'The Real Wilkie Collins,' in Bachman and Cox eds, *Reality's Dark Light: The Sensational Wilkie Collins* (Knoxville: University of Tennessee Press, 2003), p. xii.
15. As quoted by Robert Lee Wolff, *Sensational Victorian: The Life and Fiction of Mary Elizabeth Braddon* (New York: Garland, 1979), p. 324.
16. Hughes (1980), p. 23.
17. Margaret Oliphant, 'Novels', *Blackwood's* 102 (1867), p. 280. See also Wayne Burns, *Charles Reade: a Study in Victorian Authorship* (New York: Bookman, 1961).
18. Philip O'Neill, *Wilkie Collins: Women, Property and Propriety* (London: Macmillan, 1988), p. 1.

19. T. S. Eliot, 1928 'Introduction', to *The Moonstone*, by Wilkie Collins (London: Oxford University Press, 1966), p. xi.

20. Steve Farmer, 'Introduction' to Wilkie Collins, *Heart and Science*, ed., Farmer (Ontario, Canada: Broadview Press, 1996), p. 7.

21. The BBC productions of *The Woman in White* (1997) and *The Moonstone* (1996) also demonstrate the continued popularity of Collins's best-known works.

22. Harrison and Fantina (2006), p. ix.

23. H. F. Chorley, 'New Novels', *Athenaeum* 29 (1866), p. 732.

24. Charles Reade, 'Preface' to *Hard Cash* (Boston and New York: Brainard, 1910), I, p. 3.

25. George Augustus Sala, 'On the "Sensational" in Literature and Art', *Belgravia* 4 (1868), p. 455.

26. [Margaret Oliphant], 'Sensation Novels', *Blackwood's* 151 (May 1862), pp. 577, 580.

27. [Anon.], 'New Novels', *Athenaeum* (1 October 1864), p. 428.

28. Christine Ferguson, 'Sensational Dependence: Prosthesis and Affect in Dickens and Braddon', *LIT: Literature, Interpretation, Theory* 19: 1 (2008), p. 5.

29. Jonathan Loesberg, 'The Ideology of Narrative Form in Sensation Fiction', *Representations* 13 (Winter 1986), p. 115.

30. Thomas Boyle, *Black Swine in the Sewers of Hampstead: Beneath the Surface of Victorian Sensationalism* (New York: Viking, 1989), p. 146.

31. Shirley Tyler, 'Power and Patriarchal Hegemony in the Fiction of Mary Elizabeth Braddon', *Nineteenth-Century Feminisms*, 3 (Fall/Winter 2000), p. 58.

32. [W. Fraser Rae], 'Sensation Novelists: Miss Braddon', *North British Review* 43 (1865), p. 204.

33. [Anon.], 'Lady Audley's Secret', *The Times* (18 November 1862), p. 4.

34. Pamela Gilbert, *Disease, Desire and the Body in Victorian Women's Popular Novels* (Cambridge: Cambridge University Press, 1997), p. 74.

35. Alison Light, *Forever England* (London: Routledge, 1991), p. 10.

36. Richard D. Altick, *The Presence of the Present: Topics of the Day in the Victorian Novel* (Columbus, Ohio: Ohio State University Press, 1991).

37. David Punter, *The Literature of Terror: a History of Gothic Fiction from 1765 to the Present Day* (New York: Longman, 1980), p. 236; and Neil Cornwell, *The Literary Fantastic: From Gothic to Postmodernism* (Hempstead: Simon and Shuster, 1990), p. 94.

38. Andrew Maunder, 'Introduction' to *Varieties of Women's Sensation Fiction, 1855–1890*, 6 vols (London: Pickering & Chatto, 2004), I, p. 5.

39. See Kelly A. Marsh, 'The Neo-Sensation Novel: A Contemporary Genre in the Victorian Tradition', *Philological Quarterly* 74: 1 (Winter 1995), pp. 99–124.

ONE   THE RISE, FALL AND REVIVAL OF SENSATION FICTION

1. Kathleen Tillotson suggests the term 'sensation novel' was first used in September 1861 in the *Sixpenny Magazine*. See 'The Lighter Reading of the Eighteen Sixties', preface to *The Woman in White*, by Wilkie Collins (Boston: Houghton Mifflin, 1969), p. xxi. The *Saturday Review* used the label in its review of Caroline Clive's *Paul Ferroll* (1855), the story of an outwardly respectable man who has killed his wife and lives with the secret for many years. See [Anon.], 'Novels', *Saturday Review* (12 January 1856), p. 192. Lyn Pykett has located the term employed by Margaret Oliphant in her 1855 review of Collins's early novels; while Thomas Boyle indicates how it featured in mid-century responses to the theatre and in newspaper reports, mostly those describing the reactions of courtroom audiences to lurid case details. Charlotte Mitchell explains the 'sensation novel was not yet the term of abuse it was to become in the next five years, but this attack foreshadows the accusations of moral irresponsibility soon to be aimed at Wilkie Collins, Mary Braddon and Ellen Wood.' See 'Introduction' *Paul Ferroll* (Oxford: Oxford University Press, 1997), p. xi. For a short history of the term and the genre, see

Richard D. Altick, 'The Novel Experience', in *Deadly Encounters: Two Victorian Sensations* (Philadelphia: University of Pennsylvania Press, 1986), pp. 145–58.

2. The connections between fears about the 'drug-like' qualities of sensation fiction and dominant definitions of female sexuality are discussed by Kate Flint, 'The Woman Reader and the "Opiate" of Fiction 1855–1870', in Jeremy Hawthorn ed., *The Nineteenth-Century British Novel* (London: Edward Arnold, 1986).

3. George Henry Lewes, 'Farewell Causerie', *Fortnightly Review* 6 (1 December 1866), p. 894.

4. [H. L. Mansel], 'Sensation Novels', *Quarterly Review* 113 (April 1863), p. 486.

5. Mansel (1863), p. 487.

6. Alison Winter, *Mesmerized: Powers of Mind in Victorian Britain* (Chicago: University of Chicago Press, 1998), p. 224. Winter probes this effect in the context of mesmerism as she assesses how diverse reports on reading Collins's *The Woman in White* engendered a kind of magnetism in its readers.

7. [Margaret Oliphant], 'Novels', *Blackwoods Edinburgh Magazine*, 102 (September 1867), p. 259.

8. Quoted in Tillotson (1969), p. xiii.

9. Wilkie Collins, *The Woman in White*, eds Maria K. Bachman and Don Richard Cox (Ontario, Canada: Broadview Press 2006), p. 14.

10. D. A. Miller, *The Novel and the Police* (Berkeley: University of California Press, 1988), p. 146.

11. [Anon.], 'Our Female Sensation Novelists', *Christian Remembrancer* 46 (July 1864), pp. 209–36.

12. [Geraldine Jewsbury], 'New Novels', *Athenaeum* (29 July 1865), p. 147.

13. [Anon.], *Westminster Review* 86 (October 1866), pp. 269–71. Quoted in Norman Page ed., *Wilkie Collins: The Critical Heritage* (London: Routledge & Kegan Paul, 1974), p. 158.

14. John Sutherland, 'Wilkie Collins and the Origins of the Sensation Novel', *Dickens Studies Annual* 20 (1991), pp. 243–53.

15. Mary Elizabeth Braddon, *The Doctor's Wife* (London: John and Robert Maxwell, 1864), I, pp. 10–11.

16. [Anon.], 'Not a New Sensation', *All the Year Round* (22 July 1863), p. 517. The argument that 'sensationalism' is principally symptomatic of critics' anxieties is extended by Charles Dickens (unsigned, 1864), [Anon.], 'The Sensational Williams', *All the Year Round* (13 February 1864), pp. 14–15: 'Life itself is similarly sensational in many of its aspects, and nature is similarly sensational in many of her forms, and art is always sensational when it is tragic'. The piece weighs Shakespeare's likely reception as a sensation dramatist.

17. See for instance, [Margaret Oliphant], 'Modern Novelists – Great and Small', *Blackwood's* 77 (1855), pp. 554–68; Margaret Oliphant, 'Sensation Novels', *Blackwood's Edinburgh Magazine* 91 (1862), pp. 564–80; 'Novels', 94 (1863), pp. 168–83; 'Novels', 102 (1867), pp. 257–80.

18. [Margaret Oliphant], 'Sensational Novels', *Blackwood's Edinburgh Magazine*, 91 (May 1862), pp. 564–80.

19. H. A. Page, 'The Morality of Literary Art', *Contemporary Review* 5 (June 1867), pp. 169–87. See also Thomas Boyle, *Black Swine in the Sewers of Hampstead: Beneath the Surface of Victorian Sensationalism* (New York: Viking, 1989), p. 125.

20. George Eliot to John Blackwood, 11 September 1860 in G. Haight ed., *The George Eliot Letters* (New Haven: Yale University Press, 1954), IV, pp. 309–10.

21. Richard Nemesvari and Lisa Surridge, 'Introduction' to M. E. Braddon, *Aurora Floyd* (Ontario, Canada: Broadview Press, 1998), p. 13.

22. Lillian Nayder, 'Introduction' to Felicia Skene, *Hidden Depths* (London: Pickering and Chatto, 2004), p. xi.

23. Patrick Brantlinger, 'What is "Sensational" about the Sensation Novel?', *Nineteenth Century Fiction* 37: 1 (June 1982), p. 27.

24. George Henry Lewes, 'Realism in Art: Recent German Fiction' (1858), reprinted in Alice R. Kaminsky ed., *Literary Criticism of George Henry Lewes* (Lincoln, Nebraska: University of Nebraska Press, 1964), p. 87.

25. [Anon.], 'Popular Novels of the Year', *Fraser's Magazine* 68 (August 1863), p. 266.

26. [W. Fraser Rae], 'Sensation Novelists: Miss Braddon', *North British Review* 43 (September 1865), p. 100; [Anon.], (August 1863), p. 259.

27. [Anon.], 'Popular Novels of the Year', *Fraser's Magazine* 68 (August 1863), p. 261.

28. Rae (1865), pp. 104–5.

29. See George Levine, 'Realism Reconsidered', in John Halperin ed., *The Theory of the Novel* (Oxford: Oxford University Press, 1974), p. 252.

30. Hughes, (1980), p. 16.

31. Alfred Austin, 'Our Novels: The Sensational School', *Temple Bar* 29 (June 1870), pp. 410–24.

32. 'The Sensational Williams' (1864), p. 14.

33. Wilkie Collins, *Basil*, ed. Dorothy Goldman (Oxford: World's Classics, 2005), p. iv.

34. 'The Sensational Williams' (1864) pp. 14–15.

35. Quoted in Richard D. Altick, *Evil Encounters: Two Victorian Sensations* (London: John Murray, 1987), p. 4.

36. George Augustus Sala, 'On the "Sensational" in Literature and Art', *Belgravia* 4 (1868), p. 453. During this era, as Philip Edwards has noted, 'almost every novel reviewed was either sensational, or remarkable for not being so'. See P. D. Edwards, *Some Mid-Victorian Thrillers: The Sensation Novel, Its Friends and Foes* (St. Lucia: University of Queensland Press, 1971), p. 4.

37. Oliphant (1862), pp. 564–65.

38. Winifred Hughes contends that 'the popular taste in fiction closely paralleled and interacted with the theatrical convention of the period. Like the penny press, the nineteenth-century theatre belonged to the masses [...] who were its patrons.' See Hughes (1980), p. 10.

39. Altick (1987), pp. 139–40. The first self-styled 'sensation drama' was Dion Boucicault's *The Colleen Bawn* (New York, March 1860; London, September 1860), which broke records for a continuous run in London.

40. See Catherine Peters, *The King of Inventors: a Life of Wilkie Collins* (Princeton, NJ: Princeton University Press, 1991), pp. 227–45.

41. Michael Booth, *Victorian Spectacular Theatre 1850–1910* (London: Routledge, 1981); Society for Theatre Research, *British Theatrical Patents, 1801–1900* (London: Society for Theatre Research, 1996); Thomas Richards, *The Commodity Culture of Victorian England: Advertising and Spectacle, 1851–1914* (Stanford, CA: Stanford University Press, 1990), p. 55.

42. Lyn Pykett, *The Sensation Novel: from 'The Woman in White' to 'The Moonstone'* (Plymouth: Northcote Press, 1994), pp. 1–2.

43. Hughes (1980), p. 5.

44. Hughes (1980), pp. 5–6.

45. John Sutherland, 'Introduction' to *The Woman in White* (Oxford: World's Classics, 1996), p. vii.

46. H. Debenham, 'The Victorian Sensation Novel', in William Baker and Kenneth Womack eds, *A Companion to the Victorian Novel* (Westport: Greenwood Press, 2002), pp. 209–22.

47. For a detailed discussion of how this writing links up with the 'penny blood' format see S. Powell, 'Black Markets and Cadaverous Pies: The Corpse, Urban Trade and Industrial Consumption in the Penny Blood' in Andrew Maunder and Grace Moore eds, *Victorian Crime, Madness and Sensation* (Aldershot, UK: Ashgate, 2004), pp. 45–58.

48. Nicholas Rance's *Wilkie Collins and Other Sensation Novelists: Walking the Moral Hospital* (London: Macmillan, 1990), is one of the few books to acknowledge that other writers

and novels used the genre but even this follows the usual path of treating women writers as acolytes of a male mentor.

49. Quoted in Altick (1987), p. 146.

50. Mirella Billi, 'Dickens as Sensation Novelist', in Rossana Bonadei, Clotilde de Stasio, Carlo Pagetti and Allesandro Vescovi eds, *Dickens: The Craft of Fiction and the Challenges of Reading* (Edizioni: Unicopli, 2000), pp. 178–79.

51. Diana Archibald has also scrutinised *Oliver Twist* as a harbinger of the sensation novel as well as a generic hybrid that resists classification as a realist, domestic, sensational, or Newgate novel. See Diana C. Archibald, ' "Of All the Horrors [...] the Foulest and Most Cruel": Sensation and Dickens's *Oliver Twist*', in Kimberly Harrison and Richard Fantina eds, *Victorian Sensations: Essays on a Scandalous Genre* (Ohio: Ohio University Press, 2006), pp. 53–63.

52. Quoted in Walter Kendrick, 'The Sensationalism of *The Woman in White*', *Nineteenth Century Fiction* 32 (1977), pp. 30–31.

53. Quoted in Kendrick (1977), p. 31.

54. A. C. Swinburne, 'Wilkie Collins', *Fortnightly Review* (1 November 1889) in Page (1974), pp. 259, 262. *The Spectator*, reviewing Collins's *Jezebel's Daughter* reached a similar conclusion:

■ When a novelist has written so long or so much that he begins to lose the pleasure of creation, and to suspect his ideas of a lack of freshness, he will generally (if he goes on writing at all) endeavour to justify himself in doing so by claiming a motive and a value for his work loftier and more abstract than satisfied him before. His quips and cranks have grown stale, and no longer produce their former effect; but since he cannot afford to be neglected, he must needs strive to arrest attention by blustering about his 'motives'. *Spectator* (15 May 1880) in Page (1974), p. 208 □

55. Page (1974), p. 23.

56. Brantlinger (1982) p. 1.

57. Quoted in Andrew Maunder, 'Mapping the Victorian Sensation Novel: Recent and Future Trends', *Literature Compass On-line* 2 (2005) (Oxford: Blackwell), p. 1.

58. See Thomas Arnold, 'Recent Novel Writing', *Macmillan's Magazine*, 13 (January 1866), pp. 202–9.

59. Henry James, 'Alphonse Daudet' [1840–97], in *Partial Portraits* (1881), quoted in Michael Anesko, *Friction with the Market: Henry James and the Profession of Authorship* (Oxford: Oxford University Press, 1986), p. 34.

60. Maunder (2005), p. 2.

61. Quoted in Page (1974), pp. 273, 40.

62. Philip O'Neill, *Wilkie Collins: Women, Property and Propriety* (London: Macmillan, 1988), p. 1.

63. Wilkie Collins, 'Wilkie Collins's Marginalia on His Copy of Forster's *Life of Dickens*', *The World* (2 October 1889), pp. 25–34.

64. T. S. Eliot, 'Wilkie Collins and Dickens', *Times Literary Supplement* (4 August 1927); reprinted in T. S. Eliot, *Selected Essays* (London: Faber, 1976), pp. 460–71.

65. Eliot (1927), p. 460.

66. Eliot (1927), pp. 460–61.

67. Eliot (1927), p. 461.

68. Eliot (1927), p. 465.

69. O'Neill (1988), p. 3.

70. Joan De Jean and Nancy K. Miller, *Displacements: Women, Tradition, Literatures in French* (London: Johns Hopkins University Press, 1991), p. 3.

71. Suzanne Clark, *Sentimental Modernism: Women Writers and the Revolution of the Word* (Bloomington: Indiana University Press, 1991), p. 6.

72. David Goldie, *A Critical Difference: T. S. Eliot and John Middleton Murray in English Literary Criticism 1919–28* (Oxford: Clarendon Press, 1998), pp. 29–30.

73. See Linda Peterson, 'Charlotte Riddell's *A Struggle for Fame* [1883]: Myths of Authorship, Facts of the Market', *Women's Writing* 11: 1 (2004), p. 210. Charlotte Riddell (1832–1906) was a prolific Victorian novelist and short story writer.

74. Elaine Showalter, *Sexual Anarchy* (London: Bloomsbury, 1992), p. 142.

75. Gaye Tuchman and Nina E. Fortin, *Edging Women Out: Victorian Novelists, Publishers and Social Change* (New Haven: Yale University Press, 1989), p. 8.

76. Oliver Elton, *A Survey of English Literature, 1830–1880*, 2 vols (London: Edward Arnold, 1920), II, p. 220.

77. Quoted in William Stuart Scott, *Marie Corelli: The Story of a Friendship* (London: Hutchinson, 1955), p. 31.

78. Malcolm Elwin, *Victorian Wallflowers* (London: Jonathan Cape, 1934), p. 13.

79. Elwin (1934), p. 15.

80. Elwin (1934), p. 20.

81. Andrew Maunder, 'Ellen Wood as a Writer: Rediscovering Collins's Rival', *Wilkie Collins Society Journal* 3 (2000), pp. 17–31.

82. Elwin (1934), p. 232.

83. Maunder (2000), p. 20.

84. Maunder (2005), p. 3.

85. Jane Tompkins, *Sensational Designs: The Cultural Work of American Fiction* (Oxford: Oxford University Press, 1985), p. 200.

86. Rita Felski, *The Gender of Modernity* (London: Harvard University Press, 1995), p. 142.

87. See P. D. Edwards, *Some Mid-Victorian Thrillers* (Queensland: University of Queensland Press, 1971).

88. Brantlinger (1982), p. 5.

89. Newgate novels (or Old Bailey novels) were fictions published in England from the late 1820s until the 1840s that were thought to glamorise the lives of the criminals they depicted. Most drew their inspiration from the *Newgate Calendar*, a biography of notorious criminals published at various times during the late eighteenth and early nineteenth centuries.

90. The silver fork novel was a fashionable subgenre in the late 1820s and 1830s. Frequently set in the Regency period (1811–20), it was at once nostalgic in its evocation of former elegance, and censorious in judging the petty snobberies, idleness and triviality associated with aristocratic high society.

91. Brantlinger (1982), pp. 5–6.

92. Brantlinger (1982), pp. 5–6.

93. Hughes (1980), pp. 16, 18.

94. Boyle (1989), p. 3.

95. Richard D. Altick, *Victorian Studies in Scarlet* (New York: W. W. Norton, 1970), p. 79.

96. Elaine Showalter, *A Literature of Their Own: British Women Novelists from Brontë to Lessing* (London: Virago, 1982), pp. 28–29.

97. Ellen Miller Casey, 'Other People's Prudery: Mary Elizabeth Braddon' in Don Richard Cox ed., *Sexuality and Victorian Literature* (Knoxville: University of Tennessee Press, 1984), pp. 72–82.

98. D. A. Miller, 'Cage aux Folles: Sensation and Gender in Wilkie Collins's *The Woman in White*', *Representations* 14 (Spring 1986), pp. 107–36.

99. Ann Cvetkovitch, *Mixed Feelings: Feminism, Mass Culture and Victorian Sensationalism* (New Brunswick: Rutgers University Press, 1992), p. 23.

100. Andrew Maunder, *'Introduction', Varieties of Women's Sensation Fiction, 1855–1890: Volume 2 Domestic Sensationalism* (London: Pickering & Chatto, 2004), p. vii.

101. Andrew Maunder, *'General Introduction', Varieties of Women's Sensation Fiction, 1855–1890: Volume 1 Sensationalism and the Sensation Debate* (London: Pickering & Chatto, 2004), p. xii.

102. Gasson's *Guide* has become a key resource, particularly because of the bibliographical information it provides. Gasson's alphabetically arranged entries describe fictional characters and works as well as publishers, friends and associates of Collins.

103. Lillian Nayder, 'Wilkie Collins Studies: 1983–1999', *Dickens Studies Annual* 28 (1999), p. 258.

104. Harrison and Fantina (2006), p. xi.

105. Mansel (1863), p. 449.

106. Margaret Oliphant, 'Novels' *Blackwoods Edinburgh Magazine* 94 (August 1863), pp. 168–83.

107. ■ She [Ellen Wood] took the keenest interest in all great trials. She followed out the threads and points of an intricate case with the greatest clearness and insight. [...] She often said that had she been a man, she would have made a first-rate lawyer, with a passionate love for her work. □

See Charles W. Wood, 'Mrs Henry Wood. In Memoriam', *The Argosy* 43 (1887), p. 436.

108. See Robert Lee Wolff, 'Devoted Disciple: The Letters of Mary Elizabeth Braddon to Sir Edward Bulwer-Lytton, 1862–1873', *Harvard Library Bulletin* 22 (January 1974), p. 11.

109. See Andrew Mangham, *Violent Women and Sensation Fiction: Crime, Medicine and Victorian Popular Culture* (London: Palgrave, 2007).

TWO   CRIME AND DETECTION

1. Patrick Brantlinger, 'What Is "Sensational" About the "Sensation Novel"?', *Nineteenth Century Fiction* 37 (1982), p. 14.

2. Wilkie Collins, *Armadale*, ed. Catherine Peters (Oxford: World's Classics, 1989), p. 516.

3. [Anon.], 'Preface', *Punch* 44 (1863), p. iii.

4. Wilkie Collins, *The New Magdalen: A Novel* (London: Chatto & Windus, 1908), p. 124.

5. Winifred Hughes, *The Maniac in the Cellar: Sensation Novels of the 1860s* (Princeton, NJ: Princeton University Press, 1980), p. 158.

6. [Alfred Austin], 'Our Novels: The Sensational School', *Temple Bar*, 29 (June 1870), p. 419.

7. Henry James, 'Miss Braddon', in *Notes and Reviews* (Cambridge, M.A.: Dunster House, 1921), p. 110.

8. Martin Kayman, *From Bow Street to Baker Street: Mystery, Detection and Narrative* (London: Macmillan, 1992), p. 183.

9. Collins, *Armadale*, p. 657.

10. [Anon.], 'Novels and Life', *Saturday Review* (13 February 1864), p. 189.

11. John Ruskin would have endorsed this sentiment: his essay 'Fiction, Fair and Foul' attributes the sensation novel's obsession with concealment to the 'hot fermentation and unwholesome secrecy of the population crowded into large cities'. See John Ruskin, 'Fiction, Fair and Foul', in *The Works of John Ruskin*, eds E. T. Cook and Alexander Wedderburn (London: George Allen, 1912), XVI, pp. 156–58.

12. Elaine Showalter, 'Guilt, Authority and the Shadows of *Little Dorrit*', *Nineteenth Century Fiction* 34 (1979), pp. 20–40. In 'Family Secrets and Domestic Subversion: Rebellion in the Novels of the Eighteen-Sixties', Showalter argues that the power of Victorian sensationalism derives

■ from its exposure of secrecy as the fundamental and enabling condition of middle-class life, rather than from its revelation of particular scandals. The essential unknowability of each individual, and society's collaboration in the maintenance of a façade behind which lurked innumerable mysteries, were the themes which preoccupied many mid-century novelists. □

In A. Wohl (ed.), *The Victorian Family: Structure and Stresses* (London: Croom Helm, 1978), p. 104.

13. M. E. Braddon, *Lady Audley's Secret*, ed. Natalie M. Houston (Ontario, Canada: Broadview Press 2003), p. 336.

14. See Brian W. McCuskey, 'The Kitchen Police: Servant Surveillance and Middle-Class Transgression', *Victorian Literature and Culture* 28 (2000), p. 359.

15. J. W. Kaye, 'Domestic Service – Nelly Armstrong', *North British Review* 20 (1853), p. 97.

16. Anthea Trodd, *Domestic Crime in the Victorian Novel* (London: Macmillan, 1989), p. 7–8.

17. Trodd (1989), p. 8.

18. Ann Gaylin, *Eavesdropping in the Novel from Austen to Proust* (Cambridge: Cambridge University Press, 2002), pp. 114–115.

19. [Anon.], *The Lady's Maid* (London: Houston, 1877), p. 32.

20. James Williams, *The Footman's Guide* (London: Dean and Munday, 1847), p. 23.

21. Wilkie Collins, *The Moonstone*, ed. John Sutherland (Oxford: World's Classics, 1999), p. 136.

22. Wilkie Collins, *No Name*, ed. Virginia Blain (Oxford: World's Classics, 1998), p. 21. For feminist critics such as Jessica Cox, the secret that resonates through much of Collins's fiction, the unwholesome fact that narrators try to conceal by an elaborate network of lies, is illegitimacy and the unions that produce it. Collins's interest in illegitimacy had an autobiographical component: in 1869 he fathered the first of three illegitimate children by his lover Martha Rudd. *No Name* represents the apogee of his attack on the Victorian legal and social system that condemned illegitimacy, but it was by no means the first of his works to confront this issue. His previous novel, *The Woman in White*, includes two illegitimate characters (Anne Catherick and Sir Percival Glyde), and his short story, 'The Dead Hand' (1857), anticipates both *The Woman in White* and *No Name* in its treatment of illegitimacy. *Hide and Seek* (1854), and *The Dead Secret* (1857), both published some time before Collins established himself as a successful writer, address the social ramifications of illegitimacy. See Jessica Cox, 'Representations of Illegitimacy in Wilkie Collins's Early Novels', *Philological Quarterly* 83: 2 (Spring 2004), pp. 147–170.

23. John Kucich, *The Power of Lies: Transgression in Victorian Fiction* (Ithaca, NY: Cornell University Press, 1994), p. 31.

24. Welsh's later monograph, *Strong Representations: Narrative and Circumstantial Evidence in England* (Baltimore: Johns Hopkins University Press, 1991), is not about sensation and detective novels as such, but his discussion of *The Moonstone* as an index of the general rehabilitation of the principles of evidence in this period argues for the centrality of the kind of writing associated with the literary detective in the structuring and maintenance of Victorian culture. Welsh connects analysis of literary texts with other cultural materials – legal history and theory, scientific writing – to disclose how truth was being created and sustained for Victorians in a particular narrative form that included but was by no means restricted to sensation novels. See Ronald R. Thomas, 'Victorian Detective Fiction and Legitimate Literature: Recent Directions in the Criticism', *Victorian Literature and Culture* 24 (New York: AMS Press, 1996), pp. 370–71.

25. Kucich (1994), p. 37.

26. Kucich (1994), p. 21.

27. Kucich (1994), p. 15.

28. Kucich (1994), pp. 15–16.

29. Ellen Wood, *East Lynne*, ed. Andrew Maunder (Ontario, Canada: Broadview, 2002), p. 211.

30. Wood (2002), p. 297. See also Brian W. McCuskey, 'The Kitchen Police: Servant Surveillance and Middle-Class Transgression', *Victorian Literature and Culture* 28: 2 (2000), 363–368.

31. See Leonore Davidoff and Catherine Hall, *Family Fortunes: Men and Women of the English Middle-Class, 1780–1850*, 2nd edn. (London: Routledge, 2002); Sundeep Bisla, 'The Manuscript as Writer's Estate: Wilkie Collins's *Basil*, Sensation Fiction, and the Early-Victorian Copyright Act', *Genre: Forms of Discourse and Culture* 31: 3–4 (Fall–Winter 1998), pp. 269–304.

32. Jonathan Loesburg, 'The Ideology of Narrative Form in Sensation Fiction', *Representations* 13 (Winter 1986), pp. 115–138.

33. Stephen Knight, *Form and Ideology in Detective Fiction* (Bloomington: Indiana University Press, 1980).

34. Barbara Leckie, contesting Tony Tanner's assertion that adultery was 'unspeakable' in nineteenth-century society, argues that between 1857 and 1914 adultery was in fact a central preoccupation in English culture. She documents the 'visibility' of this transgressive practice in parliamentary and cultural debates, in newspaper reports of divorce trials, and in novels. Leckie analyses two sensation novels in her discussion of fictional representations of adultery: Caroline Norton's *Lost and Saved* (1863) and M. E. Braddon's *The Doctor's Wife* (1864). See Barbara Leckie *Culture and Adultery: The Novel, the Newspaper, and the Law, 1857–1914* (Philadelphia: University of Pennsylvania Press, 1999); also Randall Craig, *Promising Language: Betrothal in Victorian Law and Fiction* (Albany: State University of New York Press, 2000).

35. [H. L. Mansel], 'Sensation Novels', *Quarterly Review*, 113 (April 1863), p. 500.

36. [Anon.], 'Novels Past and Present', *Saturday Review* (14 April 1866), pp. 438–439.

37. Randa Helfield, 'Poisonous Plots: Women Sensation Novelists and Murderesses of the Victorian Period', *Victorian Review* 21: 2 (Winter 1995), pp. 161–188.

38. There are accounts of the Road Murder in Andrew Mangham, *Violent Women and Sensation Fiction: Crime, Medicine and Victorian Popular Culture* (London: Palgrave, 2007), pp. 49–63; Douglas Browne, *The Rise of Scotland Yard* (London: Harrap, 1956); John Rhode, *The Case of Constance Kent* (London: Bles., 1928); Yseult Bridges, *The Saint with Red Hands?* (London: Jarrolds, 1954); Mary Hartman, *Victorian Murderesses* (New York: Schocken, 1977). The latter two suggest that Constance Kent confessed to protect the real murderer, her father. Dickens's private theory was that Mr Kent and Elizabeth Gough had killed the child when he surprised them making love. He outlined this theory in a letter to Wilkie Collins of 24 October 1860, quoted in Richard Altick, *Victorian Studies in Scarlet* (London: Dent, 1970), p. 131.

39. Margaret Oliphant, 'Novels', *Blackwood's Magazine* 102 (September 1867), p. 257.

40. Ellen Wood, *Mrs. Halliburton's Troubles*, 3 vols (London: Macmillan, 1907), II, p. 314.

41. Trodd (1989), pp. 12–13.

42. 'Jack Shepherd' Romances refer to the sensational narratives published in newspapers, pamphlets and broadsheets, which documented the exploits of the notorious English thief of early 18th-century London, Jack Shepherd/Sheppard (1702–24). Sheppard was apprehended and imprisoned five times in 1724 but escaped four times, making him an immensely popular figure with the working classes. Sheppard's tale was revived in the nineteenth century, most notably by William Harrison Ainsworth in his third novel, *Jack Sheppard*, which was originally published in *Bentley's Miscellany* from January 1839 with illustrations by George Cruikshank, overlapping with the final episodes of Charles Dickens's *Oliver Twist*. See Matthew Buckley, 'Sensations of Celebrity: Jack Sheppard and the Mass Audience', *Victorian Studies*, 44: 3 (Spring 2002), 423–463.

43. Elizabeth Gaskell, *Mary Barton* (1848; London: Dent, 1965), p. 207. Anthony Trollope reveals the irrelevance of police mystique to a middle-class context in *He Knew He Was Right* (1869). Here it is only the protagonist, the increasingly unhinged Trevelyan, who credits the ex-policeman Bozzle with miraculous powers. Bozzle is a prime example of the sensationalist policeman who, as deplored by Gaskell and Oliphant, constructs vicious hypotheses for normal appearances: 'Men whose business it is to detect hidden and secret things, are very apt to detect things which have never been done. What excuse can a detective make even to himself for his own existence if he can detect nothing? Mr. Bozzle was an active-minded man who gloried in detecting, and who, in the special spirit of his trade, had taught himself to believe that all around him were things secret and hidden, which would be within his power of unravelling if only the slightest clue were ever put into his hand. He lived by the crookedness of people

and therefore was convinced that straight doings in the world were quite exceptional.' See Anthony Trollope, *He Knew He Was Right* (London: Oxford University Press, 1963), pp. 267–268.

44. M. E. Braddon, *Henry Dunbar* (London: John and Robert Maxwell, 1864), p. 260.

45. U. C. Knoepflmacher, 'The Counterworld of Victorian Fiction and *The Woman in White*', in *Wilkie Collins: Contemporary Critical Essays*, ed. Lyn Pykett (London: Macmillan, 1998), pp. 60–61.

46. Charles Dickens to W. H. Wills, 24 September 1858. *The Letters of Charles Dickens*, ed. Walter Dexter, 3 vols. (Bloomsbury: Nonesuch Press, 1938), III, p. 58.

47. Hughes (1980), p. 144.

48. Walter M. Kendrick, 'The Sensationalism of *The Woman in White*', *Nineteenth-Century Fiction* 32 (1977–78), p. 20.

49. Richard Barickman, Susan MacDonald, and Myra Stark, *Corrupt Relations: Dickens, Thackeray, Trollope, Collins, and the Victorian Sexual System* (New York: Columbia University Press, 1982), p. 112.

According to Barickman and his collaborators, the themes and structures of Collins's novels are 'more radical than the author seems willing to admit.' His novels end 'by insisting on redemption through marriage, though the novels themselves have undermined that solution' (p. 149).

50. See Jerome Meckier, 'Wilkie Collins's *The Woman in White*: Providence Against the Evils of Propriety', *Journal of British Studies* 22 (Fall 1982), p. 102.

51. Michel Foucault, *The History of Sexuality. Volume 1: An Introduction*, trans. Robert Hurley (New York: Vintage, 1999), p. 12.

52. D. A. Miller, *The Novel and the Police* (Berkeley: University of California Press, 1988), p. x.

53. Miller (1988), p. 42.

54. See Michel Foucault, *Discipline and Punish: The Birth of the Prison*, trans. Alan Sheridan (New York: Pantheon, 1977), pp. 202–203.

55. Miller (1988), p. 2.

56. Ronald R. Thomas, 'Victorian Detective Fiction and Legitimate Literature: Recent Directions in the Criticism', *Victorian Literature and Culture* 24 (New York: AMS Press, 1996), p. 369.

57. Thomas (1996), p. 368.

58. Miller (1988), pp. 54–56.

59. John Bender, *Imagining the Penitentiary: Fiction and the Architecture of Mind in Eighteenth-Century England* (Chicago: University of Chicago Press, 1987), p. xv.

60. Lillian Nayder, 'Robinson Crusoe and Friday in Victorian Britain: "Discipline", "Dialogue" and Collins's Critique of Empire in *The Moonstone*', *Dickens Studies Annual* 21 (New York: AMS Press, 1991), p. 213.

61. Lois McNay, *Foucault and Feminism: Power, Gender, and the Self* (Boston: Northeastern University Press, 1992), p. 38.

62. Miller (1988), p. 69.

63. Miller (1988), pp. 17, 62.

64. Elizabeth Rose Gruner, 'Family Secrets and the Mysteries of *The Moonstone*', *Victorian Literature and Culture* 21 (1991), p. 130.

65. Miller (1988), p. 162.

66. Marlene Tromp, *The Private Rod: Marital Violence, Sensation, and the Law in Victorian Britain* (Charlottesville and London: University Press of Virginia, 2000), p. 72.

67. Tromp (2000), pp. 72–73.

68. Cannon Schmitt, *Alien Nation: Nineteenth-Century Gothic Fictions and English Nationality* (Philadelphia: University of Pennsylvania Press, 1997), p. 116.

69. Schmitt (1997), p. 116.

70. Foucault (1999), p. 37.

71. Jenny Bourne Taylor, *In the Secret Theatre of Home: Wilkie Collins, Sensation Narrative, and Nineteenth-Century Psychology* (London & New York: Routledge, 1988), p. 202.

72. Miller (1988), p. 53.

73. Miller (1988), p. 41.

74. Gruner (1991), p. 138.

75. McCuskey (2000), pp. 363–365.

76. See Laurie Langbauer, 'Women in White, Men in Feminism', *Yale Journal of Criticism* 2: 2 (Spring 1989), p. 231.

77. Paul Cantor, 'Stoning the Romance: The Ideological Critique of Nineteenth-Century Literature', *South Atlantic Quarterly* 88 (1989), p. 707.

78. M. E. Braddon, *His Darling Sin* (London: Simpkin, Marshall, Hamilton, 1899), p. 112.

79. Thomas (1996), pp. 368–69.

80. T. S. Eliot, 'Wilkie Collins and Dickens', *Times Literary Supplement* (4 August 1927). pp. 525–526; reprinted in *Selected Essays: 1917–1932* (London: Faber, 1932), p. 464.

81. G. K. Chesterton, *The Victorian Age in Literature* (London: Williams & Norgate Ltd., 1925).

82. Dorothy L. Sayers, *The Omnibus of Crime* (New York: Garden City, 1929).

83. Wilkie Collins, *The Moonstone*, ed. Anthea Trodd (Oxford: Oxford University Press, 1982), p. 214.

84. Thomas (1996), p. 367.

85. Quoted in Thomas (1996), p. 367.

86. Oliphant (1862), pp. 564–580.

87. A. D. Hutter, 'Dreams, Transformations and Literature: The Implications of Detective Fiction', *Victorian Studies* 19 (1975), pp. 181–209.

88. Walter Benjamin, *Charles Baudelaire: A Lyric Poet in the Era of High Capitalism* (London, 1973), p. 40.

89. Peter Thoms, *Detection and Its Designs: Narrative and Power in Nineteenth-Century Detective Fiction* (Ohio: Ohio University Press, 1998), p. 2.

90. Thoms (1998), p. 2.

91. See Ian Ousby, *Bloodhounds of Heaven: The Detective in English Fiction from Godwin to Doyle* (Cambridge, MA: Harvard University Press, 1976) for a discussion of the limits of police competence in mid-Victorian fiction. In the comic opera *A Sensation Novel in Three Acts* (1871) by W. S. Gilbert (1836–1911), the police detective, Gripper of the Yard, frankly explains the reasons for the ineptitude of his profession within the genre.

92. Lillian Nayder, 'Wilkie Collins Studies, 1983–1999', *Dickens Studies Annual* 28 (1998), p. 276.

93. Tamar Heller, *Dead Secrets: Wilkie Collins and the Female Gothic* (New Haven & London: Yale University Press, 1992), p. 8.

94. Heller (1992), p. 8.

95. Heller (1992), p. 143.

96. Heller (1992), pp. 143–144.

97. Heller (1992), p. 155.

98. Lillian Nayder, *Wilkie Collins* (New York: Twayne, 1997), p. 42.

99. Nayder (1997), p. 41.

100. Ann Cvetkovich, *Mixed Feelings: Feminism, Mass Culture and Victorian Sensationalism.* (New Brunswick: Rutgers University Press, 1992), p. 10.

101. Cvetkovich (1992), pp. 52–53.

102. Cvetkovich (1992), p. 55.

103. Caroline Reitz, *Detecting the Nation: Fictions of Detection and the Imperial Venture* (Ohio: Ohio State University Press, 2004), pp. 46, 56–57.

104. Tamar Heller calls *The Law and the Lady* 'one of Collins's most aesthetically and ideologically complex mystery tales, centres on a female, not a male, detective, in a narrative that rewrites the Radcliffean plot of the potentially murderous husband the kind

of plot associated with the Gothic novels of Ann Radcliffe. This return to the Gothic indicates Collins's need to return to the issue – the tension between feminine marginality and male professionalism that animated his earlier fiction'. See Heller (1992), p. 167.

105. See Chris Willis, 'The Detective's *Doppelgänger*: Conflicting States of Female Consciousness in Grant Allen's Detective Fiction', in William Greenslade and Terence Rodgers (eds), *Grant Allen: Literature and Cultural Politics at the Fin de Siècle* (Aldershot, UK: Ashgate, 2005), pp. 143–153.

106. Anne Humpherys, 'Who's Doing It? Fifteen Years of Work on Victorian Detective Fiction', *Dickens Studies Annual* 24 (1996), p. 259. See also Fay M. Black, 'Lady Sleuths and Women Detectives', *Turn of the Century Women* 3 (1986), pp. 29–42.

107. Heidi H. Johnson, 'Electra-Fying the Female Sleuth: Detecting the Father in *Eleanor's Victory* and *Thou Art the Man*', in Marlene Tromp et al eds, *Beyond Sensation: Mary Elizabeth Braddon in Context* (New York: State University of New York Press, 2000), p. 256.

108. Tromp et al (2000), pp. 256–257.

THREE   CLASS AND SOCIAL (IM-)PROPRIETY

1. [Anon.], 'The Philosophy of Amusement', *Meliora: Quarterly Review of the Social Sciences* 6 (1864), pp. 193–210.

2. Francis Paget, 'Afterword' *to Lucretia; or the Heroine of the Nineteenth Century. A Correspondence Sensational and Sentimental* (London: Joseph Masters and Sons, 1868). Reprinted in *Varieties of Women's Sensation Fiction: 1855–1890: Volume I, Sensationalism and the Sensation Debate*, ed. Andrew Maunder (London: Pickering & Chatto, 2004), p. 213.

3. Paget (1868), p. 124.

4. Pierre Bourdieu, *Distinction: A Social Critique of the Judgement of Taste*, trans. Richard Nice (Cambridge, MA: Harvard University Press, 1984), p. 48.

5. In her novel *Eleanor's Victory*, M. E. Braddon impishly signals the 'strange weird attraction' of a 'sensation' picture called 'The Earl's Death'. This episode also implies the dangerous yet seductive appeal of the sensational among a predominantly middle-class readership:

■ Although the picture was ugly, there was a strange weird attraction in it, and people went to see it again and again, and liked, and hankered after it, and talked of it perpetually all that season, one faction declaring that the Lucifer-match effect was the most delicious moonlight, and the murderess of the Earl the most lovely of womankind, till the faction who thought the very reverse of this became afraid to declare their opinions, and thus everybody was satisfied. See M. E. Braddon, *Eleanor's Victory* (New York: Harper, 1863), p. 187 □

6. Oliphant (1862), p. 584.

7. E. S. Dallas, *The Gay Science* (London: Chapman and Hall, 1866), II, pp. 299–300.

8. John Ruskin, 'Fiction, Fair and Foul', in E. T. Cook and Alexander Wedderburn eds, *The Works of John Ruskin* (London: George Allen, 1912), XVI, pp. 156–58, 59, 66, 63.

9. Mansel (1863), p. 502.

10. G. H. Lewes, 'Criticism in Relation to Novels', *Fortnightly Review* N. S. 11 (1872), pp. 141–54.

11. Peter Brooks, *Reading for the Plot: Design and Intention in Narrative* (New York: Knopf, 1984), p. 36.

12. Mansel disparagingly describes the sensational 'poison' to be found in the circulating library. See Mansel (1863), p. 486; Alfred Austin refers to sensation novels as the 'worst form of mental food, if we except that which is absolutely poisonous'. See Austin, 'Our Novels: The Sensational School', *Temple Bar* 29 (July 1870), pp. 410–424; even Wilkie Collins called sensation fiction a 'deadly social poison' which 'contaminate[s] the popular literature of a clever and polished people'. See Collins, 'The Art of the Novel', *Gentleman's Magazine* 9 (October 1872), p. 393.

13. Valerie Pedlar, 'The Woman in White: Sensationalism, Secrets and Spying' in Dennis Walder ed., The Nineteenth Century Novel: Identities (London: Routledge, 2001), p. 51.

14. [Anon.], 'Novels of the Day: Their Writers and Readers', Fraser's Magazine 62 (1860), p. 210.

15. Arnold (1866), pp. 203–204.

16. Arnold (1866), p. 204.

17. Arnold (1866), p. 208.

18. Jenny Bourne Taylor, In the Secret Theatre of Home: Wilkie Collins, Sensation Narrative and Nineteenth-Century Psychology (London: Routledge, 1988), p. 4.

19. Taylor (1988), p. 4.

20. Taylor (1988), pp. 4–5.

21. Henry James, 'Miss Braddon', in Notes and Reviews (Cambridge, MA: Dunster House, 1921), pp. 115–16.

22. [H. F. Chorley], 'New Novels', Athenaeum 29 (2 June 1866), pp. 732–33. The target here is Collins's Armadale.

23. [W. Fraser Rae], 'Sensation Novelists: Miss Braddon', North British Review 43 (September 1865), pp. 98, 101.

24. Oliphant (1867), pp. 275, 280.

25. [Anon.], 'Our Female Sensation Novelists', Christian Remembrancer 46 (July 1864), pp. 209–36.

26. [Anon.], 'Not a New "Sensation"', All the Year Round (25 July 1863), p. 517.

27. Quoted in David Vincent, Literacy and Popular Culture: England 1750–1914 (Cambridge: Cambridge University Press, 1989), p. 205.

28. Dallas Liddle, 'Anatomy of a Nine Days' Wonder: Sensational Journalism in the Decade of the Sensation Novel', in Andrew Maunder and Grace Moore eds, Victorian Crime, Madness and Sensation (Aldershot, UK: Ashgate, 2004), p. 97.

29. [Anon.], 'Novels with a Purpose', Westminster Review 82 (July 1864), p. 49.

30. Austin (1870), p. 414.

31. Mansel (1863), pp. 505–6; [Anon.], 'Belles Lettres', Westminster Review 86 (July 1866), p. 126.

32. Rae (1865), p. 204.

33. Austin (1870), p. 421.

34. Jonathan Loesberg, 'The Ideology of Narrative Form in Sensation Fiction', Representations 13 (Winter 1986), pp. 115–38.

35. Loesberg (1986), p. 130.

36. Loesberg (1986), p. 135.

37. Loesberg (1986), p. 118.

38. Nancy K. Miller, 'Emphasis Added: Plots and Plausibilities in Women's Fiction', PMLA 96 (1981), p. 118.

39. Graham Law, Serializing Fiction in the Victorian Press (London: Palgrave, 2000), p. 24.

40. Deborah Wynne, The Sensation Novel and the Victorian Family Magazine (Basingstoke: Palgrave, 2001), pp. 1–3.

41. Wynne (2001), p. 2.

42. Patrick Brantlinger, The Reading Lesson: the Threat of Mass Literacy in Nineteenth-Century British Fiction (Bloomington: Indiana University Press, 1998), p. 142.

43. Cannon Schmitt, Alien Nation: Nineteenth-Century Gothic Fictions and English Nationality (Philadelphia: University of Pennsylvania Press, 1997), p. 111.

44. Schmitt (1997), pp. 111–12.

45. [Richard Holt Hutton], 'Sensational Novels', Spectator 41 (8 August 1868), pp. 931–32.

46. Austin (1870), p. 424.

47. G. H. Lewes, Edinburgh Review (1850), quoted in Richard Stang, The Theory of the Novel in England, 1850–1870 (London: Routledge, 1959), p. 184.

48. Oliphant (1867), pp. 258, 257.

49. [Anon.], 'Novels with a Purpose', Westminster Review 82 (July 1864), p. 27.

50. Frances Power Cobbe, 'The Morals of Literature', *Fraser's Magazine* 70 (July 1864), pp. 131, 129.

51. Kimberly Harrison and Richard Fantina, 'Introduction', *Victorian Sensations: Essays on a Scandalous Genre* (Ohio: Ohio University Press, 2006), p. xv.

52. Rance (1990), p. 5.

53. Jerome Meckier, 'Wilkie Collins's *The Woman in White*: Providence against the Evils of Propriety', *Journal of British Studies* 22: 1 (Fall 1982), pp. 104–36.

54. Tamar Heller, 'Recent Work on Victorian Gothic and Sensation Fiction', *Victorian Literature and Culture* 22 (1996), p. 349.

55. John Kucich, *The Power of Lies: Transgression in Victorian Fiction* (Ithaca, NY: Cornell University Press, 1994), pp. 81–82.

56. Kucich (1994), p. 118.

57. Ronald R. Thomas, 'Wilkie Collins and the Sensation Novel' in John Richetti ed., *The Columbia History of the British Novel* (New York: Columbia University Press, 1994), p. 482.

58. Ann Cvetkovich, 'Ghostlier Demarcations: The Economy of Sensation and the *Woman in White*', *Novel* 23 (1989), pp. 24–43.

59. Thomas (1994), p. 495.

60. E. Ann Kaplan, 'Maternal Melodrama: *East Lynne*' in Derek Longhurst ed., *Gender, Genre and Narrative Pleasure* (London, 1989), p. 45.

61. Geraldine Jewsbury, *Athenaeum* (3 December 1864), p. 743.

62. Winifred Hughes, 'The Sensation Novel', in Patrick Brantlinger and William B. Thesing eds, *The Blackwell Companion to the Victorian Novel* (Oxford: Blackwells, 2002), pp. 263–64.

63. Wilkie Collins, *Armadale*, ed. Catherine Peters (Oxford: The World's Classics, 1989), p. 763.

64. M. E. Braddon, *Lady Audley's Secret*, ed. Natalie M. Houston (Ontario, Canada: Broadview, 2003), p. 6.

65. At times, Collins and other sensation novelists portray loving 'families' that do not fit the traditional standard. In *No Name*, for example, the Vanstones seem in the early chapters to be a charming and apparently traditional nuclear family. Collins, however, soon reveals this family as anything but traditional, as the parents are unmarried and the daughters therefore illegitimate.

66. M. E. Braddon, *Aurora Floyd*, eds Richard Nemesvari and Lisa Surridge (Ontario, Canada: Broadview, 1998), p. 289.

67. Austin (1870), pp. 416, 421–22.

68. Austin (1870), pp. 412–13, 421.

69. Lillian Nayder, 'Transparency, Opacity and Social Boundaries', in Harrison and Fantina (2006), p. 188.

70. Bruce Robbins, *The Servant's Hand: English Fiction from Below* (New York: Columbia University Press, 1986), p. 109.

71. Leonore Davidoff, *The Best Circles: Women and Society in Victorian England* (Totowa, New Jersey: Rowman and Littlefield, 1973), p. 87.

72. Brian W. McCuskey, 'The Kitchen Police: Servant Surveillance and Middle-Class Transgression', *Victorian Literature and Culture* 28 (2000), p. 373.

73. [John R. de C. Wise], 'Belles Lettres', *Westminster Review* 84 (1865), p. 568.

74. Sandra Gilbert and Susan Gubar, *The Madwoman in the Attic: The Woman Writer and the Nineteenth Century Literary Imagination* (New Haven: Yale University Press, 1979), p. 83.

75. Eliza Lynn Linton, 'Little Women', *Saturday Review* 25 (1868), p. 545.

FOUR WOMEN, GENDER AND FEMINISM

1. Oliphant (1867), pp. 259, 275. Oliphant wrote four lengthy articles on sensation fiction, all published in *Blackwood's*. In addition to the one quoted, they are 'Modern Novelists, Great and Small', 77 (May 1855), pp. 554–68, 'Sensation Novels', 91 (May 1862),

pp. 564–84; and 'Novels', 94 (August 1863), pp. 168–83. The 1867 essay focuses most sharply on Braddon's perceived 'misrepresentation' of women. For a discussion of these articles and numerous other Victorian responses to sensation fiction, see Elizabeth K. Helsinger, Robin Lauterbach Sheets, and William Veeder, *The Woman Question: Society and Literature in Britain and America, 1837–1883, vol. 3, Literary Issues* (Chicago: University of Chicago Press, 1983).

2. Oliphant, like her sister conservatives Eliza Lynn Linton (1822–98) and Geraldine Jewsbury, shaped novels which reviewers related to the contemporary malaise: 'Mrs. Oliphant is a writer of a very different stamp from those [sensation novelists] already described, but she seems equally incapable of appreciating the motives and principles of spiritual life [...Even her *Chronicles of Carlingford*] have their sensational portions.' See [Anon.], 'Recent Novels: Their Moral and Religious Teaching', *London Quarterly Review* 27 (1866), p. 103.

3. It is a reading which has been taken up by feminist critics and it also imbues recent fictional reclamations of the genre, as well as recent film adaptations – Radja Bharadwaj's romantically inflected *Basil* (1998) and Betsan Morris Evans's determinedly feminist *Lady Audley's Secret* (2001). See also Kelly A. Marsh, 'The Neo-Sensation Novel: A Contemporary Genre in the Victorian Tradition', *Philological Quarterly* 74: 1 (1995), pp. 99–124. I discuss issues raised by Marsh's essay in Chapter Six of this Guide.

4. Oliphant (1867), p. 260.

5. Oliphant (1867), p. 274.

6. Oliphant (1867), p. 263.

7. See Leonore Davidoff, 'Class and Gender in Victorian England', in Judith L. Newton, Mary P. Ryan, and Judith R. Walkowitz eds, *Sex and Class in Women's History* (London: Routledge, 1983), pp. 17–71; Leonore Davidoff and Catherine Hall, *Family Fortunes: Men and Women of the English Middle Class, 1780–1850* (Chicago: University of Chicago Press, 1987); Elizabeth Langland, *Nobody's Angels: Middle-Class Women and Domestic Ideology in Victorian Culture* (Ithaca, NY: Cornell University Press, 1995); Mary Poovey, *Uneven Developments: The Ideological Work of Gender in Mid-Victorian England* (Chicago: University of Chicago Press, 1988). On the paradoxes that shaped Victorian masculinity, see James Eli Adams, *Dandies and Desert Saints: Styles of Victorian Masculinity* (Ithaca, NY: Cornell University Press, 1995), p. 3.

8. John Kucich points out that 'honesty' – conceived as an abstract, public virtue – was not reckoned to be one of the essential feminine traits in the Victorian period. See Kucich (1994), pp. 11–12. Nonetheless, nineteenth-century women were thought to embody what might be called 'somatic honesty.' On this point, see Mary Ann O'Farrell, *Telling Complexions: the Nineteenth-Century English Novel and the Blush* (Durham: Duke University Press, 1997).

9. Pykett (1994), p. 45.

10. Edward Bulwer-Lytton, *Lucretia* (London: Routledge, 1874), pt. 1, Epilogue.

11. These sensation heroines are foreshadowed by the underclass women who demonstrate a dangerous desire for material acquisitions: Esther in *Mary Barton* (1848), Ruth Hilton in *Ruth* (1853), and Hetty Sorrell in *Adam Bede* (1859). In all three texts, the envious yearning for material finery is sexualised so that each one's wishful attempt to ascend the social ladder only results in each becoming a 'fallen' woman.

12. Sarah Ellis, *The Women of England: Their Social Duties and Domestic Habits* (New York: J & H Langley, 1843), p. 9.

13. Lynda Hart, *Fatal Women: Lesbian Sexuality and the Mark of Aggression* (Princeton, NJ: Princeton University Press, 1997), p. 29.

14. [Anon.], 'Sensation Novels', *Medical Critic and Psychological Journal* 3 (1863), p. 519.

15. Susan David Bernstein, 'Dirty Reading: Sensation Fiction, Women and Primitivism', *Criticism* 36: 2 (Spring 1994), p. 215; see also Bernstein, 'Ape Anxiety: Sensation

Fiction, Evolution, and the Genre Question', *Journal of Victorian Culture* 6: 2 (1999), pp. 250–70.

16. [Anon.], 'Women's Novels', *The Broadway* N.S. 1 (1868), pp. 504–9. Despite glimpsing talent in some sensational works, *The Broadway* was in no doubt that '[n]ovels of this sort must be mischievous, especially to the young and impressionable, who believe all they read.' After all, '[i]f we should not like our daughters to frequent the company of rakes and [...] swindlers and murderers in real life, we cannot consistently introduce them to such society in fiction.'

17. [Anon.], 'Our Female Sensation Novelists', *Littel's Living Age* 103 (August 1863), p. 354.

18. [Anon.] (1863), p. 354.

19. Keith Reierstad, 'Innocent Indecency: The Questionable Heroines of Wilkie Collins' Sensation Novels', *Victorians Institute Journal* 9 (1980–81), p. 57.

20. See Jennifer Phegley, *Educating the Proper Woman Reader: Victorian Family Literary Magazines and the Cultural Health of the Nation* (Columbus: Ohio State University Press, 2004). When Phegley uses the term 'family literary magazine', she refers to that class of magazines typically called 'shilling monthlies' in England, including *Macmillan's* (1859), *The Cornhill* (1860), *Temple Bar* (1860), *St. James's* (1861), *The Argosy* (1865), *Tinsley's* (1867), and *St. Paul's* (1867). Such family literary magazines, Phegley contends, were aimed at culturally educating a broadly middle-class audience that included women. These magazines conceived of women as important participants in and disseminators of the nation's culture and were amenable to women writers, editors, and readers alike.

21. [Anon.], 'Contemporary Literature', *Blackwood's* 125 (1879), pp. 322–44.

22. Oliphant (1867), p. 260.

23. Kate Flint, *The Woman Reader 1837–1914* (Oxford: Oxford University Press, 1995), p. 4.

24. Flint (1995), p. 274.

25. Flint (1995), p. 277.

26. Linda Nead, *Myths of Sexuality* (Oxford: Blackwell, 1988), p. 91. See also C. Smart, 'Disruptive Bodies and Unruly Sex' in *Regulating Womanhood: Historical Essays on Marriage, Motherhood and Sexuality*, ed. C. Smart (London: Routledge, 1993), pp. 23–32.

27. Alison Light, ' "Young Bess": Historical Novels and Growing Up', *Feminist Review* 33 (1988), p. 66; Janice Radway, *Reading the Romance* (Chapel Hill: University of North Carolina Press, 1984).

28. Showalter (1982), p. 163.

29. Henry Maudsley, *Body and Mind: An Inquiry into Their Connection and Mutual Influence, Specially in Reference to Mental Disorders: Being the Gulstonian Lectures for 1870* (New York: Macmillan, 1871), pp. 27, 29, 41. In addition to his *Body and Mind*, see *The Physiology and Pathology of Mind* (1867), *Responsibility in Mental Disease* (1874), and *Natural Causes and Supernatural Seemings* (London: Kegan Paul, 1886).

30. Maudsley (1871), p. iv.

31. Maudsley (1871), p. 12.

32. For an astute study of professionalized modes of scrutiny and degeneration theories (including Maudsley's), see Stephen D. Arata, 'Strange Cases, Common Fates: Degeneration and the Pleasures of Professional Reading,' in Robert Newman ed., *Centuries' Ends, Narratives, Means* (Stanford, CA: Stanford University Press, 1996), pp. 171–90.

33. Elaine Showalter, *The Female Malady: Women, Madness and English Culture, 1850–1980* (New York: Pantheon, 1985), p. 74.

34. Helen Small, *Love's Madness: Medicine, the Novel, and Female Insanity, 1800–1865* (Oxford and New York: Clarendon Press, 1996). On mid-century mechanistic views of insanity and depression, see also Janet Oppenheim, *'Shattered Nerves': Doctors, Patients, and Depression in Victorian England* (Oxford: Oxford University Press, 1991), pp. 35–38.

35. See Joseph Melling and Bill Forsythe eds, *Insanity, Institutions, and Society, 1800–1914* (London and New York: Routledge, 1999); Andrew Scull, *The Most Solitary of Afflictions: Madness and Society in Britain, 1700–1900* (New Haven and London: Yale University Press, 1993); Andrew Scull ed., *Madhouses, Mad-Doctors, and Madmen: The Social History of Psychiatry in the Victorian Era* (Philadelphia: University of Pennsylvania Press, 1981).

36. [Anon.], 'Review of *St Martins Eve*', *Saturday Review* (31 March 1866), p. 64.

37. [Anon.], 'Madness in Novels', *The Spectator* (3 February 1866), p. 136.

38. Ellen Wood, *St Martin's Eve*, ed. Lyn Pykett (London: Chatto & Pickering, 2004), p. 134.

39. Wood (2004), p. 16.

40. Wood (2004), p. 120.

41. D. A. Miller, *The Novel and the Police* (Berkeley: University of California Press, 1988), p. 163.

42. Miller (1988), pp. 168, 178, 155–56.

43. See Lynda Hart, *Fatal Women: Lesbian Sexuality and the Mark of Aggression* (Princeton, NJ: Princeton University Press, 1997).

44. Taylor (1988), pp. 98–99.

45. Taylor (1988), p. 2.

46. Taylor (1988), p. 10.

47. Miller (1988), p. 153.

48. Taylor (1988), p. 31.

49. Taylor (1988), p. 134

50. Taylor (1988), pp. 134, 152–53.

51. Ann Cvetkovich, *Mixed Feelings: Feminism, Mass Culture and Victorian Sensationalism* (New Brunswick: Rutgers University Press, 1992), p. 7.

52. Braddon (2003), p. 107.

53. Cvetkovich (1992), p. 50.

54. Mary Elizabeth Braddon, *Lady Audley's Secret*. Ed. Natalie M. Houston (Ontario, Canada: Broadview, 2003).

55. Jill L. Matus, *Unstable Bodies: Victorian Representations of Sexuality and Maternity* (Manchester: Manchester University Press, 1995), pp. 192–93.

56. Matus (1995), p. 2.

57. Cvetkovich (1992), p. 52.

58. [Anon.], 'Our Female Sensation Novelists', *The Living Age* 78 (22 August 1863), pp. 353–54.

59. [W. Fraser Rae,], 'Sensation Novelists: Miss Braddon', *North British Review* 43 (1865), pp. 186–87.

60. Cvetkovich (1992), p. 7.

61. Elana Gomel and Stephen Weninger, 'The Tell-Tale Surface: Fashion and Gender in *The Woman in White*', *Victorians Institute Journal* 25 (1997), pp. 29–30.

62. Gomel and Weninger (1997), p. 49.

63. See also Poovey (1988). With reference to *Jane Eyre* as a 'hysterical text', Poovey suggests that '[b]ecause there was no permissible plot in the nineteenth century for a woman's anger [...] the body of the text symptomatically acts out what cannot make its way into the psychologically realist narrative' (p. 141).

64. In addition to Sander L. Gilman et al., *Hysteria Beyond Freud* (Berkeley: University of California Press, 1993), see, for instance, Evelyne Ender, *Sexing the Mind: Nineteenth-Century Fiction of Hysteria* (Ithaca, NY: Cornell University Press, 1995).

65. Julius Althaus, 'A Lecture on the Pathology and Treatment of Hysteria: Delivered at the Royal Infirmary for Diseases of the Chest', *British Medical Journal* 1 (1866), pp. 245–48.

66. Among the relevant discussions of nineteenth-century medical discourses about femininity and hysteria see Charles Bernheimer and Claire Kahane eds, *In Dora's Case: Freud-Hysteria-Feminism* (New York: Columbia University Press, 1985); Nina Auerbach,

Woman and the Demon: The Life of a Victorian Myth (Cambridge, MA: Harvard University Press, 1982), pp. 7–34; Claire Kahane, *Passions of the Voice: Hysteria, Narrative, and the Figure of the Speaking Woman, 1850–1915* (Baltimore: Johns Hopkins University Press, 1995); and Mary Jacobus, *Reading Woman: Essays in Feminist Criticism* (New York: Columbia University Press, 1986), pp. 197–274.

67. Hélène Cixous, 'Castration or Decapitation?', trans. Annette Kuhn, *Signs* 7 (1981), p. 49.

68. Tamar Heller, *Dead Secrets: Wilkie Collins and the Female Gothic* (New Haven & London: Yale University Press, 1992), pp. 153–54.

69. C. S. Wiesenthal, in an essay on *Heart and Science*, 'From Charcot to Plato', assesses these ideas in relation to Collins's 'conceptual construction of hysteria' as an affliction of the female brain, heart and womb; women can become 'victims of their own ungovernable passions' which renders them 'smothering mothers'. See C. S. Wiesenthal, 'From Charcot to Plato: The History of Hysteria in *Heart and Science*', in *Wilkie Collins to the Forefront: Some Reassessments*, eds Nelson Smith and R. C. Terry (New York, 1995), pp. 261, 265.

70. [Anon.], 'Female Novelists of the Period', *The Period* (22 January 1870), p. 99.

71. Quoted in O'Neill (1988), p. 3.

72. Showalter (1982), pp. 158–59.

73. Elaine Showalter, 'Family Secrets and Domestic Subversion: Rebellion in the Novels of the 1860s', in A. Wohl ed., *The Victorian Family: Structure and Stresses* (London: Palgrave Macmillan, 1978), p. 105.

74. Showalter (1982), p. 160.

75. Showalter (1982), p. 167.

76. Hughes (1980), pp. 120–36.

77. Ellen Miller Casey, '"Other People's Prudery": Mary Elizabeth Braddon' in Don Richard Cox ed., *Sexuality and Victorian Literature* (Knoxville: University of Tennessee Press, 1984), p. 73.

78. Showalter (1982), p. 180.

79. Catherine Peters, *The King of Inventors: A Life of Wilkie Collins* (London: Minerva, 1992), p. 122.

80. Cvetkovich (1992), p. 1.

81. Lyn Pykett, *The 'Improper' Feminine: The Women's Sensation Novel and the New Woman Writing* (London: Routledge, 1992), p. 50.

82. Pykett (1992), p. 16.

83. Pykett (1992), p. 33.

84. Helena Michie, *Sororophobia: Differences Among Women in Literature and Culture* (Oxford: Oxford University Press, 1992), pp. 59–60.

85. O'Neill (1988), p. 64.

86. Virginia B. Morris, *Double Jeopardy: Women Who Kill in Victorian Fiction* (Lexington: Kentucky University Press, 1990), pp. 109, 105.

87. Donald E. Hall, *Fixing Patriarchy: Feminism and Mid-Victorian Novelists* (New York: New York University Press, 1996), pp. 168, 174.

88. O'Neill (1988), pp. 7–8.

89. O'Neill (1988), p. 55.

90. O'Neill (1988), pp. 213–14.

91. O'Neill (1988), p. 213.

92. Alison Milbank, *Daughters of the House: Modes of the Gothic in Victorian Fiction* (New York: St. Martin's 1992), p. 14.

93. Milbank (1992), pp. 26–27.

94. Kucich (1994), p. 75.

95. See Armstrong (1987) and Poovey (1988).

96. Lillian Nayder, *Varieties of Women's Sensation Fiction 1855–1890: Volume 4* (London: Chatto & Pickering, 2004), p. xii.

97. Marianne Hirsch, *The Mother/Daughter Plot: Narrative, Psychoanalysis, Feminism* (Bloomington: Indiana University Press, 1989), p. 14.

98. E. Ann Kaplan, 'The Political Unconscious in the Maternal Melodrama: Ellen Wood's *East Lynne* (1861)' in Derek Longhurst ed., *Gender, Genre and Narrative Pleasure* (London: Unwin Hyman, 1989). See also Kaplan, *Motherhood and Representation: The Mother in Popular Culture and Melodrama* (London: Routledge, 1992). Linda Williams indicates that maternal melodrama has 'historically addressed female audiences about issues of primary concern to women.' See Williams, ' "Something Else Besides a Mother": *Stella Dallas* and the Maternal Melodrama', in C. Gledhill ed., *Home Is Where the Heart Is: Studies in Melodrama and the Woman's Film* (London: British Film Institute, 1987), p. 305.

99. Showalter (1982), p. 14.

100. Peter Brooks, *The Melodramatic Imagination: Balzac, Henry James, Melodrama and the Mode of Excess* (New Haven, CN: Yale University Press, 1995), p. x. Patrick Joyce explains that melodrama 'appealed to all, irrespective of social condition, because all were held to be equally able to read the signs of moral legibility.' See Joyce, *Democratic Subjects: The Self and the Social in Nineteenth-Century England* (Cambridge: Cambridge University Press, 1994), pp. 179, 178; Elaine Hadley, *Melodramatic Tactics: Theatricalised Dissent in the English Marketplace, 1800–1885* (Stanford, CA: Stanford University Press, 1995).

101. Kaplan (1989), p. 34.

102. Barbara Z. Thaden, *The Maternal Voice in Victorian Fiction: Rewriting the Patriarchal Family* (New York and London: Garland, 1997), pp. 122–23.

103. See Elisabeth Rose Gruner, 'Plotting the Mother: Caroline Norton, Helen Huntingdon, and Isabel Vane', *Tulsa Studies in Women's Literature* 16: 2 (Fall 1997), p. 315.

104. Pykett (1992), pp. 129–30.

105. Hughes (1980), p. 115.

106. Pykett (1992), p. 131.

107. Pykett (1992), p. 131.

108. Pykett (1992), p. 132.

109. Pykett (1992), p. 132.

110. Cvetkovich (1992), pp. 97–98.

111. Oliphant (1862), p. 567.

112. Laurie Langbauer, 'Women in White, Men in Feminism', *Yale Journal of Criticism* 2: 2 (Spring 1989), pp. 228–29.

113. Langbauer (1989), p. 229.

114. Lynda Nead, *Myths of Sexuality: Representations of Women in Victorian Britain* (London: Blackwell, 1988), p. 74.

115. Matus (1995), p. 191.

116. Matus (1995), pp. 189–90.

117. Andrew Mangham, ' "Murdered at the Breast": Maternal Violence and the Self-Made Man in Popular Victorian Culture', *Critical Survey* 16: 1 (January 2004), pp. 20–35.

118. As Marlene Tromp notes, '[*Salem Chapel*] not only employs the tactic of "startling incident" in serial publication, but draws the reader into a sympathetic relationship with a character who commits villainous acts.' See Tromp, *The Private Rod: Marital Violence, Sensation and the Law in Victorian Britain* (Virginia: University of Virginia Press, 2000), p. 156.

119. Shirley Jones, 'Motherhood and Melodrama: *Salem Chapel* and Sensation Fiction', *Women's Writing* 6: 2 (1999), pp. 239, 241.

120. Milbank (1992), p. 1.

121. [Mrs M. E. Owen], 'Criminal Women', *Cornhill* 14 (1866), p. 152.

122. John Ruskin, 'Of Queens' Gardens', *Sesame and Lilies* (New York: Chelsea House Publishers, 1987), p. 85.

FIVE DOMESTICITY, MODERNITY AND RACE(ISM)

1. *Census of Great Britain, 1851* (London: Longman, Brown, 1854), p. xxxvi.

2. The domestic space also loomed large in the theatre of the 1860s, as companies, like that led by Squire Bancroft (1841–1926) and Marie Bancroft (1829–71), employed the trappings of the home, such as pot plants and antimacassars, within their theatres to lessen the gulf between the domestic and theatrical experience. On stage too, the home was invoked in so-called cup and saucer dramas of Tom Robertson, such as *Society* (1865), *Caste* (1867), and *School* (1869).

3. See also Monica F. Cohen, *Professional Domesticity in the Victorian Novel: Women, Work and Home* (Cambridge: Cambridge University Press, 1998); Susan Johnston, *Woman and Domestic Experience in Victorian Political Fiction* (Westport, CN: Greenwood, 2001).

4. John Burnett, *A Social History of Housing, 1815–1985*, 2nd ed (London: Methuen, 1986), p. 98.

5. Braddon (2003), p. 91.

6. [Henry James], 'Miss Braddon', *The Nation* (9 November 1865), pp. 593–94.

7. Winifred Hughes argues that the

> ■ definitive feature of the sensation genre – underlying all the disparities between Wood's tearjerkers on the one hand and Charles Reade's hard-hitting "novels-with-a-purpose" on the other – is the trend to the domestication of crime, secrets, and illicit sexuality. Unlike the Gothic romance of the 1790s or the Newgate novel of the 1830s, from both of which it was partly derived, the sensation novel [...located] its shocking events and characters firmly within the ordinary middle-class home. □

See Hughes (2002), p. 261.

8. Tamara Wagner, 'Victorian Fictions of the Nerves: Telepathy and Depression in Wilkie Collins's *The Two Destinies', Victorians Institute Journal* 32 (2004), p. 190.

9. Pamela Gilbert, *Disease, Desire, and the Body in Victorian Women's Popular Novels* (Cambridge: Cambridge University Press, 1997), pp. 69–70.

10. Gilbert (1997), p. 69.

11. Walter C. Phillips, *Dickens, Reade, and Collins: Sensation Novelists. A Study in the Conditions and Theories of Novel Writing in Victorian England* (New York: Columbia University Press, 1919), pp. 13, 27.

12. Wilkie Collins, *Basil*, ed. Dorothy Goldman (Oxford: World's Classics, 2005), p. 53.

13. Lillian Nayder, *Wilkie Collins* (London: Prentice Hall, 1997), p. 72.

14. Nicholas Rance: *Wilkie Collins and Other Sensation Novelists: Walking the Moral Hospital* (London: Macmillan/Rutherford, NJ: Fairleigh Dickinson University Press, 1990), p. 53.

15. [John Tupper], 'The Subject in Art, No. II', *The Germ* 3 (March 1850), p. 121.

16. Tim Dolin and Lucy Dougan, '*Basil*, Art and the Origins of Sensation Fiction', in Maria K. Bachman and Don Richard Cox eds, *Reality's Dark Light: The Sensational Wilkie Collins* (Tennessee: University of Tennessee Press, 2003), p. 3.

17. Collins to Richard Bentley, London, 22 November 1849, *The Letters of Wilkie Collins*, eds William Baker and William M. Clarke (New York: St. Martin's Press, 1999), I, p. 59.

18. Sue Lonoff notes that *Antonina* was a '*succées d'estime*' but 'did not sell widely'. See Sue Lonoff, *Wilkie Collins and His Victorian Readers: a Study in the Rhetoric of Authorship* (New York: AMS Press, 1982), pp. 68–69.

19. Martin Meisel, *Realisations: Narrative and Pictorial Art in Nineteenth-Century England* (Princeton, NJ: Princeton University Press, 1983), p. 375.

20. Mansel (1863), p. 491.

21. Taylor (1988), p. 3.

22. Taylor (1988), p. 1.

23. Christopher Kent, 'Probability, Reality and Sensation in the Novels of Wilkie Collins', *Dickens Studies Annual* 20 (1991), pp. 259–260. In *Wilkie Collins to the Forefront: Some Reassessments*, eds Nelson Smith and R. C. Terry (New York: AMS Press, 1995), pp. 53–74.

24. Maria K. Bachman and Don Richard Cox, 'Introduction' to Wilkie Collins, *The Woman in White* (Ontario, Canada: Broadview, 1996), p. 10.
25. Susan D. Bernstein, 'Ape Anxiety: Sensation Fiction, Evolution, and the Genre Question', *Journal of Victorian Culture* 6: 2 (1999), p. 255.
26. Tim Dolin, 'Collins's Career and the Visual Arts', in Jenny Bourne Taylor ed., *The Cambridge Companion to Wilkie Collins* (Cambridge: Cambridge University Press, 2006), p. 18.
27. Dolin (2006), pp. 16–17.
28. Compare Cvetkovich (1992), p. 212, n. 4.
29. Nicholas Daly, *Literature, Technology, and Modernity, 1860–2000* (Cambridge: Cambridge University Press, 2004), p. 36.
30. Daly (2004), p. 41.
31. See also Herbert Sussman, *Victorians and the Machine: The Literary Response to Technology* (Cambridge, MA: Harvard University Press, 1968); Martin J. Wiener, *English Culture and the Decline of the Industrial Spirit, 1850–1980* (Cambridge: Cambridge University Press, 1981).
32. Daly (2004), p. 42.
33. For Mark Seltzer,

■ The cross-influences among Charcot's studies in hysteria, [the] gridding of moving bodies [in the photographs of Edward Muybridge (1830–1904)], and the graphic time-motion studies of [Etienne-Jules Marey (1830–1904)] and, somewhat later, Frank Gilbreth, [1868–1924] make visible the unlinkings of motion and volition that allow hysteria, locomotion, and machine-work to communicate with each other. See Seltzer, *Bodies and Machines* (London: Routledge, 1992), p. 17. □

34. Wilkie Collins, *The Moonstone*, ed. John Sutherland (Oxford: World's Classics, 1999), p. 380.
35. For a survey of the appearance of railways and railway accidents in Victorian fiction, see Myron F. Brightfield, *Victorian England in its Novels (1840–1870)* vol. 3 (Los Angeles: University of California Library, 1968), pp. 189–212, and Richard D. Altick, *The Presence of the Present: Topics of the Day in the Victorian Novel* (Columbus: Ohio State Univ. Press, 1991).
36. George Meredith, *Diana of the Crossways* (1885; London: Constable, 1910), p. 50.
37. Daly (2004), p. 37.
38. Stephen Knight, 'Regional Crime Squads: Location and Dislocation in the British Mystery', in Ian A. Bell ed., *Peripheral Visions: Images of Nationhood in Contemporary British Fiction* (Cardiff: University of Wales Press, 1995).
39. See Wolfgang Schivelbusch, *The Railway Journey: The Industrialization of Time and Space in the Nineteenth Century* (Berkeley: University of California Press, 1986), pp. 137–38; Jonathan Crary, *Suspensions of Perception: Attention, Spectacle, and Modern Culture* (Cambridge, MA: MIT Press, 1999); Jeffrey T. Schnapp, 'Crash (Speed as Engine of Individuation)', *Modernism/Modernity* 6: 1 (1999), pp. 1–49.
40. Daly (2004), p. 43.
41. See Valeria Tinkler-Villani ed., *Babylon or New Jerusalem: Perceptions of the City in Literature* (New York and Amsterdam: Rodopi, 2005); David L. Pike, *Subterranean Cities: The World beneath Paris and London, 1800–1945* (Ithaca and London: Cornell University Press, 2005).
42. See Walter Benjamin, *Illuminations*, ed. Hannah Arendt, trans. Harry Zohn (New York: Schocken Books, 1985), pp. 155–200.
43. [Alfred Austin], 'Our Novels: The Sensational School', *Temple Bar* 29 (June 1870), pp. 410–24.
44. Linda Dryden, *The Modern Gothic and Literary Doubles* (Basingstoke: Palgrave, 2003), p. 19.
45. Judith Walkowitz, *City of Dreadful Delight: Narratives of Sexual Danger in Late-Victorian London* (London: Virago, 1994), p. 17.
46. Walkowitz (1994), p. 18.

47. Tamara S. Wagner, 'Sensationalizing Victorian Suburbia: Wilkie Collins's *Basil*', in Richard Fantina and Kimberly Harrison eds, *Victorian Sensations: Essays on a Scandalous Genre* (Ohio: Ohio University Press, 2006), p. 210.

48. W. J. McCormack, *Sheridan Le Fanu and Victorian Ireland* (Oxford: Oxford University Press, 1980), p. 60.

49. Wynne (2001), p. 7.

50. Wilkie Collins, *The Law and the Lady*, ed. David Skilton (Harmondsworth, Middlesex: Penguin, 1998), p. 188.

51. Wagner (2007), p. 200.

52. C. F. G. Masterman, *The Heart of the Empire: Discussions of Problems of Modern City Life in England* (Brighton: Harvester Press, 1973), p. 13.

53. J. R. Seeley, *The Expansion of England: Two Courses of Lectures* (Leipzig: Bernhard Tauchnitz, 1884), p. 56.

54. See Colin Holmes, *John Bull's Island: Immigration and British Society, 1871–1971* (London: Macmillan, 1988).

55. Wilkie Collins, *Poor Miss Finch*, ed. Catherine Peters (Oxford: World's Classics, 2000), p. 118.

56. See Maryanne Cline Horowitz ed., *Race, Class and Gender in Nineteenth-Century Culture* (Rochester, New York: University of Rochester Press, 1991).

57. W. Fraser Rae, 'Sensation Novelists: Miss Braddon', *North British Review* 4 (1865), p. 202.

58. Norman Page, *Wilkie Collins: The Critical Heritage* (London: Routledge and Kegan Paul, 1974), pp. 134–35.

59. Taylor (1988), p. 4.

60. Boyle (1989), p. 225.

61. Pamela Gilbert, *Disease, Desire, and the Body in Victorian Women's Popular Novels* (Cambridge: Cambridge University Press, 1997), pp. 71–72.

62. Patrick Brantlinger, *Rule of Darkness: British Literature and Imperialism, 1830–1914* (Ithaca, NY: Cornell University Press, 1988), p. 199.

63. Florence Marryat, *Love's Conflict*, in Andrew Maunder (gen. ed.) *Varieties of Women's Sensation Fiction 1855–1890* (London: Pickering & Chatto, 2004), p. 376.

64. Lillian Nayder, 'Rebellious Sepoys and Bigamous Wives: The Indian Mutiny and Marriage Law Reform in *Lady Audley's Secret*' in Marlene Tromp et al. eds, *Beyond Sensation: Mary Elizabeth Braddon in Context* (Albany, NY: State University of New York Press, 2000), p. 32.

65. Lillian Nayder, 'Collins and Empire', in Taylor (2006), p. 139.

66. See Maria K. Bachman, ' "Furious Passions of the Celtic Race": Ireland, Madness and Wilkie Collins's *Blind Love*' in Andrew Maunder and Grace Moore eds, *Victorian Crime, Madness and Sensation* (Aldershot, UK: Ashgate, 2004), pp. 179–94.

67. *Iolani, or Tahiti as it was*, was first published in 1999 by Princeton University Press, edited by Ira B. Nadel.

68. Quoted in 'Wilkie Collins', *Appleton's Journal of Popular Literature, Science, and Art* (3 September 1870), p. 279.

69. Brantlinger (1988), pp. 30–32.

70. See Lillian Nayder, *Unequal Partners: Charles Dickens, Wilkie Collins and Victorian Authorship* (Ithaca, NY: Cornell University Press, 2002), pp. 60–99.

71. Jenny Sharpe, 'The Unspeakable Limits of Rape: Colonial Violence and Counter-Insurgency', *Genders* 10 (1991), p. 227.

72. Christopher Hilbert, *The Great Mutiny: India 1857* (Harmondsworth, Middlesex: Penguin, 1980), p. 213.

73. Collins, *The Moonstone*, p. 447.

74. Vicki Corkran Willey, 'Wilkie Collins's "Secret Dictate": *The Moonstone* as a Response to Imperialist Panic', in Fantina and Harrison (2006), p. 226.

75. [Geraldine Jewsbury], Unsigned Review, *Athenaeum* (25 July 1868), pp. 170–1.

76. See John R. Reed, 'English Imperialism and the Unacknowledged Crime of *The Moonstone'*, *Clio* 2 (June 1973), pp. 281–90. Sue Lonoff situates Collins's critique of empire in *The Moonstone* in the context of the Eyre controversy, a debate over the actions of Edward John Eyre (1815–1901) the Governor of Jamaica (1862–66), who brutally suppressed a native insurrection in 1865. See Lonoff (1982), pp. 178–79.

77. Patricia Frick, 'Wilkie Collins's "Little Jewel": The Meaning of *The Moonstone'*, *Philological Quarterly* 63: 3 (Summer 1984), p. 318.

78. Arthur Liebman and David H. Galerstein, 'The Sign of the Moonstone', *Baker Street Journal* 44 (1994), p. 73.

79. Ashish Roy, 'The Fabulous Imperialist Semiotic of Wilkie Collins's *The Moonstone'*, *New Literary History* 24 (Summer 1993), p. 658.

80. Robert Crooks, 'Reopening the Mysteries: Colonialist Logic and Cultural Difference in *The Moonstone* and *The Horse Latitudes'*, *Literature* 4: 3 (1993), p. 515.

81. See Lillian Nayder, 'Robinson Crusoe and Friday in Victorian Britain: "Discipline", "Dialogue", and Collins's Critique of Empire in *The Moonstone'*, *Dickens Studies Annual* 21 (1992), pp. 213–31.

82. Deirdre David, *Rule Britannia: Women, Empire, and Victorian Writing* (Cornell: Cornell University Press, 1995), pp. 17–18.

83. David (1995), p. 143.

84. Ian Duncan, *'The Moonstone*, the Victorian Novel, and Imperialist Panic', *Modern Language Quarterly* 55: 3 (September 1994), pp. 301–2.

85. Duncan (1994), pp. 305–6.

86. Duncan (1994), pp. 300, 305, 310.

87. Timothy L. Carens, *Outlandish English Subjects in the Victorian Domestic Novel* (London: Palgrave, 2005), p. 117

88. Carens (2005), p. 117.

89. Frances M. Mannsaker, 'East and West: Anglo-Indian Racial Attitudes as Reflected in Popular Fiction, 1890–1914', *Victorian Studies* 24: 1(Autumn 1980), p. 37.

90. Lillian Nayder, *Wilkie Collins* (New York: Twayne, 1997), pp. 122–23.

91. Homi K. Bhabha, 'The Commitment to Theory', *The Location of Culture* (London: Routledge, 1994), p. 17.

92. Collins, *The Moonstone*, p. 319.

93. See also Susan M. Griffin, 'The Yellow Mask, the Black Robe, and *The Woman in White*: Wilkie Collins, Anti-Catholic Discourse, and the Sensation Novel', *Narrative* 12: 1 (January 2004), pp. 55–73; Natalka Freeland, 'From "Foreign Peculiarities" to "Fatal Resemblance": Detecting Villainy in *The Woman in White'*, in Stacy Gillis and Philippa Gates eds, *The Devil Himself: Villainy in Detective Fiction and Film* (2002); Gabrielle Ceraldi, 'The Crystal Palace, Imperialism, and the "Struggle for Existence": Victorian Evolutionary Discourse in Collins's *The Woman in White'*, in Bachman and Cox (2003); Laurel Erickson, ' "In Short, She Is an Angel; and I Am-": Odd Women and Same-Sex Desire in Wilkie Collins's *Woman in White'*, in Marilyn Demarest Button and Toni Reed eds, *The Foreign Woman in British Literature: Exotics, Aliens, and Outsiders* (Westport, CN: Greenwood Press, 1999); Soonhee Lim, 'Wilkie Collins's *The Woman in White* and the Politics of Borderline: The Process of Deterritorialization in the Sensation Novel', *British and American Fiction to 1900*, 9: 1 (Summer 2002), pp. 217–37; Richard Nemesvari, 'The Mark of the Brotherhood: The Foreign Other and Homosexual Panic in *The Woman in White'*, *English Studies in Canada* 28: 4 (December 2002), pp. 603–27; Lillian Nayder, 'Agents of Empire in *The Woman in White'*, *Victorian Newsletter* 83 (Spring 1993), pp. 1–7.

94. [Anon.], 'Novels of the Week', *Athenaeum* (7 January 1882), p. 15.

95. [Anon.], 'Novels of the Week', *Athenaeum* (21 March 1885), p. 371.

96. Loesberg (1986), p. 115.

97. See Judith Mitchell, 'Naturalism in George Moore's *A Mummer's Wife* (1885)' in Barbara Harman and Susan Meyer eds, *The New Nineteenth Century: Feminist Readings*

of Underread Victorian Fiction (New York: Garland, 1996), pp. 159–79; Ann Heilmann, 'Emma Bovary's Sisters: Infectious Desire and Female Reading Appetites in Mary Braddon and George Moore', *Victorian Review* (2003), pp. 31–48.

SIX THE MUTATION OF SENSATION

1. Hilary Pyle, 'Review of *Sheridan Le Fanu and Victorian Ireland*', *Essays in Criticism* 33 (1980), p. 221.

2. Joseph Sheridan Le Fanu, *Uncle Silas*, ed. Victor Sage (Harmondsworth, Middlesex: Penguin, 2000), pp. 3–4. Le Fanu's *Uncle Silas*, after new editions in 1904 and 1913, went into World's Classics in 1926, though by this time all of his other novels were out of print. The 1923 anthology by M. R. James (1862–1936) *Madam Crowl's Ghost and Other Stories by Sheridan Le Fanu* was an important early step in rescuing this unjustly neglected writer from the trough of obscurity into which his corpus of work had sunk.

3. Ann Cahill extends this argument to include *The Rose and the Key* (1871) which is, she contends, similar to other Victorian sensation novels in which women are incarcerated in mental hospitals: 'What these texts have in common, as well as with their eighteenth-century counterparts, was the desire to control women, either their behaviour or their property, through incarceration.' See 'Madness and Eccentricity in Sheridan Le Fanu's *The Rose and the Key.*' *The Bram Stoker Society Journal* 10 (1998), pp. 17–29.

4. *The Times*, 14 April 1865, p. 4.

5. [Anon.], 'Review of *Uncle Silas*', *Saturday Review* (4 February 1865), p. 146.

6. See Nicholas Rance, *Wilkie Collins and Other Sensation Novelists*, p. 157. V. S. Pritchett (1900–97), in 1946, was one of the first critics to note the startling modernity of Le Fanu's 'rational' ghosts in *The Living Novel*, and so converted *Uncle Silas* into a compelling psychological thriller: 'Le Fanu's ghosts are what I take to be the most disquieting of all: the ghosts that can be justified, blobs of the unconscious that have floated up to the surface of the mind.' See V. S. Pritchett, *The Living Novel* (London: Chatto and Windus, 1946), p. 96.

7. 'Le Fanu, today, stands' according to Victor Sage, 'at the conjunction of Irish Studies, Gothic Studies and the study of the Victorian Sensation Novel.' See Sage, *Le Fanu's Gothic: The Rhetoric of Darkness* (London: Palgrave Macmillan, 2004), p. 1.

8. Patrick Brantlinger, 'What is "Sensational" about the "Sensation Novel"?', *Nineteenth-Century Fiction* 37 (1982), 5–6. In 1931 S. M. Ellis published *Wilkie Collins, Le Fanu and Others*, describing Le Fanu as 'an archaeologist, and I think it is his blend of learning with mystery and crime which created romances that hold the attention of readers who would have no liking for the ordinary sensational novel.' See S. M. Ellis, *Wilkie Collins, Le Fanu and Others* (London: Constable, 1951), p. 179. Ellis's image of Le Fanu as an archaeologist is evocative since his fiction obsessively excavates the sensational 'survivals' of a baleful past that impinge upon the modern moment.

9. See Sally Harris, 'Spiritual Warnings: The Ghost Stories of Joseph Sheridan Le Fanu', *Victorians Institute Journal* 31 (2003), p. 10. Linda Bayer-Berenbaum's definition of Gothicism is relevant here: 'Gothicism insists that what is customarily hallowed as real by society and its language is but a small portion of a greater reality of monstrous proportion and immeasurable power. The peculiarly *Gothic* quality of this extended reality is its immanence, its integral, inescapable connection to the world around us'. Linda Bayer-Berenbaum, *The Gothic Imagination: Expansion in Gothic Literature and Art* (East Brunswick, NJ: Associated University Press, 1982), p. 21.

10. Bowen writes,

■ [h]aving, for reasons which are inscrutable, pitched on England as the setting for *Uncle Silas*, he wisely chose the North, the wildness of Derbyshire. Up there, in the vast estates of the landed old stock, there appeared, in the years when Le Fanu wrote (and still more in the years of which he wrote: the early 1840s) a time lag – just such a time lag as, in a more marked form, separates Ireland from England more effectually than any sea. □

See Elizabeth Bowen, 'Introduction' to *Uncle Silas* (London: Cresset Press, 1947), p. 8.

11. See Robert Tracy, 'Undead, Unburied: Anglo-Ireland and the Predatory Past', *LIT: Literature, Interpretation, Theory* 10: 1 (1999), pp. 13–33. Tracy studies major Anglo-Irish writers to show how they adapted Irish folklore and tales of ghosts and vampires into a metaphorical expression of the Anglo-Irish anxiety about their having taken something that did not belong to them.

12. W. J. McCormack, *Sheridan Le Fanu and Victorian Ireland* (Oxford: Oxford University Press, 1980), pp. 144–45. McCormack is among the major theorists of 'Irish Gothic', having examined the field in punctilious detail, following its trajectory through the writings of Charles Robert Maturin, Le Fanu, William Carleton (1794–1869), Oscar Wilde, Bram Stoker, W. B. Yeats, John Millington Synge and Elizabeth Bowen. McCormack, introducing a section of *The Field Day Anthology of Irish Writing*, discusses at greater length the problems of method, definition and material raised by the concept of an Irish Gothic tradition. See McCormack, 'Irish Gothic and After (1820–1945)', *The Field Day Anthology of Irish Writing, Volume 2*, ed. Seamus Deane (Derry: Field Day Publications, 1991), p. 833; also McCormack, *Ascendancy and Tradition in Anglo-Irish Literary History from 1789–1939* (Oxford: Clarendon Press, 1985).

13. On the interrelationship of Le Fanu's insecurity of tenure and his fiction see McCormack (1980), p. 206.

14. Alison Milbank, 'Victorian Gothic in English Novels and Stories, 1830–1880', *The Cambridge Companion to Gothic Fiction* (Cambridge: Cambridge University Press, 2002), pp. 145–65.

15. Milbank (1992), p. 18.

16. See Andrew Smith, *Victorian Demons: Medicine, Masculinity and the Gothic at the Fin-de-Siècle* (Manchester and New York: Manchester University Press, 2004).

17. Sage (2004), p. 102.

18. Sage (2004), pp. 101–2.

19. Sage (2004), p. 130.

20. Some of Sage's preoccupations are refined from his earlier study of the theological imagination in Gothic, *Horror Fiction in the Protestant Tradition* (1988), such as the legalistic/religious status of 'witnessing' in horror fiction, attestation and the relationship of the doctrine of the resurrection to the revenants of the Gothic.

21. ■ Le Fanu's short fiction [...] is a precursory demonstration of the arbitrariness of linguistically created systems of meaning. Coming before Ferdinand de Saussure [1857–1913] and his ideas of the arbitrariness of linguistic signs, Le Fanu's texts criticise powerful systems of signification, such as medical science, by presenting circumstances that question the validity and ultimate coherence of its knowledge. □ See Mark Wegley, 'Unknown Fear: Joseph Sheridan Le Fanu and the Literary Fantastic', *Philological Review* 27: 2 (1999), 59–77.

22. See Peter Keating, *The Haunted Study: A Social History of the English Novel 1875–1914* (London: Secker & Warburg, 1989), chapter 1.

23. See Kelly Hurley, *The Gothic Body: Sexuality, Materialism and Degeneration at the Fin de Siècle* (Cambridge: Cambridge University Press, 1996).

24. Brantlinger (1982), p. 1.

25. Philip Davis, *The Victorians: The Oxford English Literary History. Volume 8. 1830–1880* (Oxford: Oxford University Press, 2002), p. 334.

26. Altick (1987), p. 3.

27. Lyn Pykett, *The Sensation Novel: From 'The Woman in White' to 'The Moonstone'* (Northcote, 1994), p. 68.

28. L. T. Hergenhan, 'The Reception of George Meredith's Early Novels', *Nineteenth Century Fiction* 19 (1964), p. 214.

29. See Arthur Waugh, *A Hundred Years of Publishing* (London: Chapman & Hall, 1930), p. 145.

30. Benjamin F. Fisher, 'A Genuine Gothic Exchange: George Meredith Pilfers Wilkie Collins's *The Dead Secret* for *Evan Harrington*', *Journal of the Georgia Philological Association* 1 (December 2006), p. 53; see also Fisher, 'Sensation Fiction in a Minor Key: *The Ordeal of Richard Feverel* [1859]', in Clyde de L. Ryals ed., *Nineteenth Century Literary Perspectives: Essays in Honour of Lionel Stevenson* (Durham, NC: Duke University Press, 1974), pp. 283–94.

31. See Suzanne Daly, 'Indiscreet Jewels: The Eustace Diamonds', *Nineteenth Century Studies* 19 (2005), pp. 69–81.

32. Anthony Trollope, *Autobiography* (London: Routledge, 1950), p. 227.

33. See Kieran Dolin, *Fiction and the Law: Legal Discourse in Victorian and Modernist Literature* (Cambridge: Cambridge University Press, 1999).

34. H. A. Page, 'The Morality of Literary Art', *Contemporary Review* 5 (1867), p. 179.

35. Adeline R. Tintner, 'Henry James and Miss Braddon: "Georgina's Reasons" and the Victorian Sensation Novel', *Essays in Literature* 10: 1 (Spring 1983), pp. 119–124.

36. Henry James to Charles Eliot Norton, 28 February 1866, in Leon Edel ed., *Henry James' Letters* (London: Macmillan, 1974), I, p. 64.

37. Quoted in Robert Lee Wolff, *Sensational Victorian: The Life and Fiction of Mary Elizabeth Braddon* (New York: Garland, 1979), pp. 10–11.

38. Michael Anesko, *'Friction with the Market': Henry James and the Profession of Authorship* (New York and Oxford: Oxford University Press, 1986), p. 13.

39. See Tamar Heller, 'Victorian Sensationalism and the Silence of Maternal Sexuality in Edith Wharton's *The Mother's Recompense* [1925]', *Narrative* 5: 2 (1995), pp. 135–42.

40. See Alfred Habegger, *Henry James and the 'Woman Business'* (Cambridge: Cambridge University Press, 1989), pp. 3–10, 23–26.

41. [Anon.], 'Review of *Hester's History*', *Spectator* 42 (24 July 1869), p. 882.

42. [Anon.], 'Review of *The Fitful Fevers of a Life*', *Spectator* 46 (22 February 1873), p. 252.

43. Paul Ward, *'Desperate Remedies* and the Victorian Thriller', *Thomas Hardy Yearbook* 4 (1973–74), pp. 72–76.

44. Lawrence O. Jones, *'Desperate Remedies* and the Victorian Sensation Novel', *Nineteenth-Century Fiction* 20: 1 (June 1965), p. 37.

45. Thomas Hardy, *The Life of Thomas Hardy*, ed. Michael Millgate (London: Macmillan, 1987), p. 63.

46. Robert Gittings, *Young Thomas Hardy* (Harmondsworth, Middlesex: Penguin, 1975), p. 138.

47. Jones (1965), p. 35.

48. Elaine Showalter, *'Desperate Remedies*: Sensation Novels of the 1860s' *Victorian Newsletter* 49 (1976), pp. 1–5.

49. Walter M. Kendrick, 'The Sensationalism of Thomas Hardy', *Texas Studies in Literature and Language* 22: 4 (Winter 1980), pp. 490–91.

50. Sally Mitchell, *The Fallen Angel: Chastity, Class and Women's Reading 1835–1880* (Ohio: Bowling Green University Press, 1981), p. 95.

51. Mitchell (1981), p. 96.

52. See Marlene Tromp et al. eds, *Beyond Sensation: Mary Elizabeth Braddon in Context* (Albany, NY: State University of New York Press, 2000); Dorice Williams Elliott, *The Angel Out of the House: Philanthropy and Gender in Nineteenth-Century England* (Virginia: University of Virginia Press, 2002); Françoise Barret-Ducrocq, *Love in the Time of Victoria: Sexuality, Class and Gender in Nineteenth-Century London* (Harmondsworth, Middlesex: Penguin, 1991); Martha Vicinus, *Independent Women: Work and Community for Single Women 1850–1920* (London: Virago, 1985); Tom Winnifrith, *Fallen Women in the Nineteenth-Century Novel* (London: Palgrave, 1994).

53. See Amanda Anderson, *Tainted Souls and Painted Faces: the Rhetoric of Fallenness in Victorian Culture* (Cornell: Cornell University Press, 1993); Bill Overton, *Fictions of Female Adultery 1864–1890: Theories and Circumtexts* (London: Palgrave, 2002); Michael Mason, *The Making of Victorian Sexual Attitudes* (Oxford: Oxford University Press, 1994); Frank Mort, *Dangerous Sexualities: Medico-Moral Politics in England since 1830* (London: Routledge,

1987); Angelique Richardson and Chris Willis eds, *The New Woman in Fiction and in Fact: Fin-de-Siècle Feminisms* (London: Palgrave, 2002).

54. Pykett (1992), pp. 5–6.

55. Wolff (1979), p. 4.

56. Albert C. Sears, 'Mary Elizabeth Braddon and the "Combination Novel": The Subversion of Sensational Expectation in *Vixen*', in Richard Fantina and Kimberly Harrison eds, *Victorian Sensations: Essays on a Scandalous Genre* (Ohio: Ohio State University Press, 2006), p. 41.

57. Wolff (1979), p. 278.

58. Gillian Beer, 'Sensational Women', *Times Literary Supplement* (11 March 1994), p. 26.

59. Pamela K. Gilbert, 'Braddon and Victorian Realism: *Joshua Haggard's Daughter*', in Tromp et al. (2000), p. 185.

60. See M. C. Fryckstedt, 'Compiling a Guide to English Fiction of the 1860s', *Publishing History* 39 (1996), p. 55.

61. See Marilyn Wood, *Rhoda Broughton (1840–1920): Profile of a Novelist* (Stamford, Lincolnshire: Paul Watkins, 1993).

62. Helen Debenham, 'Rhoda Broughton's *Not Wisely But Too Well* and the Art of Sensation', in *Victorian Identities: Social and Cultural Formations in Nineteenth-Century Literature*, eds Ruth Robbins and Julian Wolfreys (London: Macmillan, 1996), pp. 9–10.

63. Debenham (1996), p. 10.

64. Vincent E. H. Murray, 'Ouida's Novels', *Contemporary Review* 22 (1873), p. 935.

65. [Anon.], 'Contemporary Literature', *Blackwood's* 125 (1879), p. 335.

66. Pamela K. Gilbert, *Disease, Desire and the Body in Victorian Women's Popular Novels* (Cambridge: Cambridge University Press, 1997), p. 88.

67. Graham Law, 'Introduction', in *Varieties of Women's Sensation Fiction: 1855–1890 Volume 6 Newspaper Sensationalism: Dora Russell, 'Beneath the Wave' (1878)* (London: Pickering & Chatto, 2004), pp. vii–viii.

68. See Deborah Wynne, *The Sensation Novel and the Victorian Family Magazine* (Palgrave, 2001), pp. 19–22.

69. Mark Knight, 'Introduction' to Mary Cecil Hay, *Old Myddleton's Money* (London: Pickering and Chatto, 2004), p. viii.

70. Charlotte Riddell to Harry Furniss, cited in Malcolm Elwin, *Victorian Wallflowers* (London: Constable, 1934), p. 241.

71. [Anon.], 'The Novels of Miss Broughton', *Temple Bar* 41 (1874), pp. 198–99.

72. M. Shaw, 'Elizabeth Gaskell, Tennyson and the Fatal Return: *Sylvia's Lovers* and *Enoch Arden*', *Gaskell Society Journal* 9 (1995), p. 47.

73. Wilkie Collins, *Miss or Mrs? The Haunted Hotel, The Guilty River*, eds Norman Page and Toru Sasaki (Oxford: World's Classics, 1999), pp. 247, 248.

74. See Daniel Bivona, *Desire and Contradiction: Imperial Visions and Domestic Debates in Victorian Literature* (Manchester: Manchester University Press, 1990); Terry Collits, *Postcolonial Conrad: Paradoxes of Empire* (London: Routledge, 2005); Allan Conrad Christensen, *Nineteenth-Century Narratives of Contagion: 'Our Feverish Contact'* (London: Routledge, 2005).

75. Anindyo Roy, *Civility and Empire: Literature and Culture in British India, 1822–1922* (London: Routledge, 2005), p. 93.

76. Joseph Conrad, *The Collected Letters of Joseph Conrad*, eds Frederick R. Karl and Laurence Davies (Cambridge: Cambridge University Press, 1986), I, p. 137.

77. Ford Madox Ford, *Joseph Conrad: A Personal Remembrance* (New York: Octagon, 1971), p. 96.

78. Frederick R. Karl, *Joseph Conrad: The Three Lives* (New York: Farrar, Straus, and Giroux, 1979), p. 606. Wendy Lesser regards *The Secret Agent* as '[i]n some ways a parody

of the standard Dickensian plot.' See 'From Dickens to Conrad: A Sentimental Journey', *ELH* 52: 1 (1985), pp. 185–208.

79. D. A. Miller, *The Novel and the Police* (Berkeley: University of California Press, 1988), pp. 155–56.

80. Ellen Burton Harrington, 'The Anarchist's Wife: Joseph Conrad's Debt to Sensation Fiction in *The Secret Agent*', *Conradiana: A Journal of Joseph Conrad Studies* 36: 1–2 (Spring-Summer 2004), p. 51.

81. Garnett's review, 28 September 1907, reprinted in Norman Sherry, *Conrad: The Critical Heritage* (London: Routledge & Kegan Paul, 1973), p. 56. Garnett, a long-time supporter of Conrad, helped publish *Almayer's Folly* in 1895.

82. Susan Jones, ' "Stepping out of the narrow frame": Conrad's "Suspense" and the Novel of Sensation', *The Review of English Studies* 49: 195 (August 1998), p. 308.

83. Kelly A. Marsh, 'The Neo-Sensation Novel: A Contemporary Genre in the Victorian Tradition', *Philological Quarterly* 74: 1 (Winter 1995), p. 99.

84. See also John J. Su, 'Fantasies of (Re)Collection: Collecting and Imagination in A. S. Byatt's *Possession: A Romance*', *Contemporary Literature* 45: 4 (2004), pp. 684–712.

85. There is insufficient room here to record the range of contemporary fiction which employs some Victorian work as 'intertext': in other words, radically reappraising a text, performance, image, or personality from the nineteenth century. See for instance Peter Ackroyd, *Leno and the Limehouse Golem* (1994); Jonathan Barnes, *The Somnambulist* (2007); Susan Barrett, *Fixing Shadows* (2005); Louis Bayard, *Mr Timothy; A Dickensian Thriller* (2003); Peter Carey, *Jack Maggs* (1997); Michael Faber, *The Crimson Petal and the White* (2002); J. G. Farrell, *The Siege of Krishnapur* (1973); John Fowles, *The French Lieutenant's Woman* (1969); Alasdair Gray, *Poor Things* (1992); Jane Harris, *The Observations* (2006); Lloyd Jones, *Master Pip* (2006); Will Self, *Dorian, An Imitation* (2002); D. J. Taylor, *Kept: A Victorian Mystery* (2006); Colm Toibin, *The Master* (2004); Sarah Waters, *Tipping the Velvet* (1998); James Wilson, *The Dark Clue* (2001).

CONCLUSION

1. Valerie Sanders, 'Women, Fiction and the Marketplace', in *Women and Literature 1800–1900*, ed. Joanne Shattock (Cambridge: Cambridge University Press, 2000), pp. 149, 143.

2. Asa Briggs, *Victorian Things* (London: Batsford, 1988), p. 423.

3. Pamela Gilbert, *Disease, Desire and the Body in Victorian Women's Popular Novels* (Cambridge: Cambridge University Press, 1997), p. 7.

4. Lyn Pykett, 'Afterword', in Tromp et al. eds, *Beyond Sensation: Mary Elizabeth Braddon in Context* (New York: State University of New York Press, 2000), p. 279.

5. Steve Farmer, 'Introduction' to Wilkie Collins, *Heart and Science* (Ontario, Canada: Broadview, 1996), p. 1.

6. O'Neill (1988), p. 1.

7. Quoted in Farmer (1996), p. 1.

8. See Joseph Valente, ' "Double Born": Bram Stoker and the Metrocolonial Gothic', *Modern Fiction Studies* 46 (2000), 632–45; Elizabeth Signorotti, 'Repossessing the Body: Transgressive Desire in *Carmilla* and *Dracula*', *Criticism* 58: 4 (1996), pp. 607–32; Michael Davis, 'Gothic's Enigmatic Signifier: The Case of J. Sheridan Le Fanu's "Carmilla" ', *Gothic Studies* 6: 2 (November 2004), pp. 223–35; Benson Saler and Charles A. Zieger. 'Dracula and Carmilla: Monsters and the Mind', *Philosophy and Literature* 29:1 (April 2005), pp. 218–27; Alison Milbank, ' "Powers Old and New": Stoker's Alliances with Anglo-Irish Gothic', in William Hughes and Andrew Smith eds, *Bram Stoker: History, Psychoanalysis, and the Gothic* (London: Palgrave, 1998); Tamar Heller, 'The Vampire in the House: Hysteria, Female Sexuality, and Female Knowledge in Le Fanu's *Carmilla* (1872)' in Barbara Harman ed., *The New Nineteenth Century: Feminist Readings of Underread*

Victorian Fiction (1996); Carol Senf, *The Vampire in Nineteenth-Century Literature* (Bowling Green, Ohio: Bowling Green State University Press, 1988).

9. Andrew Maunder, *Bram Stoker* (Tavistock: Northcote Press, 2006), p. 132.

10. Jennifer Carnell and Graham Law, ' "Our Author": Braddon in the Provincial Weeklies', in Tromp et al (2000), pp. 127–163.

11. Margaret Oliphant, *The Victorian Age in English Literature* (London: Tait, 1892), pp. 494–95.

12. [W. Fraser Rae], 'Sensation Novelists: Miss Braddon', *North British Review* 43 (1865), p. 197.

13. Peter W. Sinnema, *Dynamics of the Pictured Page: Representing the Nation in 'The Illustrated London News'* (Aldershot, UK: Ashgate, 1998); Jennifer Phegley, *Educating the Proper Woman Reader: Victorian Family Literary Magazines and the Cultural Health of the Nation* (Ohio: Ohio State University Press, 2004). See also Andrew King, *The London Journal 1845–1883* (Aldershot, UK: Ashgate, 2004).

14. See Graham Law, *Serialising Fiction in the Victorian Press* (London: Palgrave, 2000).

15. See Barbara Onslow, *Women of the Press in Nineteenth-Century Britain* (London: Palgrave, 2000).

16. Andrew Maunder, 'Mapping the Victorian Sensation Novel: Recent and Future Trends', *Literature Compass On-Line* 2 (Oxford: Blackwell, 2005), 140, 1–32.

Bibliography

VICTORIAN SENSATION NOVELS

Braddon, Mary Elizabeth, *Aurora Floyd*, eds Richard Nemesvari and Lisa Surridge (Ontario, Canada: Broadview Press, 1998).

——, *Birds of Prey* (1867; London: Ward, Lock & Tyler, n.d.).

——, *The Black Band; or the Mysteries of Midnight*, ed. Jennifer Carnell (Hastings, UK: Sensation Press, 1998).

——, *Charlotte's Inheritance* (1868; London: Simpkin, Marshall, Hamilton, n.d.).

——, *Dead Man's Shoes* (London: Ward and Lock, 1876).

——, *The Doctor's Wife* (London: John and Robert Maxwell, 1864).

——, *Fenton's Quest: a Novel* (London: Ward and Lock, 1871).

——, *Hostages to Fortune* (London: Maxwell, 1875).

——, *John Marchmont's Legacy*, eds Toru Sasaki and Norman Page (1863; Oxford: Oxford University Press, 1999).

——, *Lady Audley's Secret*, ed. Natalie M. Houston (Ontario, Canada: Broadview Press, 2003).

——, *Lady Lisle* (1861; London: Simpkin, Marshall, Hamilton, Kent, 1891).

——, *Milly Darrell, and Other Tales* (London: Maxwell, 1873).

——, *An Open Verdict: a Novel* (London: Maxwell, 1878).

——, *Rupert Godwin* (London: Ward and Lock, 1867).

——, *To the Bitter End* (London: Maxwell, 1872).

——, *The Trail of the Serpent*, ed. Chris Willis (1861; New York: Random House, 2003).

——, *Under the Red Flag* (and other stories) (1886; London: John and Robert Maxwell, n.d.).

——, *Vixen: a Novel* (London: Maxwell, 1879).

——, *The White Phantom*, ed. Jennifer Carnell (Hastings, UK: Sensation Press, 2005).

Broughton, Rhoda. *Cometh up as a Flower*, ed. Tamar Heller (1867; London: Chatto & Pickering, 2004).

——, *Not Wisely but Too Well: a Novel* (London: Tinsley Brothers, 1867).

——, *Red as a Rose is She* (London: Bentley, 1870).

Collins, Wilkie, *Armadale*, ed. Catherine Peters (Oxford: World's Classics, 1989).

——, *Basil*, ed. Dorothy Goldman (Oxford: World's Classics, 2005).

——, *Blind Love*, eds Maria K. Bachman and Don Richard Cox (Ontario, Canada: Broadview Press, 2003).

——, *The Dead Secret*, ed. Ira B. Nadel (Oxford: World's Classics, 1999).

——, *The Evil Genius*, ed. Graham Law (Ontario, Canada: Broadview Press, 1998).

——, *Heart and Science*, ed. Steve Farmer (Ontario, Canada: Broadview Press, 1996).

——, *Hide and Seek*, ed. Catherine Peters (Oxford: World's Classics, 1999).

——, *The Law and the Lady*, ed. Jenny Bourne Taylor (Oxford: World's Classics, 1999).

——, *Man and Wife*, ed. Norman Page (Oxford: World's Classics, 1999).

——, *Miss or Mrs? The Haunted Hotel, the Guilty River*, eds Norman Page and Toru Sasaki (Oxford: World's Classics, 1999).

——, *The Moonstone*, ed. John Sutherland (Oxford: World's Classics, 1999).

——, *No Name*, ed. Virginia Blain (Oxford: World's Classics, 1999).

——, *Poor Miss Finch*, ed. Catherine Peters (Oxford: World's Classics, 2000).

——, *The Woman in White*, eds Maria K. Bachman and Don Richard Cox (Ontario, Canada: Broadview Press, 2006).

Le Fanu, Joseph Sheridan, *Uncle Silas*, ed. Victor Sage (Harmondsworth, Middlesex: Penguin Classics, 2000).

Marryat, Florence, *Confessions of Gerald Estcourt* (London: Bentley, 1867).

——, *Love's Conflict* (London: Bentley, 1865).

——, *On Circumstantial Evidence: a Novel* (London: White, 1889).

——, *Too Good for Him* (London: Bentley, 1865).

——, *Woman against Woman* (London: Bentley, 1865).

Mathers, Helen, *Eyre's Acquittal* (London: Bentley, 1884).

——, *Story of a Sin: a Sketch* (London: Chapman and Hall, 1881).

Pae, David, *Lucy, the Factory Girl; or, the Secrets of the Tontine Close*, ed. Graham Law (Hastings, UK: Sensation Press, 2001).

Reade, Charles, *Foul Play* (London: Bradbury and Evans, 1869).

——, *Griffith Gaunt: or, Jealousy* (London: Chapman and Hall, 1867).

——, *Hard Cash* (London: Sampson Low, 1863).

——, *Put Yourself in His Place* (London: Smith, Elder, 1870).

——, *A Terrible Temptation: a Story of the Day* (London: Chapman and Hall, 1871).

Russell, Dora, *Beneath the Wave*, ed. Graham Law (London: Pickering & Chatto, 2004).

Skene, Felicia, *Hidden Depths*, ed. Lillian Nayder (London: Pickering & Chatto, 2004).

——, *Strange Inheritance* (Edinburgh: Blackwood, 1886).

Wood, Ellen, *Danesbury House* (1860; London: Ward, Lock and Co., n.d.).

——, *East Lynne*, ed. Andrew Maunder (Ontario, Canada: Broadview Press 2002).

——, *Lady Adelaide's Oath* (1867), repr. as *Lady Adelaide* (London: Richard Bentley and Son, 1898).

——, *Mrs Halliburton's Troubles* (London: Macmillan, 1907).

——, *The Shadow of Ashlydat* (1864; London: R. E. King, 1905).

——, *St. Martin's Eve* (1866; London: Richard Bentley and Son, 1895).

——, *Verner's Pride* (1863; London: Richard Bentley and Son, 1896).

Yates, Edmund Hodgson, *Broken to Harness* (London: Bentley, 1864).

——, *Forlorn Hope: a Novel* (London: Tinsley Brothers, 1867).

——, *Kissing the Rod* (London: Tinsley Brothers, 1866).

——, *Land at Last: a Novel* (London: Chapman and Hall, 1866).

CONTEMPORARY CRITICISM AND THEORIZING OF SENSATION FICTION

Alexander, William, Bishop of Derry, 'Sensationalism', in *Six Sermons Preached on the Sundays after Easter 1874 in the Church of St. James's Piccadilly* (London: SPCK, 1874), pp. 75–105.

[Anon.], 'Aunt Anastasia on Modern Novels', *Tinsley's Magazine* 1 (1867), pp. 308–16.

[Anon.], Editorials in Response to the Archbishop of York, *The Times* (3 and 4 November 1864), pp. 6–9.

[Anon.], 'The Enigma Novel', *Spectator* (28 December 1861), p. 1428.

[Anon.], 'Female Novelists of the Period', *The Period* (22 January 1870), p. 99.

[Anon.], 'Homicidal Heroines', *Saturday Review* (7 April 1866), pp. 403–5.

[Anon.], ' "Lady Audley" on the Stage', *London Review* (7 March 1863), pp. 244–45.

[Anon.], 'Literary Culture of the Period', *The Period* (19 February 1870), p. 135.

[Anon.], 'Modern Novels', *Cambridge Review*, 2 (8 December 1880), p. 138.

[Anon.], 'Mrs Wood and Miss Braddon', *Littell's Living Age* (14 April 1863), pp. 99–103.

[Anon.], 'Novels, Past and Present', *Saturday Review* (14 April 1866), pp. 438–9.

[Anon.], 'Our Female Sensation Novelists', *Christian Remembrancer*, 46 (July 1864), pp. 209–36.

[Anon.], 'Our Female Sensation Novelists', *Living Age* 78 (August 1863), pp. 352–69.

[Anon.], 'Our Survey of Literature and Science', *Cornhill Magazine* 8 (January–June 1863), pp. 132–39.

[Anon.], 'Peculiarities of Some Female Novelists', *Pall Mall Gazette* (13 January 1870), p. 8.

[Anon.], 'The Philosophy of "Sensation"', *St James's Magazine* 5 (October 1862), pp. 340–46.

[Anon.], 'The Popular Novels of the Year', *Fraser's Magazine* 68 (August 1863), pp. 253–69.

[Anon.], 'Recent Novels: Their Moral and Religious Teaching', *London Quarterly Review* 27 (October 1866), pp. 100–24.

[Anon.], 'Sensation', *The Literary Times* (9 May 1863), pp. 102–3.

[Anon.], 'Sensational Novels', *Medical Critic and Psychological Journal*, 3 (1863), pp. 513–19.

[Anon.], 'Sensation! A Satire', *Dublin University Magazine*, 63 (January 1864), pp. 85–89.

[Anon.], 'Sensational Literature', *The Christian Observer*, 335 (November 1865), pp. 809–13.

[Anon.], 'The Sensational Williams', *All the Year Round* (13 February 1864), pp. 14–17.

[Anon.], 'A Sermon upon Novels', *London Review* (14 September 1867), pp. 293–94.

[Anon.], 'Thackeray and Modern Fiction', *London Quarterly Review* 22 (July 1863), pp. 375–408.

[Anon.], 'Tigresses in Literature', *Spectator* (10 March 1866), pp. 274–75.

[Anon.], 'Wilkie Collins', *Appletons' Journal of Popular Literature, Science and Art* (3 September 1870), pp. 278–81.

[Anon.], 'Women's Novels', *The Broadway*, N.S. 1 (1868), pp. 504–9.

[Anon.], 'Works of Imagination in 1864', *Literary Gazette* (14 January 1865), p. 3.

Austin, Alfred, 'On the "Sensational" in Literature and Art', *Belgravia* (February 1868), pp. 449–58.

—— 'Our Novels: The Sensational School', *Temple Bar* 29 (June 1870), pp. 410–24.

[E. B.], 'The Sensation Novel', *The Argosy* 18 (1870), pp. 137–43.

James, Henry, 'Miss Braddon', *The Nation* (9 November 1865), pp. 593–94.

[Jewsbury, Geraldine], 'Our Library Table', *Athenaeum* (3 December 1864), pp. 744–45.

[Keddie, Henrietta], 'A Word of Remonstrance with Some Novelists. By a Novelist', *Good Words* 4 (July 1863), pp. 524–26.

[Mansel, Henry Longueville], 'Sensation Novels', *Quarterly Review*, 113 (April 1863), pp. 481–514.

[Oliphant, Margaret], 'Modern Novelists, Great and Small', *Blackwoods Edinburgh Magazine* 77 (May 1855), pp. 554–68.

——, 'Novels', *Blackwoods Edinburgh Magazine* 94 (August 1863), pp. 168–83.

——, 'Novels', *Blackwoods Edinburgh Magazine* 102 (September 1867), pp. 257–80.

——, 'Sensational Novels', *Blackwoods Edinburgh Magazine* 91 (May 1862), pp. 564–80.

[Owen, Mrs. M. E.], 'Criminal Women', *Cornhill* 14 (1866), pp. 152–60.

[Paget, Francis Edward], 'Afterword' to *Lucretia. The Heroine of the Nineteenth Century. A Correspondence Sensational and Sentimental* (London: Masters, 1868).

[Rae, W. Fraser], 'Sensation Novelists: Miss Braddon', *North British Review* 43 (1865), pp. 180–204.

Sala, George Augustus, 'The Cant of Modern Criticism', *Belgravia* 4 (November 1867), pp. 45–55

[Thomson, William], 'The Archbishop of York on Works of Fiction', *The Times* (2 November 1864), p. 9.

[Wise, John Richard de Capel], 'Belles Lettres', *Westminster Review* 30 (July 1866), pp. 268–80.

SENSATION NOVEL CRITICISM

ISSUES OF GENRE

Balee, Susan, 'English Critics, American Crisis, and the Sensation Novel', *Nineteenth Century Contexts* 17: 2 (1993), pp. 125–32.

Bernstein, Susan David, 'Ape Anxiety: Sensation Fiction, Evolution, and the Genre Question', *Journal of Victorian Culture* 6: 2 (1999), pp. 250–70.

——, 'Dirty Reading: Sensation Fiction, Women and Primitivism', *Criticism* 36: 2 (1994), pp. 213–41.

Boyle, Thomas, *Black Swine in the Sewers of Hampstead: Beneath the Surface of Victorian Sensationalism* (London: Hodder & Stoughton/New York: Viking, 1989).

Brantlinger, Patrick, 'What Is "Sensational" about the "Sensation Novel"?', *Nineteenth Century Fiction* 37 (1982), pp. 1–28.

Brown, Nicola, Carolyn Burdett and Pamela Thurschwell eds, *The Victorian Supernatural* (Cambridge: Cambridge University Press, 2004).

Cvetkovich, Ann, *Mixed Feelings: Feminism, Mass Culture and Victorian Sensationalism* (New Brunswick: Rutgers University Press, 1992).

Daly, Nicholas, *Literature, Technology, and Modernity, 1860–2000* (Cambridge: Cambridge University Press, 2004).

Dames, Nicholas, *Amnesiac Selves: Nostalgia, Forgetting, and British Fiction, 1810–1870* (New York: Oxford University Press, 2001).

Edwards, P. D., *Some Mid-Victorian Thrillers: the Sensation Novel, Its Friends and Its Foes* (St. Lucia: University of Queensland Press, 1971).

Frykstedt, Monica Correa, *'On the Brink': Novels of 1866* (Uppsala: Acta University, 1989).

Haining, Peter ed., *The Penny Dreadful, or Strange, Horrid & Sensational Tales!* (London: Gollancz, 1975).

Harrison, Kimberly and Richard Fantina eds, *Victorian Sensations: Essays on a Scandalous Genre* (Ohio: Ohio State University Press, 2006).

Hughes, Winifred, *The Maniac in the Cellar: Sensation Novels of the 1860s* (Princeton, NJ: Princeton University Press, 1980).

Kincaid, James R. ed., *Victorian Identities: Social and Cultural Formations in Nineteenth-Century Literature* (London: Palgrave, 1995).

Law, Graham, *Serializing Fiction in the Victorian Press* (London: Macmillan, 2000).

Loesberg, Jonathan, 'The Ideology of Narrative Form in Sensation Fiction', *Representations* 13 (Winter 1986), pp. 115–38.

Maunder, Andrew, 'Mapping the Victorian Sensation Novel: Recent and Future Trends', *Literature Compass On-line* 2 (2005) (Oxford: Blackwell), pp. 1–32, 140.

Miller, D. A., *The Novel and the Police* (Berkeley: University of California Press, 1988).

Robbins, Ruth and Julian Wolfreys eds, *Victorian Gothic: Literary and Cultural Manifestations in the Nineteenth-Century* (London: Palgrave, 2002).

Schmitt, Cannon, *Alien Nation: Nineteenth-Century Gothic Fictions and English Nationality* (Philadelphia: University of Pennsylvania Press, 1997).

Terry, R. C., *Victorian Popular Fiction, 1860–1880* (London: Macmillan, 1983).

Wynne, Deborah, *The Sensation Novel and the Victorian Family Magazine* (New York: Palgrave, 2001).

CRITICISM OF SPECIFIC TOPICS

CRIME AND DETECTION

Eigen, Joel Peter, *Unconscious Crime: Mental Absence and Criminal Responsibility in Victorian London* (Maryland: Johns Hopkins University Press, 2003).

Humpherys, Anne, 'Generic Strands and Urban Twists: The Victorian Mysteries Novel', *Victorian Studies* 34 (Summer 1991), pp. 455–72.

Kalikoff, Beth, *Murder and Moral Decay in Victorian Popular Literature* (Ann Arbor, Michigan: UMI Research, 1986).

Kayman, Martin, *From Bow Street to Baker Street: Mystery, Detection and Narrative* (London: Macmillan, 1992).

Knight, Stephen, *Crime Fiction, 1800–2000: Detection, Death, Diversity* (New York: Palgrave Macmillan, 2004).

——, *Form and Ideology in Detective Fiction* (London: Macmillan, 1980).

Jackson, Mark ed., *Infanticide: Historical Perspectives on Child Murder and Concealment, 1550–2000* (Aldershot, UK: Ashgate, 2002).

Leps, Marie-Christine, *Apprehending the Criminal: The Production of Deviance in Nineteenth-Century Discourse* (Durham and London: Duke University Press, 1992).

Maxwell, Richard, *The Mysteries of Paris and London* (London: University Press of Virginia, 1992).

McDonagh, Josephine, *Child Murder and British Culture, 1720–1900* (Cambridge: Cambridge University Press, 2003).

Most, Glenn and William Stowe eds, *The Poetics of Murder: Detective Fiction and Literary Theory* (New York: Harcourt, 1983).

Pykett, Lyn, 'The Newgate Novel and Sensation Fiction, 1830–1868', in Martin Priestman ed. *The Cambridge Companion to Crime Fiction* (Cambridge: Cambridge University Press, 2003).

Rothfield, Lawrence, *Vital Signs: Medical Realism in Nineteenth-Century Fiction* (Princeton, NJ: Princeton University Press, 1992).

Thomas, Ronald R., *Detective Fiction and the Rise of Forensic Science* (Cambridge: Cambridge University Press, 2000).

——, 'Minding the Body Politic: The Romance of Science and the Revision of History in Victorian Detective Fiction', *Victorian Literature and Culture* 19 (1991), pp. 233–54.

Thompson, Jon, *Fiction, Crime and Empire: Clues to Modernity and Postmodernism* (Urbana and Chicago: University of Illinois Press, 1993).

Welsh, Alexander, *Strong Representations: Narrative and Circumstantial Evidence in England* (London: Johns Hopkins University Press, 1992).

FEMININITY, MADNESS AND MATERNITY

Auerbach, Nina, *Woman and the Demon: The Life of a Victorian Myth* (London: Harvard University Press, 1982).

Benjamin, Marina, *A Question of Identity: Women, Science, and Literature* (New Brunswick, NJ: Rutgers University Press, 1993).

Flint, Kate, *The Woman Reader, 1837–1914* (Oxford: Clarendon Press, 1993).

Gilbert, Pamela, *Disease, Desire, and the Body in Victorian Women's Popular Novels* (Cambridge: Cambridge University Press 1997).

——, 'Ingestion, Contagion, Seduction: Victorian Metaphors of Reading', in Tamar Heller and Patricia Moran, eds *Scenes of the Apple: Food and the Female Body in Nineteenth- and Twentieth-Century Women's Writing* (Albany, NY: State University of New York Press, 2003).

Harman, Barbara and Sutherland, Joan eds, *The New Nineteenth Century: Feminist Readings of Underread Victorian Fiction* (New York: Garland, 1996).

Hart, Lynda, 'The Victorian Villainness and the Patriarchal Unconscious', *Literature and Psychology* 40: 3 (1994), pp. 1–25.

Heilmann, Ann, 'Emma Bovary's Sisters: Infectious Desire and Female Reading Appetites in Mary Braddon and George Moore', *Victorian Review: The Journal of the Victorian Studies Association of Western Canada and the Victorian Studies Association of Ontario* 29: 1 (2003), pp. 31–48.

Helfield, Randa, 'Poisonous Plots: Women Sensation Novelists and Murderesses of the Victorian Period', *Victorian Review* 21: 2 (1995), pp. 160–88.

Hurley, Kelly, *The Gothic Body: Sexuality, Materialism, and Degeneration at the Fin de Siècle* (Cambridge: Cambridge University Press, 1996).

Langland, Elizabeth, *Nobody's Angels: Middle Class Women and Domestic Ideology in Victorian Culture* (Cornell: Cornell University Press, 1995).

Liggins, Emma and Daniel Duffy eds, *Feminist Readings of Victorian Popular Texts: Divergent Femininities* (Aldershot, UK: Ashgate, 2001).

Mangham, Andrew, *Violent Women and Sensation Fiction: Crime, Medicine and Victorian Popular Culture* (London: Palgrave, 2007).

Marland, Hilary, *Dangerous Motherhood: Insanity and Childbirth in Victorian Britain* (London: Palgrave Macmillan, 2004).

Marshall, Gail, ed., 'Psychology and the Sensation Novel', in *Victorian Fiction* (London and New York: Oxford University Press and Arnold, 2002), pp. 57–63.

Matus, Jill L., *Unstable Bodies: Victorian Representations of Sexuality and Maternity* (Manchester: Manchester University Press, 1995).

Maunder, Andrew (gen. ed.), *Varieties of Women's Sensation Fiction, 1855–1890*, 6 vols (London: Pickering & Chatto, 2004).

—— and Grace Moore eds, *Victorian Crime, Madness and Sensation* (Aldershot, UK: Ashgate, 2004).

Micale, Mark S., *Approaching Hysteria: Disease and its Interpretations* (Princeton, NJ: Princeton University Press, 1995).

Milbank, Alison, *Daughters of the House: Modes of the Gothic in Victorian Fiction* (New York: St. Martin's 1992).

Morris, Virginia, *Double Jeopardy: Women Who Kill in Victorian Fiction* (Kentucky: University Press of Kentucky, 1990).

Pykett, Lyn, *The 'Improper' Feminine: the Women's Sensation Novel and the New Woman Writing* (London: Routledge, 1992).

Russet, Cynthia Eagle, *Sexual Science: the Victorian Construction of Womanhood* (Cambridge, MA: Harvard University Press, 1989).

Shuttleworth, Sally, ' "Preaching to the Nerves": Psychological Disorder in Sensation Fiction', in M. Benjamin ed. *A Question of Identity: Women, Science and Literature* (New Brunswick, NJ: Rutgers University Press, 1993).

Stern, Rebecca, ' "Personation" and "Good Marking Ink": Sanity, Performativity, and Biology in Victorian Sensation Fiction', *Nineteenth Century Studies* 14 (2000), pp. 35–62.

Vicinus, Martha ed., *Suffer and be Still: Women in the Victorian Age* (London: Macmillan, 1972).

Zedner, Lucia, *Women, Crime and Custody in Victorian England* (Oxford: Oxford University Press, 1991).

SPECIFIC AUTHORS

MARY ELIZABETH BRADDON

Calovini, Susan, 'A "Secret" Novel of Her Own: Mary Elizabeth Braddon's Rewriting of Dickens and Collins', *Tennessee Philological Bulletin: Proceedings of the Annual Meeting of the Tennessee Philological Association* 38 (2001), pp. 19–29.

Cox, Jessica, 'From Page to Screen: Transforming M. E. Braddon's *Lady Audley's Secret'*, *Journal of Gender Studies* 14: 1 (March 2005), pp. 23–31.

Ferguson, Christine, 'Sensational Dependence: Prosthesis and Affect in Dickens and Braddon', *LIT: Literature, Interpretation, Theory* 19: 1 (2008), pp. 1–25.

Kaplan, Joel H., 'Exhuming Lady Audley: Period Melodrama for the 1990s', in James Redmond ed. *Melodrama* (Cambridge: Cambridge University Press, 1992), pp. 143–60.

Liggins, Emma, 'Her Mercenary Spirit: Women, Money and Marriage in Mary Elizabeth Braddon's 1870s Fiction', *Women's Writing* 11: 1 (2004), pp. 73–87.

Mangham, Andrew, 'Hysterical Fictions: Mid-Nineteenth-Century Medical Constructions of Hysteria and the Fiction of Mary Elizabeth Braddon', *Wilkie Collins Society Journal* 6 (November 2003), pp. 35–52.

Marks, Patricia, ' "The Boy on the Wooden Horse": Robert Audley and the Failure of Reason', *Clues: a Journal of Detection* 15 (1994), pp. 1–14.

Nemesvari, Richard, 'Robert Audley's Secret: Male Homosocial Desire and "Going Straight" in *Lady Audley's Secret*', in Thomas, Calvin ed. *Straight with a Twist: Queer Theory and the Subject of Heterosexuality* (Urbana: University of Illinois Press, 2000).

Odden, Karen, ' "Reading Coolly" in *John Marchmont's Legacy*: Reconsidering M. E. Braddon's Legacy', *Studies in the Novel* 36: 1 (Spring 2004), pp. 21–40.

Peters, Fiona, 'Mad, Bad, or Difficult? Mary Elizabeth Braddon's *Lady Audley's Secret* and the Enigma of Femininity', in Margaret Sönser Breen ed. *Truth, Reconciliation, and Evil* (New York and Amsterdam: Rodopi, 2004).

Phegley, Jennifer, ' "Henceforward I Refuse to Bow the Knee to Their Narrow Rule": Mary Elizabeth Braddon's *Belgravia* Magazine, Women Readers, and Literary Valuation', *Nineteenth-Century Contexts* 26: 2 (June 2004), pp. 149–71.

Schroeder, Natalie, 'Feminine Sensationalism, Eroticism, and Self-Assertion: M. E. Braddon and Ouida', *Tulsa Studies in Women's Literature* 7: 1 (1988), pp. 87–103.

Sturrock, June, 'Murder, Gender, and Popular Fiction by Women in the 1860s: Braddon, Oliphant, Yonge', in Andrew Maunder and Grace Moore, eds *Victorian Crime, Madness and Sensation* (Aldershot, UK: Ashgate, 2004).

Tromp, Marlene, Pamela K. Gilbert and Aeron Haynie eds, *Beyond Sensation: Mary Elizabeth Braddon in Context* (Albany, NY: State University of New York Press, 2000).

Voskuil, Lynn, 'Acts of Madness: Lady Audley and the Meanings of Victorian Femininity', *Feminist Studies* 27: 3 (Fall 2001), pp. 611–39.

Wiesenthal, C. S., ' "Ghost Haunted": a Trace of Wilkie Collins in Mary Elizabeth Braddon's *Lady Audley's Secret*', *English Language Notes* 28 (1991), pp. 42–44.

Wolff, R. L., *Sensational Victorian: the Life and Fiction of Mary Elizabeth Braddon* (New York & London: Garland, 1979).

WILKIE COLLINS

Bachman, Maria K., and Don Richard Cox eds, *Reality's Dark Light: the Sensational Wilkie Collins* (Tennessee: University of Tennessee Press, 2003).

Baker, William, *Wilkie Collins's Library: a Reconstruction* (Westport: Greenwood Press, 2002).

Barickman, Richard, Susan Macdonald, and Myra Stark, *Corrupt Relations: Dickens, Thackeray, Trollope, Collins and the Victorian Sexual System* (New York: Columbia University Press, 1982).

Clarke, W. M., *The Secret Life of Wilkie Collins* (London, 1988).

Ellis, S. M., *Wilkie Collins, Le Fanu and Others* (London, 1931).

Gasson, Andrew, *Wilkie Collins – An Illustrated Guide* (Oxford: Oxford University Press, 1998).

Gaylin, Ann, 'The Madwoman outside the Attic: Eavesdropping and Narrative Agency in *the Woman in White*', *Texas Studies in Literature and Language* 43: 3 (Fall 2001), pp. 303–33.

Gomel, Elana, 'The Tell-Tale Surface: Fashion and Gender in *The Woman in White*', *VIJ: Victorians Institute Journal* 25 (1997), pp. 29–58.

Heller, Tamar, *Dead Secrets: Wilkie Collins and the Female Gothic* (New Haven & London: Yale University Press, 1992).

Hendershot, Cyndy, 'A Sensation Novel's Appropriation of the Terror-Gothic: Wilkie Collins' *The Woman in White*', *Clues* 13: 2 (1992), pp. 127–33.

Huskey, Melynda, 'No Name: Embodying the Sensation Heroine', *Victorian Newsletter* 82 (Fall 1992), pp. 5–13.

Jones, Anna, 'A Victim in Search of a Torturer: Reading Masochism in Wilkie Collins's *No Name*', *Novel: a Forum on Fiction* 33: 2 (Spring 2000), pp. 196–211.

Kent, Christopher, 'Probability, Reality and Sensation in the Novels of Wilkie Collins', *Dickens Studies Annual* 20 (1991), pp. 259–80.

Ledwon, Lenora, 'Veiled Women, The Law of Coverture, and Wilkie Collins's *The Woman in White*', *Victorian Literature and Culture* 22 (1994), pp. 1–22.

Lonoff, Sue, *Wilkie Collins and His Victorian Readers: a Study in the Rhetoric of Authorship* (New York: Garland, 1982).

Mangham, Andrew ed., *Wilkie Collins: Interdisciplinary Essays* (Cambridge: Scholars Press, 2007).

Maynard, Jessica, 'Black Silk and Red Paisley: the Toxic Woman in Wilkie Collins's *Armadale*', in Gary Day ed. *Varieties of Victorianism: the Uses of a Past* (London: Macmillan, 1998), pp. 63–79.

Miller, D. A., 'Cage aux Folles: Sensation and Gender in Wilkie Collins's *The Woman in White*', *Representations* 14 (Spring 1986), pp. 107–36.

Nayder, Lillian, *Wilkie Collins* (New York: Twayne, 1997).

O'Neill, Philip, *Wilkie Collins: Women, Property and Propriety* (London: Macmillan, 1988).

Page, Norman ed., *Wilkie Collins: the Critical Heritage* (London: Arnold, 1974).

Pedlar, Valerie, 'Drawing a Blank: the Construction of Identity in *The Woman in White*', in Dennis Walder ed. *The Nineteenth-Century Novel: Identities* (London: Routledge, 2001).

Peters, Catherine, *The King of Inventors: a Life of Wilkie Collins* (London: Minerva, 1992).

Pykett, Lyn, *The Sensation Novel from 'The Woman in White' to 'The Moonstone'* (Plymouth: Northcote House in association with the British Council, 1994).

——, *Wilkie Collins: Authors in Context* (Oxford: Oxford University Press, 2005).

——, *Wilkie Collins, New Casebooks: Contemporary Critical Essays* (London: Macmillan, 1998).

Rance, Nicholas, *Wilkie Collins and Other Sensation Novelists: Walking the Moral Hospital* (London: Macmillan/Rutherford, NJ: Fairleigh Dickinson University Press, 1990).

Reierstad, Keith, 'Innocent Indecency: the Questionable Heroines of Wilkie Collins' Sensation Novels', *VIJ: Victorians Institute Journal* 9 (1980), pp. 57–69.

Reitz, Caroline, 'Colonial "Gwilt": in and around Wilkie Collins's *Armadale*', *Victorian Periodicals Review* 33: 1 (Spring 2000), pp. 92–103.

Smith, Nelson and R. C. Terry eds, *Wilkie Collins to the Forefront: Some Reassessments* (New York, 1995).

Stave, Shirley A., 'The Perfect Murder: Patterns of Repetition and Doubling in Wilkie Collins's *The Woman in White*', *Dickens Studies Annual* 25 (1996), pp. 287–303.

Sutherland, John, 'Wilkie Collins and the Origin of the Sensation Novel', *Dickens Studies Annual* 20 (1991), pp. 243–53.

Talairach-Vielmas, Laurence, 'Victorian Sensational Shoppers: Representing Transgressive Femininity in Wilkie Collins's *No Name*', *Victorian Review: the Journal of the Victorian Studies Association of Western Canada and the Victorian Studies Association of Ontario* 31: 2 (2005), pp. 56–78.

Taylor, Jenny Bourne ed., *The Cambridge Companion to Wilkie Collins* (Cambridge: Cambridge University Press, 2006).

——, *In the Secret Theatre of Home: Wilkie Collins, Sensation Narrative, and Nineteenth-Century Psychology* (London & New York: Routledge, 1988).

Thoms, Peter, *The Windings of the Labyrinth: Quest and Structure in the Major Novels of Wilkie Collins* (Athens, Ohio: Ohio University Press, 1992).

CHARLES DICKENS

Billi, Mirella, 'Dickens as a Sensation Novelist', in Rossana Bonadei ed. *Dickens: the Craft of Fiction and the Challenges of Reading* (Unicopli, Milan: Italy Publication, 2000).

Nayder, Lillian, *Unequal Partners: Charles Dickens, Wilkie Collins, and Victorian Authorship* (Ithaca, NY, and London: Cornell University Press, 2002).

Surridge, Lisa, ' "John Rokesmith's Secret": Sensation, Detection, and the Policing of the Feminine in *Our Mutual Friend*', *Dickens Studies Annual: Essays on Victorian Fiction* 26 (1998), pp. 265–84.

THOMAS HARDY

Allingham, Philip V., 'Sensation Novel Elements in The *London Graphic*'s Twenty-Part Serialisation of Hardy's *The Mayor of Casterbridge* (January through May, 1886)', *The Thomas Hardy Year Book* 31 (1990), pp. 34–64.
Jones, Lawrence O., '*Desperate Remedies* and the Victorian Sensation Novel', *Nineteenth-Century Fiction* 20: 1 (June 1965), pp. 35–50.
Radford, Andrew, *Thomas Hardy and the Survivals of Time* (Aldershot, UK: Ashgate, 2003).
Showalter, Elaine, '*Desperate Remedies*: Sensation Novels of the 1860s', *Victorian Newsletter* 49 (1976), pp. 1–5.
Ward, Paul, '*Desperate Remedies* and the Victorian Thriller', *Thomas Hardy Yearbook* 4 (1973–74), pp. 72–76.

SHERIDAN LE FANU

Burwick, Frederick, 'Romantic Supernaturalism: the Case Study as Gothic Tale', *Wordsworth Circle* 34: 2 (2003), pp. 73–81.
Cahill, Ann, 'Madness and Eccentricity in Sheridan Le Fanu's *The Rose and the Key*', *The Bram Stoker Society Journal* 10 (1998), pp. 17–29.
Cooke, Simon, 'Dangerous Subversives: the Role of Painters in Sensational Fiction', *Victorians Institute Journal* 31 (2003), pp. 157–72.
Gibbons, Luke, ' "Some Hysterical Hatred": History, Hysteria and the Literary Revival', *Irish University Review* 27: 1 (1997), pp. 7–23.
Hennelly, Mark M., Jr. 'Framing the Gothic: from Pillar to Post-Structuralism', *College Literature* 28: 3 (2001), pp. 68–87.
Howes, Marjorie, 'Misalliance and Anglo-Irish Tradition in Le Fanu's *Uncle Silas*', *Nineteenth-Century Literature* 47: 2 (September 1992), pp. 164–86.
Hughes, William, 'The Origins and Implications of J. S. Le Fanu's "Green Tea" ', *Irish Studies Review* 13: 1 (2005), pp. 45–54.
McCormack, W. J., *Dissolute Characters: Irish Literary History through Balzac, Sheridan Le Fanu, Yeats and Bowen* (Manchester: Manchester University Press, 1983).
——, *Sheridan Le Fanu and Victorian Ireland* (Oxford: Oxford University Press, 1980).
Milbank, Alison, 'From the Sublime to the Uncanny: Victorian Gothic and Sensation Fiction', *Costerus* N.S. 91 (1994), pp. 169–79.
——, 'Milton, Melancholy and the Sublime in the "Female" Gothic from Radcliffe to Le Fanu', *Women's Writing* 1: 2 (1994), pp. 143–60.
Sage, Victor, *Le Fanu's Gothic: the Rhetoric of Darkness* (London: Palgrave, 2003).
Tracy, Robert, 'Undead, Unburied: Anglo-Ireland and the Predatory Past', *LIT: Literature, Interpretation, Theory* 10: 1 (1999), pp. 13–33.
Walton, James, *Vision and Vacancy: The Fictions of J. S. Le Fanu* (Dublin: University College Dublin Press, 2007).
Wegley, Mark, 'Unknown Fear: Joseph Sheridan Le Fanu and the Literary Fantastic', *Philological Review* 27: 2 (1999), pp. 59–77.
Zuber, Devin P. 'Swedenborg and the Disintegration of Language in Sheridan Le Fanu's Sensation Fiction', in Kimberly Harrison and Richard Fantina eds, *Victorian Sensations: Essays on a Scandalous Genre* (Ohio: Ohio University Press, 2006).

ELLEN (MRS HENRY) WOOD

Barefoot, Guy, '*East Lynne* to *Gas Light*: Hollywood, Melodrama and Twentieth-Century Notions of the Victorian', in Jacky Bratton, Jim Cook and Christine Gledhill, eds *Melodrama: Stage Picture Screen* (London: BFI Publications, 1994).

Elliott, Jeanne, 'A Lady to the End: the Case of Isabel Vane', *Victorian Studies: a Journal of the Humanities, Arts and Sciences* 19 (1976), pp. 329–44.

Gruner, Elisabeth Rose, 'Plotting the Mother: Caroline Norton, Helen Huntingdon, and Isabel Vane', *Tulsa Studies in Women's Literature* 16: 2 (Fall 1997), pp. 303–25.

Heller, Tamar, 'Victorian Sensationalism and the Silence of Maternal Sexuality in Edith Wharton's *The Mother's Recompense*', *Narrative* 5: 2 (May 1997), pp. 135–42.

Langbauer, Laurie, 'Women in White, Men in Feminism', *The Yale Journal of Criticism: Interpretation in the Humanities* 2: 2 (Spring 1989), pp. 219–243.

Liggins, Emma, 'Good Housekeeping? Domestic Economy and Suffering Wives in Mrs Henry Wood's Early Fiction', in Emma Liggins and Daniel Duffy, eds *Feminist Readings of Victorian Popular Texts: Divergent Femininities* (Aldershot, UK: Ashgate, 2001).

Losano, Antonia, '*East Lynne, The Turn of the Screw*, and the Female Doppelgänger in Governess Fiction', *Nineteenth Century Studies* 18 (2004), pp. 99–116.

Mangham, Andrew, '"I See It; But I Cannot Explain It": Female Gothicism and the Narrative of Female Incarceration in the Novels of Mrs Henry Wood', in Karen Sayer and Rosemary Mitchell, eds *Victorian Gothic* (Leeds, England: Leeds Centre for Victorian Studies, 2001).

Maunder, Andrew, '"I Will Not Live in Poverty and Neglect": *East Lynne* on the East End Stage', in Kimberly Harrison and Richard Fantina, eds *Victorian Sensations: Essays on a Scandalous Genre* (Ohio: Ohio State University Press, 2006).

——, '"Stepchildren of Nature": *East Lynne* and the Spectre of Female Degeneracy, 1860–1861', in Andrew Maunder and Grace Moore, eds *Victorian Crime, Madness and Sensation* (Aldershot, UK: Ashgate, 2004).

McCuskey, Brian W., 'The Kitchen Police: Servant Surveillance and Middle-Class Transgression', *Victorian Literature and Culture* 28: 2 (2000), pp. 359–75.

Odden, Karen, 'Re-Visioning the "Vision from a Fairer World than His": Women, Creativity, and Work in *East Lynne* and *Mrs Doubtfire*', in Diane Long Hoeveler and Donna Decker Schuster, eds *Women's Literary Creativity and the Female Body* (London: Palgrave, 2007).

Phegley, Jennifer, 'Domesticating the Sensation Novelist: Ellen Price Wood as Author and Editor of the *Argosy Magazine*', *Victorian Periodicals Review* 38: 2 (Summer 2005), pp. 180–98.

Rosenman, Ellen Bayuk, '"Mimic Sorrows": Masochism and the Gendering of Pain in Victorian Melodrama', *Studies in the Novel* 35: 1 (Spring 2003), pp. 22–43.

RELATED HISTORICAL AND THEORETICAL CRITICISM

Altick, Richard D., *The Presence of the Present: Topics of the Day in the Victorian Novel* (Columbus: Ohio State University Press, 1991).

Anderson, Amanda, *Tainted Souls and Painted Faces: The Rhetoric of Fallenness in Victorian Culture* (Ithaca: Cornell University Press, 1993).

Armstrong, Nancy, *Desire and Domestic Fiction: a Political History of the Novel* (London: Oxford University Press, 1987).

Bailey, Peter, *Leisure and Class in Victorian England: Rational Recreation and the Contest for Control, 1830–1880* (London: Routledge, 1978).

Baldick, Chris, *The Social Mission of English Criticism, 1848–1932* (Oxford: Clarendon Press, 1988).

Bodenheimer, Rosemarie, *The Politics of Story in Victorian Social Fiction* (Cornell: Cornell University Press 1988).

Brantlinger, Patrick, *Rule of Darkness: British Literature and Imperialism, 1830–1914* (Cornell: Cornell University Press, 1988).

Eliot, T. S., 'Wilkie Collins and Dickens', *Times Literary Supplement* (4 August 1927). pp. 525–26; reprinted in *Selected Essays: 1917–1932* (London: Faber, 1932).

Ferguson, Christine, *Language, Science and Popular Fiction in the Victorian Fin de Siècle: the Brutal Tongue* (Aldershot, UK: Ashgate, 2006).

Foucault, Michel, *Discipline and Punish: the Birth of the Prison*, trans. Alan Sheridan (New York: Pantheon, 1977).

Freeman, Nicholas, *Conceiving the City: London, Literature, and Art 1870–1914* (Oxford: Oxford University Press, 2007).

Gallagher, Catherine, *The Industrial Reformation of the English Novel: Social Discourse and Narrative Form* (California: University of California Press, 1985).

——, and Thomas Laqueur, eds, *The Making of the Modern Body: Sexuality and Society in the Nineteenth Century* (Berkeley: University of California Press, 1987).

Gilmour, Robin, *The Victorian Period: the Intellectual and Cultural Context of English Literature, 1830–1890* (London: Longman, 1993).

Hadley, Elaine, *Melodramatic Tactics: Theatricalized Dissent in the English Marketplace, 1800–1885* (Stanford: Stanford University Press, 1995).

Harman, Barbara Heal, and Susan Meyer eds, *The New Nineteenth Century: Feminist Readings of Underread Victorian Fiction* (New York: Garland, 1996).

Joyce, Patrick, *Visions of the People: Industrial England and the Question of Class, 1840–1914* (Cambridge: Cambridge University Press, 1990).

Kranidis, Rita S., *Subversive Discourse: the Cultural Production of Late Victorian Feminist Novels* (New York: St. Martin's Press, 1995).

Larson, Jil, *Ethics and Narrative in the English Novel, 1880–1914* (Cambridge: Cambridge University Press, 2001).

Logan, Deborah Anna, *Fallenness in Victorian Women's Writing: Marry, Stitch, Die, or Do Worse* (Columbia: University of Missouri Press, 1998).

Lootens, Tricia, *Lost Saints: Silence, Gender and Victorian Literary Canonization* (Charlottesville: University Press of Virginia, 1996).

Nunokawa, Jeff, *The Afterlife of Property: Domestic Security and the Victorian Novel* (Princeton, NJ: Princeton University Press, 1994).

Oulton, Carolyn W., *Literature and Religion in Mid-Victorian England: from Dickens to Eliot* (London: Palgrave, 2003).

Poovey, Mary, *Making a Social Body: British Cultural Formation, 1830–64* (Chicago: University of Chicago Press, 1995).

——, *Uneven Developments: the Ideological Work of Gender in Mid-Victorian England* (Manchester: Manchester University Press, 1998).

Shanley, Mary Lyndon, *Feminism, Marriage, and the Law in Victorian England, 1850–1895* (Princeton, NJ: Princeton University Press, 1989).

Showalter, Elaine, *A Literature of Their Own: British Women Novelists from Brontë to Lessing* (Princeton, NJ: Princeton University Press, 1977).

Singer, Ben, *Melodrama and Modernity: Early Sensational Cinema and its Contexts* (New York: Columbia University Press, 2001).

Thompson, Nicola Diane, *Reviewing Sex: Gender and the Reception of Victorian Novels* (New York: New York University Press, 1996).

Tucker, Herbert F., *A Companion to Victorian Literature and Culture* (Malden, MA: Blackwell, 1999).

Walkowitz, Judith, *City of Dreadful Delight: Narratives of Sexual Danger in Late-Victorian London* (Chicago: University of Chicago Press, 1992).

USEFUL WEBSITES – ALL DETAILS ARE CORRECT AT THE TIME OF GOING TO PRESS

GENERAL INTEREST WEBSITES:

http://www.lang.nagoya-u.ac.jp/~matsuoka/Victorian.html (accessed on 17 July 2008)
  [The Victorian Literary Studies Archive with helpful links to concordances and other research-related sites]
http://members.aol.com/MG4273/sensatio.htm (accessed on 17 July 2008)
  [A thorough guide to Victorian Sensation writing]
http://www.victorianweb.org/genre/sensationbib.html
  [A selected bibliography of secondary criticism on the Victorian Sensation Novel]
http://vos.ucsb.edu/browse.asp?id=2751 (accessed on 17 July 2008)
  [Voice of the Shuttle contains excellent information on selected Victorian sensation writers as well as recent criticism]
http://www.victorianprose.org/ (accessed on 17 July 2008)
  [Though not devoted entirely to the sensation genre, this Victorian Prose Archive boasts good links and information about conferences, newsgroups and online research journals]
http://andromeda.rutgers.edu/%7Ejlynch/Lit/victoria.html (accessed on 17 July 2008)
  [Contains a comprehensive list of links to important research sites on Victorian literature, including the sensation genre]
http://www.indiana.edu/~letrs/vwwp/ (accessed on 17 July 2008)
  [The Victorian Women Writer's Project, whose goal is to provide accurate transcriptions of works by British women writers of the nineteenth century]

AUTHORS-SPECIFIC WEBSITES:

http://www.wilkie-collins.info/bibliography.htm (accessed on 17 July 2008)
  [A resource which contains supplementary information about Wilkie Collins's important contribution to the detective genre, as well as his connection with Charles Dickens]
http://www.jslefanu.com (accessed on 17 July 2008)
  [A detailed and informative database on J. Sheridan Le Fanu]
http://www.sensationpress.com (accessed on 17 July 2008)
  [A specialist press which provides carefully annotated scholarly editions of neglected novels and short story collections by sensation writers such as M. E. Braddon]
http://www.mrshenrywood.co.uk (accessed on 17 July 2008)
  [A website devoted to the life and work of Ellen Wood]

Index